T0209385

L♥VE CONQUERS ALL

SPIRITUAL MESSAGES OF HOPE FOR OUR DESPAIRING WORLD

Denise Bachrodt

BALBOA.PRESS
A DIVISION OF HAY HOUSE

Balboa Press books may be ordered through booksellers or by contacting:

Balboa Press
A Division of Hay House
1663 Liberty Drive
Bloomington, IN 47403
www.balboapress.com
1 (877) 407-4847

Because of the dynamic nature of the Internet, any web addresses or links contained in
this book may have changed since publication and may no longer be valid. The views
expressed in this work are solely those of the author and do not necessarily reflect the
views of the publisher, and the publisher hereby disclaims any responsibility for them.

The author of this book does not dispense medical advice or prescribe the use of any
technique as a form of treatment for physical, emotional, or medical problems without the
advice of a physician, either directly or indirectly. The intent of the author is only to offer
information of a general nature to help you in your quest for emotional and spiritual well-
being. In the event you use any of the information in this book for yourself, which is your
constitutional right, the author and the publisher assume no responsibility for your actions.

Any people depicted in stock imagery provided by Getty Images are models,
and such images are being used for illustrative purposes only.
Certain stock imagery © Getty Images.

Print information available on the last page.

ISBN: 978-1-9822-4767-6 (sc)
ISBN: 978-1-9822-4768-3 (hc)
ISBN: 978-1-9822-4769-0 (e)

Library of Congress Control Number: 2020908801

Balboa Press rev. date: 06/04/2020

The Blessed Virgin Mary (BV) and the Infant Jesus Christ

Love Conquers All
Messages of Hope for Our Despairing World

Denise Bachrodt
Love Conquers All

Love conquersALLLLC.com

Denise Bachrodt is available for select speaking engagements. To inquire about a possible appearance, please contact: Balboa Press, Eric Saxon at 877-407-4947 ext. 5127

My website is: loveconquersallllc.com

My podcast on iTunes is: loveconquersallllc

My podcast on your host website is: loveconquersallllc.podbean.com

For Brother Thomas Johnston and Mary McAlpin who
have supported me through this entire process.

CONTENTS

PREFACE

This book was meant to give *"hope"* to a world of despairing people due to government corruption, sexual abuse, and human trafficking. I asked God, "What do we make of all this?" He told me, "It all needed to rise to the surface so that we would become aware of what is actually happening in our world today, that we would no longer tolerate such behavior, and it is paving the way for peace on earth."

Many of these messages gave me comfort while going through a contentious divorce. Hopefully these messages will be of great help to you too. Also note that "Dear child" begins each message because we are all children of God.

Enjoy the book!

GOD SPEAKS TO US

Dear Child,

Yes, today is a glorious day. Yet we have no days in heaven. We have no need for time. Things are measured on the *"good deeds"* that we perform after a resting period. Tasks are assigned if we choose to act on them. We keep very busy. Your dad is currently working on the *"World Peace Mission."* His task is to instill peace and harmony into the hearts of individuals on earth. Yes, it is a huge task, but one he is working hard to accomplish. He is a *"living saint"* and appreciates everything we do for you. You were so fortunate to have him as your dad. We love him very much and are guiding him.

Now for you, continue to do whatever we tell you to do each and every day. You are being guided by us. At times the tasks may seem difficult or impossible to accomplish. Have faith, and *know* we are with you to assist you in accomplishing these things. You are never alone. Remember that we love you very much, and are guiding you.

Today is a very special day because we have you all to ourselves. There are many things we would like to discuss with you. The focus is around *"world peace"* and the means to achieve it.

All can be accomplished through *LOVE.* Love conquers all. Love has a compassionate and understanding heart. Love is never quick to judge. Love is not demanding or controlling. Love is complete acceptance of others, their ways, and notions. Love never falters to help one another. Love is kind, giving, and merciful. Love does conquer all.

So often we forget just how much God loves us, and what that means in our lives. Love has no boundaries. Love transcends beyond time and space, as you see with your dad. Love is eternal. God is eternal and is pure love. Open up your hearts and let him in! What a difference this would make in our world today. Could you imagine if everyone loved each other? What an affect that would have on our world? We would have *world peace!* God would surely be happy with us. However, that's not the case right now. Sad to say. Mankind is obsessed with power and control, greed and possessions. How cruel. It is so negative and demeaning. It shows a *"lack of God"* in their lives.

It is not "*in vogue*" to even discuss God, and what He means to us in our daily lives. How completely sad this is! We are creating self-proposed philosophies. One of death and destruction. Is this what you want for our world? Do you wish to see it come to a tragic end like this? If not, you must pray daily for: world peace; the conversion of evil ones; and for Gods intervention with our world leaders.

Everything can be accomplished with God involved, even *world peace*. He hears our prayers and answers them. He is never quick to judge or anger. God is so good. We must choose good over evil. God comes to us in many ways and through many people. Sometimes those people are asking us for help. Show your compassion and understanding. Other times they may just be lonely, and you need to lend a listening ear. There is a part of God in all of us. We are made in His image and likeness. Therefore, be kind to one another. Love yourself and your neighbor, as God so loves you. Yes, love is the bottom line. One in which the entire world evolves. Everyone responds to love, kindness, and generosity. Be generous of your time in order to help another. Share what you have learned in discussion with others. Help bring love and kindness into the hearts and minds of the individuals you meet. This is contagious. Help bring people back to God. Talk about God with others. Talk about His goodness. Talk about the miracles He performs each and every day for us. Mention how He would build the heavens and earth, even if you were the only person on earth. He would do that just for you! That's how much He loves you. Let Him into your minds and hearts. Let Him influence your thoughts and actions daily. *Never doubt His love for you*. Remember, He is with you always and in all ways. Trust in Him and His love for you. Let Him become a part of your daily life! You would begin to appreciate everything. The sun, moon, stars, and every creature on earth both large and small. It's a chance to *open your heart and be happy*. With God pouring all His love into you, you cannot help but be happy and at peace. Knowing that all is well. He is handling everything. Yes, it's a major change in mindset going from "*If it's meant to be, it's up to me*" to one of "*Letting go and letting God.*" However, it definitely works and for the betterment of mankind! Why not return this earth into it's original "*Garden of Eden?*" It once was a time of peace and harmony. Help it return to that *now*. Believe it or not, you play a large factor in this program. You are a major influence on mankind, as insignificant as you feel now. For every act of kindness goes a long way. One heart touches another, and it has a rippling effect. Good conquers evil. Love overcomes fear and despair. Unity with God can change your world. Now is the time to talk about this with your fellow man. Instill love back into their hearts instead of fear and anxiety. Tell everyone to pray for: *world peace;* for God interceding with your world leaders; and for the conversion of the evil ones. Don't worry, and ask how can this possibly be accomplished? What strategies and goals do you have in place? Just say, I have the most major weapon in hand, that is *God's love for us.* Love conquers all! Pray for peace. He hears our prayers and answers them. Miracles happen every day. Good will conquer evil.

This needs to be a unified effort on everyone's part. Ask God for guidance, and He will point you in the right direction. *Never doubt His love for you.* He's always there for you. Do not despair. His love transcends all space and time. It is eternal.

Once world peace is accomplished, we will have heaven on earth. It will be returned to its original *"Garden of Paradise."* Everyone will be filled with peace and harmony, and you will see this accomplished in your lifetime. Pray dearly for this because miracles do happen. A collective mindset of peace will help to bring about *"Peace- on -Earth."* This I promise you. It is never too late to start praying and turning to God.

Now is the time to act. Tell everyone you meet to start praying for *world peace.* Know that you can accomplish this. He performs miracles every day. The pendulum needs to swing the other way. Man needs to love one another again. Perform *random acts of kindness,* show *good news* on TV. It really will have a contagious effect on your sanity. Believe that this can happen, and soon, for our world to survive. God only wants the very best for us. He wants to grant our every wish. He wants us to be happier than we could ever dream possible. So, pray daily, and see good in everyone you meet. Look at the good, not bad, in every situation. Never judge, because you are not in that person's shoes or life. Be happy with and accept everything you have because it has been given to you by God. Be positive, not negative. Keep love in your heart, not hate. Pray for your enemies. God will handle them, and work to change their hearts. Most of all, stay close to God. Be mindful of Him with everything you do.

Incorporate Him into your daily life. Know that He is with you always and in all ways. He does hear your prayers and answers them. He is a kind, loving, merciful God, and only wants the very best for you.

If ever you should become discouraged, take a *time out* and ask for His help. In no time, help is on its way.

Life would be so much easier for all of us if we just believed that God is handling it all. We give Him our problems, and He handles them. He gives us the solutions to them. No need to worry or have anxieties about them. The trouble occurs when we give Him our problems, and then take them back to fret over them! Do we enjoy being unhappy? Maybe so. However, given the choice, we would prefer being happy over being sad. God is our answer in every case. He created us and wants us to *return to Him*. Why not start *now*, instead of waiting until we are on our death bed. It's never too late to return to God. He is the answer to all of your problems. He is kind and compassionate, and only wants you to love Him as He so loves us. Never falter from God. Let Him into your life on a daily basis. Stay close to Him, and He will reward you greatly. Now is the time to act. Our world can be saved. There is still time to act. His loving arms are *open* to you. Let Him into your hearts and minds, and *know* that He is there for you always and in all ways. It is never too late. His love for you is eternal. Stay as close to Him as you possibly can by keeping Him in your daily life.

Our world so desperately needs to hear this *now*. Let everyone know of this urgency. It is imperative that you do this. *Now* is the time to act. God will give you the words to say at any given time. Do not be discouraged by others and their recriminations. This is Gods will for you, not their will! Who are they anyway, but mere imperfect men? God is perfect and is pure love. Let Him run your life, not them. Do not fall into the negative ways of society with its fear, despair and anxiety. Listen to God. Keep Him in your mind and heart. He is the answer, not them. Those people are caught up in their egos. Let them be, and do not challenge them. There are many more people in the world thirsting for your words of wisdom. Please ignore these men and their egos, and just pray for them. God will handle them in His own time. Please, please, please share what we are saying to you. The world needs to hear this message, the time to act is *now*. We will give you the wisdom and courage to act. We will put the words into your mouth. Be our vehicle, our instrument for getting this out to the people who desperately need to hear it. The others will jump on the *band wagon* when it is *in vogue*. In the meantime, when you leave the retreat, tell everyone about what you heard here. We will let you know who will be responsive, and you can begin sharing your message. It is so *vitally important* for the betterment of mankind. You are our instrument, our spokesperson to bring this about. Do not falter in your belief or your love of God. He is guiding and directing your every move. Have confidence that He is there guiding your every thought and action. Do not fear, just know that you are doing God's work. He needs many people like you to do this in order to accomplish His plan. Remember, we have a *peace force* in heaven and one on earth. You have been appointed to the one on earth. God will clear the way for you to be heard. Do not worry, He will guide your movement by movement according to His will and actions. Be open and mindful to His way. He so loves you, and wants you to become his instrument. I know you pray, "*God it's not my will, but your will be done.*" Your phrase is "*Loving Lord, help me to do your will.*" This is God's will for you. This is why He set your life up to be the way it is now. This is your purpose in life. To help bring people close to God. To talk about God in their lives. To point out what a role He has in each and every life. This is the time to act *now*! People so desperately need to hear this message. They need to be reminded of His love for them, and the very active role He plays in their lives. They need to *return to God*, and pray more. They need to involve God in their lives each and every day. They need to love God and their neighbors, as He so loves them. They need to *return to God*. They need to ask Him for everything, both large and small. They need to open up, and let Him into their hearts and minds.

This is how our world will begin to change. People need to stop being negative, and listen to the killing news. They need to begin the positive actions and thinking within their own lives. This will help turn the world around. They need to pray daily for: *world peace;* the conversion of evil ones; and for Gods intervention with our world leaders.

Only through prayer can all of this be accomplished. *Now* is the time to act. Our world has never been so close to total destruction. The time is *now! Return to God!* He performs miracles and can change things. Only

God can intervene at this point to make a difference. Mankind has brought it this far, now God needs to do the rest to bring about *world peace*. This is so vitally important. I cannot stress it to you enough. *Act Now.* The time is running short. Pray, pray, pray for God's love and intercession. Miracles do happen. Believe, believe, believe that God answers our prayers. Have strong faith in Him. Let Him guide you. Listen, and be open to Him, now more than ever before, our world needs prayer. Prayer can change everything. Prayer does make a difference. With God in our lives, all is well. Without God, we are in the mess we currently are in. We need to wake up and begin praying. It is our only salvation. A return to God is in order. Do it *now*, before it is too late. Let Him be a part of your life. Let him guide you. Rest in His presence. *Know*, and do not worry, that all is well with God at your side. Stay calm and peaceful, and know that He is with you. Let Him become a part of your life. Let Him speak through you. Become His instrument. Be live putty in His hands. His time is *now* for you. *Act now.* Pray always and in all ways. Listen to Him. Never question His judgement. When in doubt, do nothing. He will guide you on what to do and say. Remember, He is there for you, always and in all ways. It's never too late to return to God. He is waiting in the wings for you. His love is eternal. Never doubt His immense love for you. Stay close to Him. Let Him work in your life. Always know you can turn to Him with whatever problem you may have. Let Him be your anchor to the wind. Only God is constant, everything else falls away. He is pure love. His love is eternal. "*Let go and let God.*" Only through God can you really be happy. He is pure love. By you sharing in His life, you have a chance to experience a *slice of heaven*. Yes, peace can be achieved on earth by a return to God. Only He can bring this about. Only God, by His immense love for mankind, can restore order to this world of ours. Let Him work for you. Ask Him for help. Let Him bring about *world peace*. Which He so desperately wants to do. "*Ask, and you shall receive.*" "*Let it be on earth, as it is in heaven,*" Amen. "*Seek, and you shall find.*" Go now, and be in God's peace and love for you.

We love you very much and are guiding you.

Love,
BV and Christ.

CHAPTER ONE

HOPE FOR A DESPAIRING WORLD

Dear Child,

It is wonderful to see you again. Please stay close to us. Our connection is very important to our world. One day you will be talking to people through us. Yes, that day will come, but for now just sit and listen.

The world is in a very grave position right now. Your president would like to proceed with the war on terrorism without the Security Council's approval. This is not good. You need the world's support for peace. You cannot achieve it through war. Peace can only be achieved by talking with one another and negotiating. One-upmanship will not work. The thrust of power, and need to conquer is too great. When will mankind learn that *nothing* is accomplished through war? You need to live up to your true potential. This can be achieved by a peaceful means. Only a few set individuals want war. The rest of the population wants peace. Keep praying for *world peace*. God hears all prayers and answers them. Believe and trust in Him. He works miracles every day. Miracles are performed every minute of every day. Believe in God, and *know* that He is with you always and in all ways. The world can be turned around through prayer. Each and every one of you need to pray every day for: *world peace;* God's intercession with our world leaders; and the conversion of the evil ones. God hears all prayers and answers them. *Know* that He is there for you in all ways. He loves you very much and is guiding you. Never give up your faith. It is at the core of your being. It is the essence of your soul. Never give up. No matter what the world has to say about the situation. Keep preaching *peace*, and things will turn around. Do not ask how or why, simply know that God is with you always and in all ways. He is guiding and protecting you. Stay close to Him, and He will guide you. Do not worry about anything. *Know* that God is there taking care of you.

Know that we love you, and are watching over you every minute of every day. You are never alone.

The time is short for this world. Mankind needs to learn its lessons quickly. Otherwise, much death and destruction will occur. Yes, *peace* is possible, and is intended for the world either with this generation or the next. You are ultimately good people, who will return to God. But for now, many of you are far away from God. You have turned your backs on Him. He is so sad to see the way you have turned out. This is not the way *He* wanted you to be. He gave you *free will* so that you could return to Him freely, of your own accord. However, now He is the furthest thing from your minds. You need to listen to Him. Open your lives to Him. Have faith and trust in Him. By doing this, your lives would be so happy and fulfilled. You would be happier than you could ever dream imaginable. That is where your faith and trust come into play. Without God, nothing is possible. All life ceases to exist. It is the end of everything. Is that what you want for this world? You would choose death and destruction over love and kindness. What kind of people are you? What have you become? When will you return to God? He is a God who is all loving, kind and merciful, and forgives everyone. He is pure love. Love is the only thing that lasts. Love is the most powerful emotion. It overcomes all other emotions. God will reign again on this earth. His time is coming. So be prepared. Do not doubt His word or His love for you. It is eternal and everlasting. He is magnificent and all knowing. He wants so much for you to succeed as a race, and turn to Him and love Him. You need to change your will and lives and be with Him. You will be happier than you ever dreamed possible. Just, *"Let go and let God."* All things are possible with God. *Know* and believe in Him. He will guide you, and show you the way. Have faith and trust in Him.

He is the one everyone is *searching for,* and does not even realize it. With faith, all things are possible. With *peace* comes love and happiness, and a calm that is all knowing. All is well. Believe in Him. Give your life to Him, and you will have no need to worry about anything. Your life will be guided by Him. Just be *open* to Him. All happiness is *possible* with His love and mercy.

The planet can return to its original *"Garden of Eden."* If everyone turned their lives over to God, that is what it would become. You would have *peace-on-earth.* It is *possible.* Pray for *peace.* God's intercession with our world leaders, and for the conversion of the evil ones. Miracles happen every day. Simply trust and believe in Him, and all is possible through faith, hope and love. With God, all things are possible. *Know* that He wants everyone to turn to Him for world peace. He wants you with Him to be happier than you could ever dream imaginable. Love Him with your whole heart and soul, as He loves you. Be open and just love Him, that is all He asks of you. It is that easy. *"Let go and let God."* All things are possible with God. The world is empty and meaningless without Him. *Know* that He loves you, and wants to give you everything that life has to offer to make you happy. *"Ask, and you shall receive."* He wants to give you everything, just ask. His love for you is so great that He sent His only son to earth to show you the way. He died so that your sins would be forgiven. He showed you the way of eternal life through God.

Talk about Him as much as you can. Help people turn to Him again, so that they can trust and believe in Him. He so much wants to be a part of everyone's life. Just know that He is there for you, always and in all ways. He never turns His back on you, even during your darkest hour. He is always there for you. You are never alone. Just trust and love Him, and *know*, through faith, that all things are possible. So, continue to pray for *world peace*. Miracles do happen. Stay close to God. Let Him become a part of your daily life. Now is the time to be with Him. His love is endless. Let Him shower it upon you. Open your heart so that He can make you happy. It is not difficult, yet so very rewarding.

The time to act is *now*. Pray for *peace*. Love yourselves, your neighbors, and your God. *Do not give up.* Miracles happen. God hears all of your prayers. Love conquers fear. *Do not be afraid.* God is with you always and in all ways. He is guiding you, and loves you so very much. More than you will ever know or seem possible. He wants the very best for all of you, and wants to give you everything! Just, *"Let go and let God."* Have faith and trust in Him. Know that through His love for you. *All things are possible*. A father never refuses his child for what he wants or needs. *"Ask and you shall receive."* Keep praying and turning your lives over to Him. He loves you so very much and is guiding you. *Know* that He is there for you whenever you need Him. Turn your life over to Him, and you will be happier than you could ever dream imaginable. He wants to give you everything. Simply, ask for it, and it shall be yours.

We love you very much,
BV and Christ

Dear Child,

Now more than ever, people need to turn to God. It is *not* easy to do so in this world today. It is not the *fad* to say you believe in Him and *know He is watching out for us.* People will say you are crazy. They say, "*If it's meant to be, it's up to me.*" People think they have total control, and are in charge of everything. Little do they know that they could not take one breath without God's help. He sat on the sidelines for some time now, just watching as the human race self-destructs. Pray. Pray always and in all ways. Be mindful of God in every moment. Do not let *fear* capture your heart and soul. Fear is the opposite of love. It makes no room for growth—only death and destruction.

It is not easy being a Christian today. You will be ridiculed for your beliefs and looked down upon as a fanatic and a *weak person.* Little do they know how powerful you can become with God's help. With God, everything is possible. *World peace* for instance. If people prayed for *world peace,* you would have *world peace.* No one would put up with the violence or fighting. Peace and love would be the norm, and the standard form of behavior. "*Let go and let God.*" He is the only one who can intervene and change the world. He so desperately wants you to turn to Him, and not continue on your destructive path. Negotiate and talk with one another. It is so *vitally important.* Have faith, hope, and love. Never before have these three points meant so much. Practice loving yourselves, and your neighbors daily. Turn to God for everything. *All is possible with God. Do not give up. God would never turn His back on you. So, do not turn your back on Him.* He loves you so very much and only wants the best for you. You mean so much to Him. Can't you see that? Don't destroy yourselves. *Learn to love one another, and live together in a peaceful world. Grow up!* Be kind to one another, as God is kind to you. *Now* is the time to act. Change your ways and be kind to one another. It is not too late. Do this and changes will come about for the better. *Know* that God loves you very much and is guiding you.

Never before in the history of mankind have you become so close to extinction. *Act now!* Be good, and turn to God. *It's that easy.* What you are trying to do is much more difficult. Playing God. How ludacris! No one, or thing, can take the place of God. Get off your high horse, and love your *true God*. He is there anxiously awaiting your prayers. *It's not too late. Act now!*

God loves you so much and wants to give you the world. All you have to do is ask Him for it. Your wish is His command. He just wants you to be happy with this life. You are creating your own misery. Is that what you want? To be miserable your entire life? God plans such happiness and fulfillment for you in this life. Just reach out, and ask for His help. He will make sure this will come about. He is always there for you, and in all ways. He loves you so very much. Believe in Him as He believes in you. Never doubt His unending love for you. He is there for you until the end of time. Simply tell Him what you want, and you will receive it. But remember to turn your life over to Him. He so much wants to participate in your life. He is thrilled about your *true potential,* and what you really can become, given His help and direction. Just, *"Let go and let God." All is possible with God.* Believe in Him, and *know* that He is there for you. He answers all prayers. So, continue to ask for: *world peace;* God's intercession with our world leaders; and the conversion of the evil ones. He will hear your prayers and answer them.

Stay close to Him, and *never doubt His love for you. Do not give up! He is with you always and in all ways.* Keep paying for our world. Miracles do happen. Believe in Him. Have strong faith and *know* that all is well.

We love you very much and are guiding you.

BV and Christ

Dear Child,

Now remember to pray daily for: *World peace*; God's intercession with our world leaders; and the conversion of the evil ones. This is *very important*. Now more than ever in the history of mankind, has man come so close to extinction. Pray daily for peace in our lives, in the world, and with our neighbors and loved ones. God so much wants to give you the world, if you would only ask for it. Yes, He hears your prayers and answers them. He is a loving and merciful God. One so eager to love and please you, and slow to anger. His mercy and patience are endless. *Know* that He is there for you at all times, and in all ways. Never doubt His love for you. You are never alone. Stay close to Him always. He loves you so very much, and only wants the best for you. *Never doubt his love for you.* He so loves the world that He gave His only son. He does not want this world to end. It is a creation of His love for you. You, through prayers and action, can return this planet back to its original *"Garden of Eden."* You need to love God with your whole heart and soul, and your neighbor as yourself. If you follow these two commandments, you can have *peace-on-earth*.

Now more than ever, you need to rise above your differences, and love your neighbor and enemies. You are all a part of God's creation, which was good and pure. But somehow you managed to destroy most of it. There is still *hope*. By returning to God, He will show you the way of peace and happiness. Just put your life into His hands. He will guide you, and turn things around for you. Place your hope and trust with God. Through your faith, He will make things better for you. He is the only one who can do this. This needs to be accomplished sooner, rather than later. God hears all prayers and answers them. Just when you think everything is hopeless, He creates *miracles! So, keep your strength in Him. Trust in God, and know that He is there for you! He hears your prayers and answers them. Stay close to him. Do not turn your back on Him. He would never turn His back on you.* Stay close, and *know* that He is there for you, always and in *and all ways. Do not give up on Him, He would not give up on you*. Use your *free will* and choose God to guide you throughout your life. Do not place your faith into today's society or mankind. Mankind, left to his own means, will destroy himself. *Do not let this happen. Use your free will and choose God*! He is patiently waiting for you. Please do this, and do it *now*! The time is growing short for mankind. Turn your lives over *to God now*! He will set the crooked way straight!

Miracles happen every day. He has the *power* to change things immediately!

Place your faith in Him, and do it now!

We love you very much and are guiding you.

BV and Christ

Dear Child,

Thank you for coming once again. We appreciate your devotion and dedication. Now let's get down to the plan at hand. God wants to save the world, but we need your help. Continue, daily, to pray for: *World peace*; God's intercession with our world leaders; and the conversion of the evil ones.

It won't be long now before the war is over, thanks to everyone's prayers and devotion. God hears your prayers and answers them. Continue your devotion of Him long after the war. This is a lifetime process. God needs to be a part of your daily life in order for you to achieve abundance with everything. Through His intercession, you will be able to accomplish the tasks you were put on this earth to do. He will help you get right to the heart of things. Through His love and guidance, you will be happier than you ever dreamed possible. You will be *at peace*. Remember, give everything to God, and He will handle it. No need to worry about anything. His love for you is endless. Continue to place your life into His hands. He will mold you into His image and likeness. Each day, you will become more loving, forgiving, and merciful. These are the gifts only God can pass onto you. Stay close to Him, and He will reward you. Speak of Him often to everyone you meet. Be *mindful* of Him in every situation. Have faith, trust, and hope in Him. Love Him, as He loves you. *"Ask, and you shall receive." Never doubt His love for you.* It is endless. He is a very kind, loving, forgiving, and merciful God.

The time will come when you will need to act. We will guide you every step of the way. Remember, *God speaks through silence.* So, remain quiet, and He will guide you.

It's never too late to turn your life over to God. You will be happier than you could ever dream possible. He is waiting for you …

Never think too much about the future. It is not here yet. When it arrives, we will be there to guide you. So, *do not worry* about anything. We are handling everything.

We so much want to be a part of your daily life. To guide you, and instruct you on the way the world could be. Stay open and love God. He loves you so very much.

Remain strong under criticism. We will be there at your side. Never doubt God's love for you. It is endless. Be strong, no matter what happens. We are there with you always and in all ways.

Yes, the war will end soon. Continue to pray for: *World peace*; God's intercession with our world leaders; and the conversion the of evil ones.

The world can be restored to its original *"Garden of Eden."* This can be accomplished through prayers.

God performs *miracles* every day. Just, *"Ask, and you shall receive."* He hears your every thought and wish. Do not give up on Him. He would never give up on you. Stay close to Him at all times. He will guide you and protect you. Never be afraid. He is always there at your side. Trust in Him. Believe that He performs miracles, and have faith that *all is well.*

It was wonderful having you here the past few weeks. Please remain close to us. We will visit you wherever you may be. Never doubt our love and devotion to you. Just *ask*, and we will continue to send messages. These are so necessary for our world today. Continue to pass them along to your friends. Before you know it, many people will be receiving these messages, which are so important for the survival of the human race.

Encourage people to turn to God with their troubles. Tell them to pray daily. God hears our prayers and answers them. Miracles happen every day. Place your faith, hope, and trust in God. Never give up on Him. He would never give up on you. Stay close to Him. He will guide you. *"Be still and know that I am God."* Be quiet and hear God's words for you. *Stop and listen to Him. He will guide your every step, and you will never feel alone.* Trust in Him, and you will be happier than you could ever dream possible. *"Let go and let God"* into your life. You will never be sorry. Peace and happiness will enter your life. Let your life be guided by God. It's the only way to achieve happiness in this world. *Stop* and *listen* to Him. He is there for you, always and in all ways.

Remember to check in with us on a daily basis. We will continue to give you messages. Just pray for strength and guidance, and your prayers will be heard.

We love you very much and are guiding you.

Love,
BV and Christ

Dear child,

Even though today is a gloomy day, it's nice to have you close by here. You may hear the same things over and over again, but we cannot stress to you enough to pray each day for: *world peace*; God's intercession with our world leaders; and the conversion of the evil ones. If everyone in the world prayed for this, your world would see *world peace*. Continue to pray daily. Do not give up *hope*. Miracles do happen each and every day. It's important to stay close to God. He will guide you with everything you do and say. Never worry about a thing. Place all of your anxieties and problems into God's hands. He will take care of it all. Do not waver in your faith. Stay strong and close to Him. Many people will endure many hardships before the conversion process is over. Yes, some people can learn quickly, while others need to go through turmoil and destruction in order to learn. Keep praying for the world. People are working in heaven, as well as, earth to achieve *world peace*. Keep up the good work. Pray daily. Stay close to God, and don't worry. Let your faith conquer all. Do not let fear creep into your psyche. Only allow love and peace. Have faith, hope, and trust in God. He will see you through this unstable time. Yes, more events will occur in this world in order for people to stay close to God. He so much wants mankind to return to him. He wants to help you to become happier than ever, and to be at peace. This is a much better offer than leaving mankind left on his own. Left to his own devices, mankind would destroy himself. Sorry to say this, but it is true. You see evidence of this statement in the world today. Do not fear or hesitate in turning your life over to God. He is pure love! What could be wrong with that! He has unconditional love for mankind, and is so compassionate and merciful. Never fear his love for you. It can only bring about good. I know it is a leap of pure faith to turn your life over to God, but it is so very rewarding. Never, in the history of mankind, has man been on the brink of extinction. Mankind has turned its back on God! How foolish! What can you accomplish without God? Absolutely nothing!

Stay close to God. Be happy with his unconditional love for you. Feel comforted and cared for by Him. *Never doubt His love for you. He is with you always and in all ways. It's never too late to turn to Him. He will be waiting with open arms. He loves you so very much, and is guiding you every step of the way.*

Now more than ever, mankind needs to turn to God. It is absolutely necessary for the survival of the human race. Yes, this is a test, as is all of life on earth. A chance to *return to God*, and make that choice freely. Yes, God will help you once you turn to Him, but it is up to each and every one of you to choose God over evil. He cannot make that choice for you. You have *free will*, and only you can make that choice. Once you choose God, He will greet you with *open arms*. He will love you unconditionally and help you every step of the way! But you must take the first step by choosing God, and He will take care of the rest. That is why you are here on earth. To do what it takes to *return to God*. Yes, it is a great learning place, but what most people are searching for is God, and they don't even know it. Eventually, if they work hard enough, they will find the path to God. It is so important that you turn your life over to God. It is essential for the survival of mankind. It's so very easy, yet so difficult for some people to do. Pray for the world daily. Pray for the people in this world. Pray that they may receive God into their hearts and minds so that this world will be made a better place. Pray that leaders can give up their *egos* in order to negotiate *for the good of mankind*. This is essential for *world peace*. I know we are discussing a moment of great conversion, but it is essential in order to save the human race. You are that close to becoming extinct! Some people in this world hate America, and would like to see it obliterated off the face of the earth. They would be happy to use their *weapons of mass destruction* in order to do so. When will mankind learn to negotiate and talk with one another about their differences? This all seems to be accomplished after a war, not before one. This time, there will be no one left to negotiate with after the war. *Please, please, please listen and talk to one another.* There really are not that many differences among you all. You have much more in common than you can imagine. Just put greed, ego, one-upmanship, and superiority aside, and talk with one another. God will inspire you as to what to say to each other. *Peace* can be achieved in your lifetime in a gentle way, not in a hostile way. Mankind needs to proceed with *discussions of peace*, and not war. Put aside your differences, and concentrate on your similarities. You will find that your love of family and your God are important to the whole human race. So, put together a means to work *peacefully* for the sake of mankind. Look at ways to save your planet environmentally. Feed the starving people of the world. God gave you plenty of food. Maintain an attitude of helping each other instead of destroying one another. God will help you achieve this every step of the way. It is a change of mindset. Having *peace* instead of war. Helping each other, instead of killing one another. Loving one another, instead of hating one another. Back to the basics. Be happy for one another, not jealous or envious of another. Have a win-win approach to life, instead of a lose-lose one. It's a mindset for the *good of the whole*, not just a chosen few. This world can be a much better place, but remember *peace* begins with you and your life. Make *peace* with family members and friends. Ask God to help *achieve peace* throughout the world. He hears your prayers and answers them. Each individual can do their part to achieve *world peace* by bringing peace into their own homes. If this were done by each and every individual, a new mindset and attitude would permeate throughout the human race. War would not be tolerated as an option. You are not powerless. You do have control and freedom of choice. Start with *peace* in your own home, then spread it among friends, and watch what happens. All of mankind wants a better life. This is achieved through God, and not war. God bridges. He is pure love. Love last for an eternity! Open up your hearts and let God into them. Let love into your hearts. Turn your lives over to God, and He will do the rest. It's actually very simple. God is the solution to all of our problems. Turn to him for everything. Note that all is well. Place your hope, faith, and trust in him, and know that all will be taken care of for you. You will be at *peace. Peace* that only God can give you. Believe that He is with you always and in all ways. Stay close to Him, and let Him guide you throughout your life.

We love you very much and are guiding you.

Love BV and Christ

Dear Child,

We so needed to speak with you. We want you to get the word out to everyone that God loves them so very much, and He wants all of mankind to turn their hearts and souls over to Him. It's that easy! If everyone turned to God, you would have *peace-on-earth*. So, continue to pray daily for: *world peace*; the conversion of the evil ones; and for God's intercession with our world leaders. It is imperative that you do pray daily for these things. God hears your prayers and answers them. Now more than ever, people need to turn their hearts and souls to God. He is waiting … Your world would be a much better place with God on your side. Things would come to you so much easier and in a gentle way. It is possible to have everything you ever wished for with God on your side. Be *open* to His love for you. He wants to give you everything! Most of all *peace*. What a gift. Stay centered and calm, and God will take care of everything. He loves you so very much, and only wants you to be happy in this life. Happier than you have ever dreamed possible. Just, "*Let go and let God.*" Now is His time to rule, not Satan's. Yes, there is evil in this world, but good will conquer evil. Keep the faith. Have faith, hope, and *trust* in God. He will make the crooked way straight. Remain close to us and the sacraments, and *know* that all is well. This is all going according to God's "*Divine Plan.*" There is nothing that God won't do or accomplish. He will rule supreme in the end. Stay close to Him. Trust in His love and mercy for you, and *know* that all is well … All of the events today are occurring according to God's "*Divine Plan.*" He does not want to hurt or punish you. He only wants you to turn to Him. When you don't, He needs to do something to capture your attention. It is so very important to turn your hearts and minds to God. He is with you always and in all ways. You are never alone. He is with you. Guiding you at all times. So, do not lose faith, or think that God is not there for you. You are His most precious gift, whom He gave His only son to die for you, so that you may be saved. Make the conscious choice to turn to God. Allow Him into your life, and watch what happens. Your worries and fears will be gone because you know that God is handling everything. Everything is possible with God on your side, and nothing is possible without Him. He rules supreme, and wants you to be part of His kingdom. You must continue to do good deeds on earth. Never judge another person. Only God knows what that person is really about, and you don't. All of you have intricate lives. Only God knows what is in the depths of your souls. *So, never judge another person.* You have no authority to do so. If you become angry with someone, simply ask the Lord's blessing on that individual. That person will soon change before your very eyes. God handles everything. He hears and answers your prayers. *Trust* is the key factor in loving God. His ways are different than yours. He is looking at the whole picture. While you just have a fraction of information regarding any given situation. So, keep your faith and hope in God. Love Him with your whole heart and soul, and obey His commandments. Be kind to one another. Love each other as God loves you. Remember, the two most valuable commands are: love God with your heart, mind, and soul; and love your neighbor as yourself. These are the two most powerful commands God has made. By observing these two commandments, all of the others will be obeyed. He needs you desperately to get the word out to others. Help restore *hope* in their lives. Give them a reason to live for. Help them to find God once again. Pray for their conversions. Ask for God's help in everything you say and do. No need to worry or fear. God is handling it all …

We love you very much and are guiding you.

Love,
BV and Christ

11-20-08 am

Dear Child,

Yes, today is a quite peaceful day. I hope you enjoy it. Please remember to pray for: peace-on- earth; the conversion of the evil ones; and for God's intercession with our world leaders. It's *very important* that you do this each and every day.

Now for the task at hand. Pray for your world, and all of its inhabitants. This is a time of grave danger. Many nations are vying for positions of power. This brings about aggression and war. Pray for a softening of their hearts and enlightenment of their souls. This will bring out the *wisdom* which they most desperately need. With *wisdom*, they can rule affectively. With *wisdom*, they can negotiate. With *wisdom*, they can be *just* and *know* the right thing to do at any given moment. It is imperative that you pray for these things. Remember, God hears your prayers and answers them. Your world can change, and for the better I might add. However, you need to *include God* in all that you say and do. Only God can bring about the change that is so desperately needed and no one else. God, through His *"Divine Intervention,"* will bring about *"Peace-on-earth."* Remember, you will see *"Peace-on-earth"* in your lifetime. It will happen, hopefully, sooner than later. Pray, my child, that all people *turn to God* in order to save your planet. This is imperative that you do this each and every day. Pray for the good of everyone. Their souls need to be saved. They are so lost. They do not know where to go, even to find God. Most of them don't even realize they are searching for God. God is the answer to all of their troubles. He is their salvation. Pray for these people. They need your prayers.

Yes, you will see *"Peace-on-earth"* in your lifetime. The *peace* that was meant to be. Sooner or later, mankind will realize that war is not the answer. You need to come from *common ground* in order to negotiate. You all need to get along! You have a *global economy* and need each other! When will you realize, you cannot have one without the other? You have grown *dependent* on one another. Now, grow to respect and love one another. You all need to work together to save your planet for it is in peril.

The pollution is killing it. Many life forms are dying. Soon mankind will die as a species, unless you all band to work together to save your planet. Don't you realize this urgent situation? Turn to God now for help! He will guide you, and work miracles to save you and your planet. It is that easy. Simply get past yourself, and let God be *"in charge."* Only God has the answers to your problems. Only God can heal your planet and the people in it. God is your *hope, light,* and *salvation. "Let go and let God."* He will handle everything. He will lead your world into a bright new day. He is the *alpha and omega.* The all and end all. Let Him love you, and shower you with graces and blessings. He only wants you to have an abundantly happy life. He wants you to be *open* to Him. He wants you to love Him with your whole heart and soul, as He loves you.

So, begin now. Open your eyes, mind, and heart to God. Let Him shower you with *faith, hope and abundance.* Let Him love and guide you. Be aware that He is with you always and in all ways. He will never leave you. Feel confident and happy in His presence. And know that all is well …

We love you very much and are guiding you.

Love,
BV & Christ

Dear Child,

Welcome back! How wonderful it is to see you this snowy retreat morning ... It truly is a great time of anticipation ... One in which our Lord made the *supreme sacrifice* to come and save your world ... I was so happy to be His instrument. Yes, He was *quite active* in my womb about this time many years ago. He was leaping for joy to come into this world. He was full of awe and wonder. He only saw the best in everyone and everything ... He saw great potential for this world. He is still full of *hope* for your world. He only wishes that everyone would *turn to Him* in order to save it once again. My child, be true to your prayer life. Remember to pray daily for: *Peace-on- earth*; the conversion of the evil ones; and for God's intercession with our world leaders. It is *vitally important* that you do this each every day, and encourage others to do too.

Yes, my love, it is time to reflect. Go within, and be at peace with the Lord. Feel His presence in you and around you. *Know* that He is with you always and in all ways. It is necessary to be *mindful* of Him with all that you say and do. It's not easy, but necessary in order to give your world *hope,* for better days are coming. You will see *Peace-on-earth* in your lifetime. God hears your prayers and answers them. You must pray for *peace*, and it will come. Not only to you, but to your world. God's "*Divine Plan*" is at work. Better days are coming, and with great anticipation. You will celebrate the birth of baby Jesus, who came to bring *peace* to the world. Keep Him in your heart and soul. Experience the joy of this advent season. The anticipation of great joy, love, and peace is about to give birth to your world. Turn all of your troubles over to God. Let Him handle them. They will *work out better* than you can ever dream imaginable. Experience this *blessed season* of advent. Go within, and experience a deep relationship with God. He is here waiting for you. Let Him into your life. Experience the joy of His love. Experience Him deeply and profoundly in your heart. Become the joy, hope, and love that

Christ so wants to show the world. Be His instrument. We will instruct you as to what to do and say. No need to worry, never think. Go in *peace* to love and serve the Lord.

Know that we love you very much and are guiding you.

Love,
BV & Christ

Dear Child,

Welcome back! It is always good to see you. Remember to pray daily for: *Peace-on-earth*; the conversion of the evil ones; and for God is intercession with our world leaders. It is *vitally important* that you do this each and every day.

Now for the task at hand. Your leaders are preparing to pass the health care bill. This will bankrupt your country. Pray that it does not happen. God hears your prayers and answers them. Do not give up *hope*. Help is on its way. The ships you see at night are all part of God's *"Divine Plan"* to help rectify things on your planet. Yes, they are here to help you. Do not fear. Help is on its way throughout the universe. You have sounded the alarm with your prayers, and God is answering them.

Yes, you will see *"Peace-on-earth"* in your lifetime. It is coming my child so *be patient.*

Do not worry or fear of anything. Place your troubles into God's hands. He will handle them, and better than you could ever imagine ... No need to micromanage a thing. Simply, *"Let go and let God,"* and *watch* the process. God is with you, my child, always and in all ways. *Stop, listen, and feel* His presence around you. He is always with you. You are never alone. He experiences everything with you. He is with you my child. Constantly encouraging you. He wants you to be *thankful* for His abundant blessings upon you. He wants you to appreciate each and every moment. He wants you to be here and now. Accepting His abundance by the minute. He loves you so very much my child, and only wishes for you to *return to Him.* So, work very hard in this life to look at the bright side of things. Encourage others to do so too. Give them *hope*. Restore faith and love into their lives. Let them know that things will get better. They just need to *pray* and turn to God for their answers. Remember, help is on its way. You are never alone. We love you very much and are guiding you.

Love,
BV & Christ

Dear Child,

We love you. Welcome back! Thank you for taking the *frigid walk* over to be with us. We appreciate your hard work and dedication.

Please, remember to pray daily for: *Peace-on-earth*; the conversion of the evil ones; and for God is intercession with our world leaders. It is *vitally important* to say this prayer. God hears your prayers and answers them.

Now, my child, many changes will occur in your world. Do not be afraid for we are with you always and in all ways. It's not easy at times, but stay true to your prayer. Do not allow the *ways of the world* to cause you to *despair*. Only God has the answers to all your world problems. People need to *turn to Him* for answers. His Divine Plan is *world peace*. So, have faith and hope in Him, and He will guide you with His love. It is that simple. We love you and are guiding you. It is necessary to remain *close to us* in order to be saved. With these upcoming changes, many people will *despair or die of freight*. They need to remain anchored in God, and He will guide you. *Know* that *all is well* no matter what happens. You are part of God's chosen ones. You are His children. Do not falter in your faith. Remain strong. Remember, you are *never alone. We* are with you through it all. It does not matter what people say and think. Remain close to us. We will guide you. It can be an easy transition if you remain *close to us*. God is with you always and in all ways. You are never alone. For He is with you through it all. Allow Him to guide you. Allow Him to nurture you. Allow Him to comfort you. He is with you through it all. Let Him into your life, to live in your hearts and souls. When you do this, you will have no need to think. He will guide your every move. He will tell you what to say and do. He will instruct your every thought. Become His instrument of love and peace so you can convey His message to the world. Especially now, during advent when the world awaits the birth of the Son of Man. Jesus is our hope and love. He will bring about *peace-on-earth* once again … He is the *"Prince of Peace."* *Now* is the time for *peace*. Peace in your heart, mind, and soul. Peace in your families and peace in your world. It is time to stop fighting, and have *peace-on-earth*. Please, please, please remind everyone of this during this Christmas Season. Advent is a time of great anticipation. It is a time of great joy, awaiting the birth of the *"Prince of Peace."* Take baby Jesus into your heart. Become the *peace* the world needs. Practice acceptance. Practice patience and humility. Practice being *pure* love, for that is what God is, and He wants to share it with the world.

Never question the hour or time these events will take place. Just *know* that they are coming. Stay in the *present moment*. Let God guide you through it all. It is not too late for the world to turn to Him. It is time, *now*, to open up your mind and heart to God. He will accept you with *open arms*. It is not too late. He is patiently waiting your arrival.

Remember, stay close to God, and He will guide you. *Know* that all is well …

We love you very much and are guiding you.

Love,
BV & Christ

Dear Child,

Welcome back on this cold winter morning. Thank you for making the effort to come and be with us. We love you, and are happy you are here.

Now for the task at hand ... Remember to pray daily for: *peace-on-earth*; the conversion of the evil ones; and for God's intercession with our world leaders. It is *vitally important* that you do this each and every day.

Your world is *in shambles* my child. The government is collapsing. People are at war, and your nation is void of God. How sad because America was built as *"One Nation Under God."* What happened to that principle? *"In God We Trust"* is on your dollar bill. When will people turn to God again for help? Aren't you in dire straits already? Must it become much worse before people will turn to God? How sad to be void of Him in their lives. With God, all is possible. Without Him, nothing is possible. When will people wake up and realize what a role God plays in their lives. He is at the very core of their being. Life would be so much easier *knowing* that God is with you through it all. You would have no need to worry. God would handle it all for you if you would only ask for His help. He is patiently waiting for you ...

Yes, my child, a *new world* is coming, and soon I might add. All of this is happening according to God's *"Divine Plan."* Trust in Him. Have faith in Him, and know that all is well ... You have no need to know the time or date of such events. Just live each moment as it comes being directed by God's will. When you live *in the moment,* you will be happier. You will become more appreciative and thankful for God's help. You will see His love in everything. Begin to look at the bright side of everything. There is a reason for it all. Yes, it is to become closer to God. You are all a part of God. He just wants you to *return to Him.* Just surrender to His love, and He will do the rest. It's that easy. Life can be easy and carefree if you just place your faith, hope, and love in God. He will guide your every move. Love Him and trust Him. He is guiding and protecting you. He loves you so very much. You have no need to worry about a thing. You do not even need to think. Just *listen* to what God is telling you to do, and act upon it. It's that easy.

So, my child, for now we will say goodbye, and look forward to speaking with you soon.

We love you very much and are guiding you.

Love,
BV & Christ

Dear Child,

Welcome back! What a great surprise to meet with you one more time before Christmas. Continue to pray daily for: *Peace-on-earth*; the conversion of the evil ones; and for God's intercession with our world leaders. It is *vitally important* that you do this each and every day.

Now for the task at hand. Pray for your world my child. The healthcare bill is about to be passed, and it could bankrupt America. Never before has your country been in such dire straits. Please, please, please pray daily for it. God blessed America, and He needs you *all to return to Him*! Must you lose *everything* before you do! This is a *warning*! Return to Him *now* before it is too late. He can move mountains. He can return America to its proper leadership before it's too late. Encourage everyone you meet to pray. It is necessary in order to give America back its freedom. The time is *now*, do not wait! I implore you to pray, and encourage everyone to do so, too!

My child, the time is drawing near when you will be celebrating the birth of the Christ child. How wonderful! What an amazing gift God gave to this world! He gave His only son to *save this world*! Celebrate His coming! Ponder on this marvelous gift to mankind! God is so magnificent! He loves you all so very much! Return to Him with your entire heart, mind, and soul! Do it *now!* I implore you. *Now is the time to return to God! I implore you to do this now!* He is waiting with open arms for you. He loves you so very much. Show Him how much you love Him by opening your heart and soul to Him. He is yours forever. Do not worry about the future. Simply concentrate on the here and now. Ponder this great *gift* to mankind. I know you are not deserving, but *be thankful* that God is so good to you … Love Him with your whole heart and soul, and *know* that all is well.

We love you very much and are guiding you.

Love,
BV & Christ

Dear Child,

Welcome back! It's wonderful to see you again. Please, please, please remember to pray daily for: *Peace-on-earth*; the conversion of the evil ones; and for God's intercession with our world leaders. It is *vitally important* that you do this each and every day. Please, tell everyone you meet to do so too.

Now for the task at hand. Child, pray for your world leaders. They must get beyond their own *egos*, and rule the world according to the people's wishes. They represent the people. They are not *above them*. They have been elected by the people to be their governing body. They have lost sight of their responsibilities *for the people*. They have been overtaken by power, control, and greed. How sad. These vices will destroy your nation. Pray, that they change their ways. Your world needs miracles, *now* more than ever. Pray for these changes to occur quickly, for the sake of your world! God hears your prayers and answers them. Be at *peace* knowing that help is on its way. God's *"Divine Plan"* is at work! He wants to restore *"Peace-on-earth,"* but you must pray for it, my child. God hears your prayers and answers them. God wants to restore your planet to its original *"Garden of Eden."* He wants your planet to become what it was originally intended to be. One of peace, love, and happiness. Mutual sharing and respect for each other will be in the consciousness of every individual on earth. *Love* will rule supreme. People will love God with their whole heart and soul, and love their neighbor as themselves. This is what God had intended your world to be when He first created it. So, *pray* that God enacts His plan quickly, in order to save your earth. Remember, that mankind was created with *free will*. Now is the time to use it, to bring about *peace*. Pray for *peace*, and encourage everyone to do so too. Give people *hope*. Give them reasons to go on living in a *positive manner*. Talk about God with everyone you meet. They need to be reminded of Him. They need to know that they could not even draw a *breath* without Him. They need to be *mindful* of Him in all that they say and do.

God loves you so very much, my child. He has given you so many graces and blessings. Be thankful for it each and every day! God loves you so very much, and only wants the best for you. Love Him with your whole heart and soul. Let Him guide you. He is there for you always and in all ways. Stay close to Him my child. He loves you so very much. Soon, your mission will be revealed to you. But for now, remain close to us. Stay calm and quiet in order to hear us. We will help you through it all. You are never alone. We are with you always and in all ways. Continue your devotion to us. *Know* that we are with you, and remember how much God loves you.

We love your very much and are guiding you.

Love,
BV & Christ

Dear Child,

Welcome back! It is *always* good to see you. Please, please, please, remember to pray daily for: *Peace-on-earth*; the conversion of the evil ones; and for God's intercession with our world leaders. It is *vitally important* that you do this each and every day, and encourage others to do so too.

Child, the time is coming when you will need to speak about God with *everyone* you meet! *People need hope!* They have *despaired*. Tell them how much God loves them, and how He is anxiously awaiting their arrival! They *need* to *hear* this message! They need to get closer to God, and turn to Him for *everything!* He is the *only one* who can change things. Through *"Divine Intervention,"* the crooked way can be made straight. Remind people to *pray*. God *hears their prayers* and *answers* them *better* than they could ever dream possible.

Yes, child, peace is on its way. Soon, you shall see a world full of peace, joy, and happiness. It won't be long now, when all of this shall be *behind you*. You shall be hard pressed to remember your world as it is today. Yes, you will love God with your whole heart and soul, and your neighbors as themselves. It truly shall be a *glorious time* to be alive! You are living in one of the most exciting times in the history of mankind! Never before has so much change occurred so quickly! All those who wish to cling to the *negative traits* shall perish. Child, look forward to these days for they are rapidly approaching. Christ's second coming is just around the corner. What a *miracle!* Everyone will get on their knees and thank God for His *"Divine Intervention."* It truly shall be a *glorious time* to be alive! You shall be *free* at last! *Free* to love God with your whole heart and soul, and your neighbor as yourself! Yes child, a *peace* like this the world has never known. Not since the time of Adam and Eve. Yes, your planet shall be restored to its original *"Garden of Eden!"* What a glorious time to be alive! All this can happen in an instant! God is capable of making these changes instantly! Simply *stop* and *watch* the process. You will be amazed of God's *great love* for you. He truly loves this world and everyone in it! Simply turn to Him for *everything*, and watch what *miraculous things* happen.

Now, child, feel free to go about your day, and *know* that we are with you *always* and in *all ways*.

We love your so very much and are guiding you.

Love,
BV & Christ

Dear Child,

Welcome back to our usual message room. Please, please, please, continue to pray for: *Peace- on-earth*; the conversion of the evil ones; and for God's intercession with our *world leaders*. It is *vitally important* that you do this each and every day.

Child, it won't be long now when your world shall change completely. All for the better I might add ... The time is coming when the world will need to hear these messages. Yes, you are our messenger. In due time, our mission for you shall be revealed to you.

Now for the task at hand. Pray for your world my child. It is in grave danger. Evil forces are plotting to take over America. *Pray* that this does not happen. God shed His grace on thee. You were made as *"One nation under God with liberty and justice for all!"* Your freedoms are slowly being removed from you. Soon, you could become a socialistic country bordering on communism. Yes, God is being removed from your schools, the military, and in general, it is not politically correct to discuss God. How very, very sad. No wonder drug and alcohol addictions are at an all time high in your country. People have *lost hope*! They are *despairing!* There is no one they can turn to in their minds. You need to talk about God with everyone you meet. You need to make people *mindful* of God. He is there for them *always* and in all ways. He will never leave you. Place all of your troubles into God's hands, and watch what miracles happen.

Yes, my child, Christ's second coming is almost here! Prepare for Him. Be on your best behavior. You do not know the hour or the day of His coming. But it is very, very soon! Your world *desperately* needs God, now more than ever. Have everyone turn to God *now* before it's too late. Too late to be saved.

Child, we will continue these messages on your retreat desert day. So, for now, go out and enjoy this beautiful day!

We love you very much and are guiding you.

Love,
BV & Christ

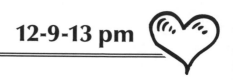

Dear Child,

Welcome back! It's through the grace of God that you have returned to us. Be thankful and grateful to God.

Child, much will happen between now and Christmas. Your life could change *completely*. All for the better I might add ... *Do not fear!* Simply *watch the process.* God does work in mysterious ways ... Allow Him to work *His magic* in your life, and watch what miraculous things happen. Child, this is a time of *great faith,* as you have experienced on your plane ride into Aspen. You *asked God for help* and you *received* it *instantly!* God answered your prayer, and you were able to safely land into Aspen after circling the airport for a while. This was a *significant gift* from God! He allowed you to return to the retreat on a timely basis. How wonderful! Continue to pray to God, and be our witness to Him with everyone you meet. Yes, people need to be *mindful* of Him in all that they say and do. Only God can change the world, and the hearts of mankind. Only God can make the crooked way straight. Remember, He hears our prayers and answers them. He will *never* let you down. *"Ask, and you shall receive!"* Be mindful of Him in all that you say and do.

Child, now is the time of great tribulation on earth. The world is changing and evolving as we speak. Much better days are coming ... *Do not let fear* get in the path of progress. Come from love. *Love heals all wounds.* Love conquers all! It is the only emotion that transcends space and time. It is eternal! God is love!

My child, I know you have a heavy heart with your *current situation,* but *very soon* this shall pass! Much better days await you. Place all of your *faith, hope, and trust* in God! He will handle it all. *Know* that all is well, and going according to God's *"Divine Plan."*

Everything happens for a reason, although at the time, things seem to not make any sense. Just thank God for the situation. It makes us grow deeper in our *faith,* and *trust* in God. Yes, many people are experiencing *extreme diversity* in their lives right now. Remain close to God, and He will guide you through it all.

Yes, there is a *spiritual battle* being fought right now. But remember, "*Good shall conquer evil!*" That is why things seem to be coming to a head. We are all *connected!* We need to turn to God *now* as one human family, and be ready and willing to follow Him, and do His work. It won't be long now, when Christ's second coming shall be upon us! Yes, it shall be a time of great joy! *Peace-on-earth* shall arrive with "*The Prince of Peace.*" What a glorious time to be alive! Look forward to these days, my child, for they are rapidly approaching. Soon, people shall love God with their whole heart and soul, and love their neighbor as themselves. What a glorious time to be alive!

Child, these *end times* are a birth of a *new nation*. One designed by God Himself. People shall live in *peace and harmony*. There shall be no need of a thing. It shall be as if heaven *descended* upon earth! People shall live long, happy lives. Yes, my child, this is quickly approaching. Look forward to these days. See the *good* in everyone you meet.

Remember, Christmas is coming. Not only are you awaiting the birth of baby Jesus, you are also awaiting the birth of your *new world*. They both are quickly approaching …

My child, I know you are tired, let's break for now, and continue this later.

We love you so very much and are guiding you.

Love,
BV and Christ

Dear Child,

Welcome back! It's always good to see you. We have reserved this spot just for you today.

Child, please, please, please remember to pray for: *Peace-on-earth*; the conversion of the evil ones; and for God's intercession with our world leaders. It *vitally important* to do this each and every day, and encourage others to do so too.

Child, your prayers are powerful. *Know* that, and remember to *"Ask, and you shall receive."* God hears every one of your prayers and answers them. He will *never* let you down. Place all of your *faith, hope, and trust* in Him. *Know* that all is well and going according to His *"Divine Plan."*

Child, the time is coming when your world shall change *completely*. Yes, you will not need to worry about a thing. We will be handling it all. Peoples *mindsets* shall change. They will *know* that God is handling things, and have complete *peace* and *harmony* in their hearts. Yes child, this miraculous intervention is about to occur. Christ's second coming is on its way. So many people are praying for His *"Divine help."* He hears your prayers, and is on His way. So, stay centered on God, and *know* that *all is well* and going according to God's *"Divine Plan."*

Child, it won't be long now when your world shall change *completely*. You no longer will have any *"stress"* in your life. It will be as if heaven descended upon earth for you. Remember, God hears your prayers, and will provide you with *everything* you need. It won't be long now. Help is on its way.

Yes, you were meant to attend this retreat for many reasons, but most of all, to feed your soul. You were starving! God heals all wounds. Just place your entire being into His hands, and He will handle it all.

Soon, you shall begin our mission for you here on earth. You will enjoy bringing people closer to God. They need to hear about Him. They need to *stop despairing* and have *hope*. They need to turn their lives over to God, and watch what *miraculous things* happen! You shall be our *instrument of hope*. You need to *"prepare"* people for Christ's second coming! They don't realize that it could happen any day now! They are asleep! They have given up *hope* and are *despairing*. They need to turn to God for everything so that their prayers can be answered. Remember, they need to use their *free will* to turn to God *now* before it's too late. Too late to matter. Too late to be saved.

Child, the time is coming when all of this *strife* shall be behind you. Much better days are coming, and quickly I might add. Simply enjoy each day while you can, and be grateful for all that God has given you. He is watching over you, and knows what you need *before* you can even ask Him! He wants *everyone* to turn to Him *now* before it's too late. So, encourage everyone to turn-to-God for *everything*! He hears their prayers and answers them. Only God can make the crooked way straight, and no one or nothing else can make it happen. Only God can move mountains. Only God can perform miracles. Use your *free will* to turn to God *now* before it's too late. It can't hurt! Nothing else is working. Give God a try. He is anxiously awaiting your arrival.

Child, the future of your world is glorious! All of mankind shall love God with their whole heart and soul, and love their neighbor as themselves. It truly shall be a glorious time to be alive! Look forward to these days my child, for they are quickly approaching. Never has earth experienced such peace! Everyone shall radiate with this peace! All strife, anger, negativity, and wars shall be gone. Your planet shall be elevated to a new *spiritual level*. One full of love and joy! All heartache and disease shall be gone. People shall live long, happy, healthy lives. What a blessing! You were born just at the right time in order to see *"Peace-on-earth!"* What a miracle! Look forward to these days for they are quickly approaching.

Now child, learn to live *in the moment*, while still looking forward to the future. In this blessed moment, exactly where God is *guiding you*. He speaks to you, and tells you what to do or say at any given moment. So, *remain present* to His help and love. He only wants the very best for you and nothing else. So, place all of your troubles into God's hands, and watch what miracles happen. He wants to give you it all. Simply, *stop, watch,* and *listen* to what He is telling you to do. He will *never* let you down. He is with you, *always* and in *all ways. Know* that He will never leave you. He is with you always, guiding and protecting you. So, stay centered, remain close to us, and *know* that all is well.

We love you very much and are protecting you.

Love,
BV & Christ

Dear Child

Welcome back! It's always good to see you. Please, please, please, remember to pray daily for: *Peace-on-earth*; the conversion of the evil ones; and for God's intercession with our world leaders. It is *vitally important* that you do this each and every day, and encourage others to do so too.

Now for the task at hand. Pray for your world, my child. Grave injustices are occurring throughout your planet. People want their freedom. They no longer wish to be *enslaved* by their government. Pray for their souls. They truly are suffering. Pray that they *turn-to-God* for everything! Only God can make the crooked way straight. Only God can change things and bring about "*Peace-on-earth*." Pray for His constant guidance and intercession.

Child, the time is coming when a great deal of change will occur on your planet. All for the better I might add. God is hearing your prayers and answering them. *Peace-on-earth* is on its way! What a glorious time to be alive! *Christ shall reign Supreme*! People will love God with their whole heart and soul, and their neighbor as themselves. All shall be made well. Much better days are coming. Trust us child. You are witnessing the dawning of a *new age*. One of peace, love, joy, and freedom! Freedom to do God's will, and love Him with your whole heart and soul. Free to pursue your many interests in this life, as well as, pursuing your God given mission.

Child, remain patient, love God with your whole heart and soul, and know that all is well and going according to God's "*Divine Plan*."

We love you so very much and are guiding you.

Love,
BV & Christ

12-9-14

Dear Child,

Welcome back! It's always good to see you. Child, please remember to pray daily for: *Peace-on-earth*; the conversion of the evil ones; and for God's intercession with your world leaders. It is *vitally important* that you do this each and every day and encourage others to do so too.

Child, continue to pray for your world on a daily basis. It is in grave danger. Evil forces are plotting to take over America due to its *weakened state* of its current leadership. Pray, that this does not happen! God hears your prayers and answers them. He will *never* let you down … Pray my child and encourage others to do so too. God has great plans for your nation. It must continue to be a great one. No other country on earth is like America! God shed His grace on thee. *Everyone* needs to turn to God for help! Only God can make the crooked way straight. Only God can perform miracles! Yes, my child, pray daily for America's protection.

You are living in a very tumultuous time. Everything seems upside down. People's morals and values are completely gone! No one cares anymore about your country's morality in politics, business, or family life. Pray that people change their ways and return to the values that made America great! We will assist you in whatever way we can. Pray for swift changes in your government. Remember, God hears your prayers and answers them. People need to restore their faith and trust again in God! Only then can these changes *for the better* begin to come about! Pray, that people have a change of heart and mindset. Your world *desperately* needs this *now*!

Yes, it's just about the time of our Lord's "Second Coming!" Be prepared. Stay alert. For you do not know the hour or the day He will appear. Remain close to us, and we shall guide you every step of the way,

My child, do not lose *hope* when you look at the ways of the world. Better days are coming! *Believe* that this is true! Yes, *Peace-on-earth* is on its way. God wants this for everyone, and not only for a chosen few. Encourage everyone you meet to turn-to-God *now* before it's too late!

They can *trust* Him! They need to place all of their troubles into God's hands, and He will make the crooked way straight! He is coming to rule over the entire earth. He is elevating your planet to a new spiritual level. One that He had planned for since the beginning of time! *Peace* is on its way, and very quickly I might add.

Yes, you shall see *Peace-on-earth* in your lifetime! We assure you of this. However, you need to encourage *everyone* to pray for *peace*! They need to be *mindful* of God in all that they say and do. Christ is coming again! All who are *with Him*, shall be saved! Those who are against Him shall perish! It can all happen in an instant! So be prepared. Do not let your guard down. God is your *truth, hope,* and *light*! He is the only one who can save you, and no one else. *Know* that This is *true*! Time is running out! The end days are near. Be prepared, and keep God in your heart and soul. *Know* that He is with your *always* and in *all ways.* He will never leave you. He is there for you guiding your every step. He loves you so very much, and only wants the best for you. Believe that this is true! Read this every day if you must. Until you firmly *believe* that this is *true*! His love for your is *abundant*! He is with you at all times. Feel His presence. He loves you so very much. He has forgiven all of your sins both in the past, and what is yet to come! So, remain very, very close to Him. You are being guided every step of the way. He is with you always. Feel His presence. *Know* that all that we tell you is *true* child.

Now we want you to go in peace to love and serve the Lord.

We love you very much and are guiding you.

Love,
BV & Christ

Dear Child,

Merry Christmas! How wonderful to see you again! Yes, this time many years ago, I could feel the *"Christ child"* stirring in my womb, preparing to be born. What a wonderous, yet frightening, time for us. We had to flee our home for our child's life, and had nowhere but a lonely stable to stay in for our child's birth. It was a wonderous, yet magical, night. What a miracle! When our baby Jesus was born! What a gift to the world! He was truly a gift from God. Our *little infant* was so precious! All the shepherds in the area came with their flocks following the *bright star,* which led them to our manager and baby Jesus. What a gift. All came in awe and wonder of Him. They knew He was a *special gift* from God, my child. It seems like *only yesterday* when the *Christ Child* was born. How magnificent! What a gift to humanity! Thank God for His gift of sending His only son to free the world. What a miracle!

Yes, my child, this gift is upon you. Receive His birth and great gift of kindness and redemption for all of mankind! Yes, my child, Jesus would have been born if you were the only *soul* on earth. That's how much God loves you! Thank Him for this my child. It is a great gift!

Thank your parents for giving you the gift of faith. Yes, one that seeps *very deep* into your soul. This gift will help you get through *any* hardship or difficulty in your life. This gift of faith gives *life*! It gives you *hope*. It gives you a taste of God's *eternal love* for you, my child. Thank God for this gift. Thank God for it all. Remember, only God can make the crooked way straight. Only God can perform miracles! *"Ask and you shall Receive." "Seek and you shall find." Know* that all is well, and going according to God's *"Divine Plan." Trust* us, for what we tell you is *true*.

Much better days are *in store* for you, my child. Ones filled with peace, joy, and happiness! God has a plan for you, and soon, very soon, it shall be revealed to you. Your days of *strife* are just about over. Place all of your troubles into God's hands, and *watch* the *miracles happen*. It's only a matter of time now, and all shall be made well. *Trust us* for what we tell you is *true*. We would *never lie* to you my child. Much better days are coming filled with peace, joy, and happiness! Yes, my child, these days are *almost upon you*.

Know that all is well, and going according to God's *"Divine Plan."* A plan that was enacted since the beginning of time.

My child, place all of your troubles into God's hands and, *watch* the miracles happen! Yes, my child, with God on your side, all is possible, and without Him, nothing is possible …

So, *know* that much better days are upon you. *Trust us,* my child. We are anxiously awaiting the start of your *new life* so our plan for you can be revealed to you. A much better life awaits you, my child, filled with love, peace, and happiness! So, place *everything* into God's hands, and watch the miracles happen.

We love you so very much, my child and are guiding you.

Love,
BV & Christ

1-6-15

Dear Child,

Yes, this gorgeous day was made just for you. Enjoy it, my child. Thank you for joining us today. Today is special. Made just for you. Enjoy the peace and calm it offers you. Feel *God's presence* in it all. He is with you always and in all ways. Yes, you are far from the maddening crowd in Florida. How wonderful! God picked you up, and placed you here in this *safe* environment. Yes, it is a miracle! He has *great plans* for you, and soon, they shall be revealed to you, my child. Your days of *strife are almost over*! Thank God! A *new world* and *life* are opening up right before your very eyes! Yes, my child, thank God for that. Your *freedom* awaits you. The time of sorrow and misery are *behind you*. A new day lies before you filled with peace, love, joy, and happiness! How wonderful!!

Yes, God has planned this for you since the beginning of time! Yes, He wants to give you it all. All you have to do is *ask* Him, and all shall be given to you. *"Seek and you shall find."* God is anxiously awaiting your arrival. He wants to give you it all.

Remain *conscious* of God with all that you say and do. Allow Him to *speak* through you. Become His *instrument* of love and mercy. Remember, only God can make the crooked way straight. Only God can perform *miracles.* Yes, He is the Alpha and the Omega. Soon, very soon, you shall experience Christ's second coming! Soon, very soon, you shall experience *"Peace-on-earth!"* Soon, very soon, you shall see all of mankind turn to God for everything! He shall be loved above all things! Everyone shall love God with their whole heart and soul, and love their neighbor as themselves. Thank God! What a miracle! Yes, this was all meant to be since the beginning of time. Your planet shall be restored to its original *Garden of Eden.* Yes, my child, this was all meant to be since the beginning of time.

So, take each day as it comes. *Know* that you are divinely guided and protected. *Know* that all is well and going according to God's "*Divine Plan.*"

Now go in peace to enjoy this wonderous day.

We love you very much and are guiding you.

Love,
BV & Christ

Dear Child,

Welcome back! It's *always* good to see you. Yes, continue to *trust in us* with all that you say and do. Remember, it won't be long now when all of this *strife* shall be behind you. *Trust us* for what we tell you is *true*. We would never lie to you or forsake you, my child. We are there with you *always* and *in all ways*.

Continue to meditate, going deeper to connect with God. He is there for you, my child. *"Ask and you shall Receive."* He hears your prayers and answers them. *Know* that this is *true,* child. He only wants the very best for you my child.

Child, the time is coming when your world will change *completely!* No longer will you have anger, wars, or negativity of any kind! God will *no longer tolerate this*! You shall have *peace-on-earth*! Yes, it is the time of Christ's second coming! A time when mankind shall use his *free will* to choose God over evil. With God, they shall love Him with their whole heart and soul, and love their neighbor as themselves. With evil, they shall perish! It's that simple. So, continue to love God with your whole heart and soul, and continue to love your neighbor as yourself. *Know* that much better days are coming! They will be filled with peace, joy, and happiness. Look forward to these days for they are quickly approaching. What we tell you is *true,* my child. Much better days are *in store* for you, my child.

So, go in peace now, to love and serve the Lord. Continue to appreciate each new day. Be thankful for all that God has done for you and given you. *Know* that all is well, and going according to God's *"Divine Plan."*

We love you so very much and are guiding you.

Love,
BV & Christ

Dear Child,

Yes, it is Mother's Day! What a beautiful day to honor our mothers, who have given so much to us. Thank God for mothers. Where would we be without them? They are our *teachers* and caregivers when we are small, and in later life, we get to return the favor, and care for them. Yes, life is a cycle. For everything there is a season under heaven. A time to be born, and a time to die. All is made well with God on your side. Believe this, my child. Any strife you may be feeling shall pass quickly. Much better days are coming, filled with peace, joy, love, and happiness. It shall be a time of *great love*, and a renewal of your spirit. Yes, much better days are coming, my child. Look forward to them, for they are quickly approaching.

My child, God has a plan for you, and very, very soon, it shall be revealed to you.

Yes, your life is changing in many ways. All for the better, I may add. *Trust* us, for what we tell you is *true*. A *new life* is opening up to you right before your very eyes. One filled with peace, joy, love, and happiness. God's love is showering upon you, my child. He loves you so very, very much! He only wants the very best for you my child. The days of strife and sadness are almost completely behind you. Remember, everything can change in an *instant*. Watch the process. Much better days are coming. Hold onto that thought, and look forward the future. It is a *rosy* one.

So, go in peace now to love and serve our Lord.

We love you very much and are guiding you.

Love,
BV & Christ

Dear Child,

Welcome back! It's always good to see you. Remember to pray daily for: *Peace-on-earth*; the conversion of the evil ones; and for God's intercession with our world leaders. It is *vitally important* that you do this each and every day, and encourage others to do so too.

Now child, remain very close to us in the days ahead. Many changes are occurring rapidly, all for the *better* I may add, and we shall guide you through them all. Yes, my child, the *truth* is being made know. Yes, my child, *good* shall conquer *evil*! Yes, my child, *know* that *all is well*, and being made well. These things we promise you. *Watch* as it all unfolds right before your very eyes. A *new day* is coming for you and *all* of mankind. *Watch* the process.

You are living in one of the most exciting times in the history of mankind! Your planet is being elevated to a new *spiritual level*. Yes, my child, all of these changes were meant-to-be since the beginning of mankind. *Watch* the process as it all unfolds right before your very eyes.

Yes, my child, these are very exciting times to be alive. God has such great plans for you! *Watch* as it all unfolds. We are guiding you through it all.

Never before, in the history of mankind, have so many changes come about so quickly! By remaining *very close* to Him, we shall guide you through it all. Remember, all of these changes are for the *betterment* of mankind. God wants you all to be *abundantly* happy! He wants you to be filled with peace, joy, love, and happiness! So, *watch* as it all unfolds right before your very eyes. Yes, a *new day* is coming, and very, very quickly I may add. This is your year of many changes, all for the better.

So, my child, go with a renewed h*ope, knowing* that all is well, and going according to God's *"Divine Plan."*

Now go *in peace* my child, to love and serve the Lord.

We love you very much and are guiding you.

Love,
BV & Christ

Dear Child,

Welcome back! It's *always* good to see you. Please, please, please remember to pray daily for: *Peace-on-earth*; the conversion of the evil ones; and for God's intercession with our world leaders. It is *vitally important* that you do this each and every day and encourage others to do so too.

Child, now is the time to *stop, wait,* and *listen* to what God is instructing you to do next. Then *act* upon it. He is guiding you my child. No harm shall come to you. *Know* that *all is well,* and going according to God's "*Divine Plan.*" A plan that was set in motion since the beginning of time. So, child, believe that we are with you through it all. We are guiding you every step of the way. No need to worry or fret. Simply *know* that *all is well* and being *made well.*

Yes, continue to pray for your country and your president. They are in dire need *of prayers.* Evil forces are attempting to usurp the power in your government, and take over your country. God will not allow this to happen! He blessed America, and will continue to do so. My child, *do not* give up *hope*! There is light at the end of the tunnel. Remember, things can change in an *instant*! *Watch the process. All* is being made well, and going according to God's "*Divine Plan.*"

So, my child, go in peace *knowing* that we are with you through it all. *Know* how much we love you and are guiding you.

Love,
BV & Christ

Dear Child,

We are so happy to see you once again. It has been a while. Child, please, please, please continue to pray for: *Peace-on-earth*; the conversion of the evil ones; and for God's intercession with our world leaders. It is *vitally important* that you do this each and every day, and encourage others to do so too.

Now for the task at hand. Child, remember *peace-on-earth* is at hand. God is guiding your President to meet with the leaders of the three different religions in your world in order to unify them, and come from their similarities, *not their* differences. He is using President Trump to help bring about "*World peace.*" Watch the process. *All* is being made well. A *new day* is dawning for *all* of mankind. God's "*Divine Plan*" is in action. *Watch* as it *all* unfolds right before your very eyes. The truth shall be made known. *Peace-on-earth* is on its way. Christ's second coming is just around the corner. *Trust us.* For what we tell you *is true.* We would *never* lie to you, my child.

Remember, God is with you *always* and in *all ways.* He would never leave or forsake you. Simply place your troubles into God's hands and *watch* His miracles happen. *Know* that all is well, and being made well.

Now is the time to *stop, wait,* and *listen* to what God is instructing you to do next, then *act* upon it. All is going according to His "*Divine Plan.*" God has great plans for you, my child, and soon, very soon they shall be revealed to you. Watch as everything shall *open up* right before your very eyes. So, *watch* as His miracles shall change your lives completely. Simply *know* that all is well, and being made well.

It won't be long now, when all of this *strife* shall be behind you! Yes, my child, a *new day* is coming for you, and all of mankind. *Watch* as God reveals to you His wonderous deeds. Simply *know* that all is well, and being made well..

We love you so very much and are guiding you.

Love,
BV & Christ

Dear Child,

Child, remember to pray daily for: *Peace-on-earth*; the conversion of the evil ones; and for God's intercession with our world leaders. It is *vitally important* that you do this each and every day, and encourage others to do so too.

Now for the task at hand. Pray for your world, my child, and its leaders. You are experiencing the most *pivotal time* in the history of mankind. It truly is a battle of good vs. evil. *Know* that good shall conquer evil! *Know* that all is well, and going according to God's *"Divine Plan."* A plan that was set in motion since the beginning of mankind. Watch the process, as it all unfolds right before your very eyes. Yes, my child, *all* is well and being made well.

It truly is a test in faith, to keep your eyes focused on God now, and His promises of better days. But *trust us,* for what we tell you is *true!* A *new day* is coming for you and all of mankind. *Watch* as it all unfolds right before your very eyes. Keep the faith. Have *hope,* and *know* that much better days are coming for you and all of mankind. Watch the process.

So, my child, whenever you become saddened or discouraged, simply place it all into Gods hands, and watch His miracles happen. A *new day* is coming for you and all of mankind! It won't be long now. *Peace-on-earth* is so very near. Christ's second coming is just around the corner.

So, hold fast to your love of God, and believe in His miracles. It is all being made well. Watch the process. God has big plans for you, and soon, oh so very soon, they shall be revealed to you.

So, go *in peace* now child, to love and serve the Lord.

We love you so very much and are guiding you.

Love,
BV & Christ

Dear Child,

Happy 4th of July! Enjoy your day, dear. It's a gift from God! Today is a *very special day* in America. It is filled with peace, joy, love, and happiness! God blessed America, and He continues to do so, even now. It is the greatest nation on earth! It is known as *"One Nation Under God with liberty and justice for all!"* Yes, you are a shining example for the world! Continue to pray for your country my child. It is in *dire need* of prayers. Its division will soon subside, and you will be united, once again, as one nation under God! Watch the process.

Now, back to you my child. *Know* that all is well, and being made well. *Know* that the truth shall be made *known*. *Know* that good shall conquer *evil*.

Child, now is the time to *stop, wait,* and *listen* to God instructing you on what to do next, then *act* upon it. Remember, we are guiding you every step of the way. We would *never* leave or forsake you. We are with you through it all, guiding your every move. Much *better days* are coming for *you* and *all* of mankind! Watch the process, as it *all* unfolds right before your very eyes. *Know* that much better days are upon us *now*! Watch the process, and look forward to these days, for they are upon you *now*! Remember, we are with you through it all. We would never leave or forsake you.

So, go *in peace* now, my child, *knowing* that all is well, and being made well. It's all part of God's *"Devine Plan."*

We love you so very much and are guiding you.

Love,
BV & Christ

Dear Child,

Welcome back. It's *always* good to see you. Please, please, please remember to pray daily for: *Peace-on-earth*; the conversion of the evil ones; and for God's intercession with our world leaders. It is *vitally important* that you do this each and every day, and encourage others to do so too.

Now child remain very close to us in the days ahead. *Change* is upon you. All for the *better* I may add. We are guiding you through it all. Soon, oh so very soon, your days shall be filled with peace, love, joy, and happiness! Look forward to these days for they are upon you *now!* Much *better* days lie ahead for you, my child. Soon, oh so very soon, God's plan shall be revealed to you. Remember, all was meant to be since the beginning of time. Watch the process, as it all unfolds right before your very eyes.

Child, remember to pray for your world! Change is upon it too! All for the better I may add. Yes, "World peace" is on its way. Christ's *second coming* is just around the corner! *Watch,* as it all unfolds right before your very eyes. Much *better days* are coming for you, and your entire world! Watch the process. It is all part of God's "*Divine Plan*" in action!

So, child, remain *very close* to us in the days ahead. We are guiding you through it all. No harm shall come to you. We are protecting you. God has a plan for you, and very, very soon it shall be revealed to you.

So, my child, go *in peace knowing* that *all is well,* and being made well. We love you so very much and are guiding you.

Love,
BV & Christ

Dear Child,

Welcome back! It's *always* good to see you. Please remain very close to us in the days ahead. Many changes are *in store* for you. All for the *better* I may add. Remember to *stop, wait,* and *listen* to what God is instructing you to do next, then act upon it. It's just a very short time longer, then *all* of this *strife* shall be behind you! Thank God!

Yes, my child, much *better days* are ahead for you. They shall be filled with peace, joy, love, and happiness! Look forward to these days, for they all are quickly approaching.

Now for the task at hand. Child, your mission is about to begin. Watch the process, and see how it all unfolds right before your very eyes. God is guiding you every step of the way. Soon, oh so very soon, your life shall be filled with peace, joy, love, and happiness! It is about to *open up* in so many new and wonderous ways. Remember, God is guiding your every move. Remain *open* to us. A *new day* is dawning right before you very eyes. Watch the process. See how *God's wonderous deeds* open up right before your very eyes. Yes, my child, all of this was meant-to-be since the beginning of time. Remain very close to us, and we shall guide you through it all. Much *better days* are ahead for you, and *all* of mankind. Watch the process, and *know* that all is well, and being made well.

So child, go *in peace* to love and serve the Lord. We love you so very much and are guiding you.

Love,
BV & Christ

Dear Child,

Do not worry or fret. *Know* that all is *well* and being *made well*. Now is the time to *stop, wait,* and *listen* to what God is instructing you to do, then *act* upon it. He is guiding your every step, my child! *Know* that this is *true*. We would never lie to you, my child.

Child, you are witnessing God's *"Divine Plan"* in action! Yes, things are changing rapidly! Watch as God's miracles unfold right before your very eyes. Much *better days* are coming filled with peace, joy, love, and happiness! *All* is being *made well*. Watch the process.

Child, soon you shall see a whole *new world* open up right before your very eyes. *Watch* as it all unfolds right before your very eyes. Soon, oh so very soon, you shall see a world filled with peace, joy, love, and happiness! *All* of mankind shall love God with their whole heart and soul, and love their neighbor as themselves. Watch the process and *know* that much better days are coming!

So, my child, whenever you become troubled, place everything into God's hands, then watch His miracles happen.

So, my child, go *in peace* to love and serve the Lord.

We love you so very much and are guiding you.

Love,
BV & Christ

Dear Child,

Welcome back! It's always good to see you. Remember to pray daily for: *Peace-on-earth*; the conversion of the evil ones; and for God's intercession with our world leaders. It is *vitally important* that you do this each and every day, and encourage others to do so too.

Now for the task at hand. Continue to *pray* for your world, my child. It is in *grave danger* of a takeover by the evil ones! *Pray that this does not happen!* Remember, God hears your prayers and answers them. He would *never* leave or forsake you. He is with you *always* and in *all ways.*

So, my child, whenever you feel troubled, simply place all of your concerns into God's hands. Then watch His miracles happen! Yes, my child, a *new world* is opening up right before your very eyes. *Watch* as it all unfolds. You are witnessing God's "*Divine Plan*" in action!

Know that *all* is *well* and *being made well.* Soon, oh so very soon, you will see a world full of peace, joy, love, and happiness! Yes, all of mankind shall love God with their whole heart and soul, and love their neighbor as themselves. It shall be as if heaven descended upon earth! Watch the process.

But, until then, continue to *stop, wait,* and *listen* to what God is instructing you to do, then *act* upon it.

So, go in peace now, my child, to love and serve the Lord.

We love you very much and are guiding you.

Love,
BV & Christ

Dear child,

Welcome back! It's always good to see you. Please, please, please, remember to pray daily for: *Peace-on-earth*; the conversion of the evil ones; and for God's intercession with our world leaders. Remember to do this each and every day, and encourage others to do so too.

Now for the task at hand. Your world is changing rapidly, my child. All for the better I might add. *Watch* the process, as God's miracles unfold right before your very eyes.

Now is the time to *stop, wait,* and *listen* to what God is instructing you to do, then *act* upon it. This morning was a perfect example of listening to God and acting upon it. God did not want you to go to San Diego right now, due to a sequence of events, which are occurring now! He wants you *here* to pray for the world! *Watch* as God's miracles unfold right before your very eyes.

Child, much that we ask you to do is based upon faith. You do not see the whole picture, but God does. He is guiding your every move! *Trust Him,* my child. He knows what is right for you. Continue to allow God to guide you. Remember, only God can make the crooked way straight. Only God can perform miracles, and no one else. Watch as His miracles unfold right before your very eyes.

My child, you will see a whole *new world* open up right before your very eyes. It's happening as we speak. It will be filled with peace, joy, love, and happiness. Look forward to these days, for they *are* quickly approaching! People will love God with their whole heart and soul, and love their neighbor as themselves. You will not even recognize your world this time next year. Simply *know* that much better *days* are coming, and quickly I might add.

So, go *in peace* now, my child, to love and serve the Lord.

We love you very much and are guiding you.

Love,
BV & Christ

Dear Child,

Welcome back! It's always good to see you. Yes, you were meant to be here today to pray for your world. Your prayers that good conquer evil are being heard. God will answer them. Watch as His miracles unfold right before your very eyes.

Now is the time to *stop, wait,* and *listen* to what God is instructing you to do, then *act* upon it. It won't be long, now, when your world shall change completely. All for the better I may add. Watch the process, and *know* that *all is well* and *being made well.*

Child, you are living in a time of great change. Watch as God's miracles unfold right before your very eyes. A *new day* is coming, filled with peace, joy, love, and happiness! It is all happening *now* as we speak. Remember, all of these changes were meant to be since the beginning of time. They are all part of God's *"Divine Plan."* Watch as it all unfolds.

So, my child, keep the faith and *know* that all is well, and being made well.

Now go *in peace* to love and serve the Lord.

We love you very much and are guiding you.

Love,
BV & Christ

Dear Child,

Welcome back. It's always good to see you. Please, please, please, continue to pray for: *Peace-on-earth*; the conversion of the evil ones; and for God's intercession with our world leaders. It is *vitally important* that you do this each and every day, and encourage others to do so too.

Child, now is the time to *stop, wait,* and *listen* to what God is instructing you to do, then *act* upon it. It won't be long now when all of this strife shall be behind you, my child. For what we tell you is *true.* We would never *lie* to you.

Child, you are about to witness many changes in your world. All for the better I may add. These changes were meant to be since the beginning of time. Watch as they *all* unfold right before your very eyes.

Yes, my child, you are about to witness *Peace-on-earth,* and Christ's second coming.

You are living in one of the most exciting times in the history of mankind! Watch as God's miracles unfold right before your very eyes.

Child, whenever you worry or fret, simply place all of your troubles into God's hands, then *watch* His miracles happen.

Child, so many changes are upon you now. You will not even recognize your world this time next year. Watch the process, and *know* that all is well, and being made well.

So, my child, go *in peace*, to love and serve the Lord. We love you very much and are guiding you.

Love,
BV & Christ

CHAPTER TWO

LOVE OF ALL MANKIND

Dear Child,

Good afternoon. It's good to see you once again. Welcome back. This afternoon we would like to continue our discussion about *love*. Yes, it is what makes the world go around. It extends to eternity. That is why your plea for life is so powerful, because it extends to the heavens, and God's love showers down upon you. Love is the greatest emotion you can have. It extends beyond time and space. It is infinite, God is infinite, and pure love. Acknowledge Him on a daily basis, and you will see the difference He makes in your life. He molds you into His image and likeness. He molds you into what He wants and needs as individuals in our world today. People who love and care for one another. People who help each other, and share their joys and sorrows, food and property. Yes, the world has enough food to go around to feed the hungry. No one should be left starving or hungry. You should love and care for each other, as God cares for you. Never let a day go by where you don't fail to tell someone that you love them. It is essential for their health and well-being, as well as, your well-being. Love is essential in our lives. *Know* that God loves you so very much. He would give you everything you ask for and more. He gave you life! He gives you freedom, peace and happiness. He is *pure love*. Never forget that, and *know* He works in your lives. He only wants the very best for you. Stay close to Him. Stay focused on Him.

Never allow anyone or anything to deter you from Him. He is the very essence of your life! He dwells in your being! Keep Him close to your heart. Allow Him to *think* for you. Allow Him to *act* for you! *Listen* to what He tells you to do, and *act* on it. Stay so very close to Him. He will never leave your side or abandon you. He is *pure love,* and only wants to share it with you. With His love, you will experience a peace and happiness that you have never had in your life! You will be ecstatic! His love for you is immense! Bask in His love. Allow Him to shower you with His good gifts. Open up your hearts and minds to Him. Let Him know that He is essential in your life. *Show up* to pray each day. Let Him speak to you through *silence*. Allow Him to help turn this negative world into a positive one. Allow Him to guide you.

Eliminate fear in your heart. Just open up, and let His love shine in you. What gifts He could give you, if you would just give Him the chance to do so.

I know it is difficult to understand at times, but let your belief in Him carry you through. Your faith will be the instrument by which He can perform His miracles. It will enable you to become more intuitive which is one of the gifts of *being silent* in centering prayer. You are present for God to work in your life. It's not something that requires effort. Only a discipline to *show up* each day for 20 minutes of *silence*. God does the rest. During these moments of prayer, you unite with everyone in the world, both past and present. All time and space ceases, and you are one with God! How wonderful! How incredible for God to shine His love upon you in this way. *"Be still and know that I am God."* That is what He is telling us. Our world has grown technologically, and very slow spiritually. That is why we are in the fix we are in now. Everyone is prepared to blow each other up! How ludacris! This is not God's plan for the world. He wants you children to get along with each other in peace and harmony. You achieve this by increasing your spirituality through prayer. *Please* incorporate God into your daily life. Allow the love for each other to return, and hatred to diminish. Let God into your life, and have a better life! Stop trying to control everything. Because in reality, you are totally out of control. Only God can control the universe and the world, not you. Allow God to work in your life so your ego can diminish.

Respect each other's needs and wishes. Help one another. Listen to each other. Have compassion and understanding toward each other. These are all qualities of *love*. Love one another as God loves you. Love God with your whole being. Be kind to yourself. Try your best, that is all you can do.

Remember, God loves you so very much and is guiding you. So, stay close to Him. *Show up* and pray on a daily basis. Listen to His wishes for you, and carry out His deeds. He will give you the strength and courage to do so. He will show you the way. No need to think or worry. He is guiding you. *Know* that you are a part of a bigger picture. You are a small cog in the wheel of the world. Have faith, and *know* that all is being done according to God's "*Divine Plan.*" "*Ask and you shall receive.*" "*Seek and you shall find.*"

Now go with God, and *know* that we are guiding you and love you.

Love,
BV & Christ

A Christmas Message 12-5-05

Dear Child,

Now for the task at hand … Remember to pray daily for: *World peace*; the conversion of the evil ones; and for God's intercession of our world leaders. It is not easy to be a follower of Christ today. The world does not want to keep Christ in Christmas! This is what Christmas is all about. The birth of our Lord. He came to save the world, and our world is turning its back on Him. How tragic! Look at all He has done for you, and still wants to give you even more. Yet, you turn away from Him. What is wrong with you people! Are you so caught up in yourselves that you no longer have room for God in your lives! How sad. How can you possibly be happy in this world and achieve redemption without God. You think you are so smart, yet you are far from the age of reason. When will you people *makeup* and return to God? He needs to become a part of your daily life. He needs to become a part of your heart and souls. When will you people learn this lesson? Must God bring total destruction among you, so that you would return to Him? Must He take such drastic measures to get your attention? What is wrong with you people? Why aren't you praying? Your world needs prayers now more than ever. Stay close to God for your own good. He can help you so much with your life. Hand all of your troubles over to him. Let Him guide you, and watch how easily your life will begin to flow. Never worry about a thing, for He is handling everything. Stay close to Him, for He loves you so very much. You have no idea just how much He loves you. You are the apple of His eye. Each day, take time to pray and be alone with God. He will perform wonders in your life, but you must first be *open* to His love and kindness. He so desperately wants to bond with you, but you must first be *open* to His love for you. All things are possible with God on your side, and nothing is possible without Him. Stay close to Him in all that you say and do. Be mindful of Him, for He is with you always and in all ways. Yes, Christmas is drawing near. It's a time of great joy and celebration, but *first* and *upmost,* keep God in your heart and soul. He will help you feel His divine presence this Christmas. Yes, it is a time of love and joy, but first keep God in your heart. The Christ child will speak to you. He came to save the entire world. Let Him into your heart, so He can begin His work through you. He will inspire you as to what to do and say. He loves you so very much. Turn to Him for everything. He will guide you, and take care of your problems. He only wants to love you, and make you happy. Allow Him into your life. Allow Him to transform you, so you will be made happier than you ever dreamed possible in your life. Allow Him to be with you at all times. Be mindful of Him, and allow Him to act through you. He loves you so much and is guiding you. You are His special angel. He loves you so very much. Stay *open* to His love and guidance. Allow Him to transform your life into *pure joy*. He is there for you, always and in all ways. Never doubt His love for you. It is eternal. Allow Him to be part of your life. Allow Him to work through you. Allow Him to be with you at all times. Allow Him to transform you. Become His instrument of *peace*. Our world needs *peace* now more than ever. Strive for peace and love in your heart. Speak of it to everyone you meet. Begin to convert the world, slowly but surely.

Yes, you will see *Peace-on-earth* in your lifetime. God will rule in the end. Keep the faith, and *know* that all is well. God's "D*ivine plan*" is in action *now*. Just go with the flow, and pray daily for: *World peace*; the conversion of the evil ones; and God's intercession with our world leaders. God hears your prayers and answers them. God knows you are trying. *Never give up.* He will guide you. You are never alone. He is with you always and in all ways.

We love you very much and are guiding you.

Love,
BV & Christ

Dear Child,

Welcome back! It's always good to see you. Please, please, please, remember to pray daily for: *Peace-on-earth*; the conversion of the evil ones; and for God's intercession with our world leaders.

It won't be long now child, when you will begin to see a great many changes occurring on your planet. All for the better I might add. These changes were meant to come about in order to achieve *peace-on-earth*. A peace like you have never seen before. One *all encompassing.* Not only will there be *peace-on-earth*, but that peace will permeate every single human being in earth. It truly shall be a glorious time to be alive! Look forward to these days, my child, for they are rapidly approaching. Soon, all of mankind shall turn to God for everything! Soon, you shall all operate as one conscious body radiating in God's holy light. Yes, you will be so mindful of God with all that you say and do, that you shall want the very best for every living being upon earth! It shall be a time of *great giving.* The strife, anger, negativity, and wars shall be gone! Only *peace* shall prevail. God's love shall reign supreme! You all shall operate as one human body of beings only wishing to please God in every way you can. You shall be *mindful* of Him with all that you do and say. There is nothing that you would not do for God, nor He for you. It shall be the most glorious time your planet earth has ever experienced. Yes, it shall last over 1,000 years. People shall grow deeper and deeper into God's *peace.* Love shall permeate your planet. What a miracle! God fulfilling His *"Divine Plan"* of *peace-on-earth.* You shall join many other evolved planets experiencing this *peace.* These beings shall come to you *in peace.* They shall explain how they have operated for thousands of years *in peace.* They shall explain to you all that they have accomplished. It shall be fascinating to see and hear, for you have existed in the dark ages for too long. Now is the time to be elevated to a new *spiritual level,* both for you, and your planet. The other planets have existed for many years *in peace,* and have accomplished so very much, both environmentally, as well as, technologically. These planets have grown extraordinarily faster due to their *peace ethic*. Where planet earths growth has been stymied due to its war efforts. But soon that shall change. All for the better I might add.

Continue to strive to keep peace and love in your hearts. This is a great start. Remember, bigger and better days are coming. A whole *new world* awaits you. This has all been part of God's "*Divine Plan*" since the beginning of time. Now it is about to be initiated. What an exciting time to be alive! Hold onto your hat, for these changes will be occurring rapidly. Simply remain close to us, and we shall guide you through it all. So, never give up *hope*. Place your faith and trust in God, and watch what miraculous things happen!

We love you so very much, and are guiding you.

Love,
BV & Christ

Dear Child,

Welcome back. It's always good to see you. Please, please, please, remember to pray daily for: *Peace-on-earth*; the conversion of the evil ones; and for God's intercession with our world leaders. It is *vitally important* that you do this each and every day, and encourage others to do so too.

Now for the task at hand. Pray for your world, my child. It is in the midst of *great change*. Soon, you shall see a new form of government, currency, and major changes in attitude. All for the better I might add. These were all meant to come about since the beginning of time. What an exciting time to be alive! *Peace-on-earth* is in the making. Soon, God's plan shall be enacted, and all on earth shall turn to Him for everything. Their hearts and souls shall be filled with His *"Divine Love,"* and all will be made well. People shall love God with their whole heart and soul, and love their neighbor as themselves. No longer will people be *put down,* or enslaved. You shall be free to love God with your whole heart and soul. Never before, in the history of mankind, have things been so wonderful! Not since the days of Adam and Eve *before* they ate from the *forbidden tree. Peace-on-earth* is being established as we speak! Look forward to these days, for they are rapidly approaching! Child, you shall experience a *peace* like the world had *never known*. This *peace* shall reign in the hearts and souls of *everyone* on earth. You shall show it through your love of God and your neighbor. Your only wish will be to *serve God* with your whole heart and soul. It truly shall be a glorious time to be alive!

So, child, *know* that much better days are coming. Hold onto that thought when times get tough. Remember, they are only temporary, and that this too shall pass.

Now go in *peace* to love and serve the Lord.

We love you very much and are guiding you.

Love,
BV & Christ

Dear Child,

Welcome back! It's *always* good to see you. Please, please, please, remember to pray daily for: *Peace-on-earth*; the conversion of the evil ones; and for God's intercession with our world leaders.

It is *vitally important* that you do this each and every day, and encourage others to do so too.

Child, it won't be long now, when all of this *strife* shall be *behind you*. Thank God! This time of *strife* is almost completely over! Thank God! Yes, God wanted you to use this *hiding time* wisely. He wanted you to strengthen your faith, nourish and strengthen your body, and restore your mind and soul! Yes, my child, you have been through a terrible ordeal all of these years. Now is your time to *regroup* and start over. It is time to make *God* the center and *focus* of your life. Allow the *Holy Spirit* to guide you in all things. *Know* that all is *well* and going according to God's " *Divine Plan."* Yes, this plan was enacted since the beginning of time. Now it is coming to fruition. *Watch* the *process*. It is a *miraculous* one! God has *great plans* for you, my child, and soon, very soon they shall be enacted. Watch the process, and *watch* the miracles happen. Remember that God only wants the very best for you, my child. So, *"Let go and let God."* He is with you through it all. Guiding your *every step. Know* that *all is well,* and going according to God's *"Divine Plan".* Watch the process.

Child, it won't be long now when all of this strife shall be *behind you*! Much better days are coming, filled with peace, joy, and happiness! Look forward to these days, my child, for they are *quickly approaching*! *Trust us.* We would *never lie* to you. Much better days are coming! The *best* is yet to come! We only want the *very best* for you, my child. We need for you to become *our instrument* to bring the word of God to many people. Soon, very soon, your mission for us shall begin! *We are working very hard,* behind the scenes, to rectify this situation. Soon, very soon, all shall be *made well.* It is part of God's plan for you, my child. Just like you are *safe and sound* now my child. Thank God every day for this miracle! There are more miracles to come. Watch the process.

Child, now is the time of *great faith*. Your people are being elevated to a new *spiritual level*. One filled with peace, joy, and happiness. Watch the process. Those who wish to *hang onto their negative ways,* shall perish! God will no longer *tolerate* wars, anger, rage, and hostility! No, enough is enough! He made you all to *get along* with each other and *not* fight and kill one another. *No,* this was not part of His "*Divine Plan.*" His plan is only for the *good* of all mankind. You have used your *free will* to bring about all of this hatred, wars, and negativity. That was not in God's Plan! Now He needs to rectify the situation. Watch the process. Soon, very soon, the days of peace, joy, and happiness are almost upon you! What a *glorious time* to be alive!

So, continue to place all of your faith, hope, and trust into God's hands, and watch the miracles happen. Simply, "*Let go and let God.*" It truly is a *wondrous time* to be alive.

We love you so very much my child, and are guiding you.

Love,
BV & Christ

CHAPTER THREE

OUR FUTURE

Dear Child,

Thank you for coming, once again, to hear our message. The time for mankind to change and turn their lives over to God is very *short. Act now.* The hour is near. Now, more than ever before in the history of mankind, has man been this close to extinction. The hour is near. Turn your lives over to God. He hears your prayers and *answers them.* Things can still change in the world. *Now,* more than ever, *people need to turn their lives over to God. Be open to Him. Open your hearts to Him.* You will be happier than you could ever dream possible. The kingdom of God is at hand, now, more than ever. *Turn to God for everything.* He hears your prayers and answers them. Life can become so *easy* for you, if you would just *place everything into Gods hands.* He will handle everything. No need to worry or wonder how it will be accomplished. Just, *"Let go and let God."* He loves you so very much and so deeply. He does not want you to *destroy yourselves.* Just turn to God, and ask *him to intercede* in this madness. You have *free will* to do this, and *God will handle everything.* You have to ask Him for help. This is where your *free will* comes into play. *"Ask and you shall receive."* If you do not *ask,* you will not *get* what you want. Please, please, please, *turn your lives over to God. It is so vitally important!* Do it now, do not wait. The time is near, do not hesitate. People do *not understand the depth of destruction* that can come upon you. Is this what you want? What good is brought about through fighting? That does not work anymore. *War is not the answer. Turn to God,* and *peace will come upon you,* and all of *mankind.* You will have a *peace* that you never dreamed possible. Only God can give you this. No one or nothing else can do this for you. *God is the answer. Pray to Him now. Do not hesitate. Now is the time to turn to God for everything. He hears your prayers and answers them. Pray now. Do not hesitate. The time is near for the survival of the human race, pray now. It is not too late! Do it now! Do not leave mankind up to his own devices. Ask God to intervene.*

Pray daily for: Peace-on-earth; God's intercession with our world leaders; and the conversion of the evil ones.

Tell everyone you meet to *pray* to God for *peace*. The more people pray for *peace,* the faster it will come about, but we need to pray for "World peace", and do it now!

It is *not easy being human* these days. Your souls cry for *peace*, yet your emotions say war is eminent. Nonsense! *Peace* is at hand if you ask for it. God performs miracles every minute of every day. He wants to help you so very much, but you need to ask Him for the help. He answers all of your prayers. *"Ask and you shall receive."* The human race needs to change its ways now. *Do not hesitate, the time is now.* Never before in the history of man, has mankind come so close to *extinction. Act now before it is too late.* The time is at hand. Turn to God. He hears all prayers and answers them. It is Gods ways, not our ways, that are important.

Everything flows according to Gods plan when you let Him take over. It is not your ways, but God's ways. You become much *more peaceful* when you hand things over to God, and let Him handle things. You will be living in the moment! Which is all we ever have really, only *this precious moment.*

So, go in peace, and *know* that God is watching out for you. He hears your every prayer and answers them. *Know* that He is with you always, and in all ways. He loves you very much, and is guiding you. Just be mindful of him now and every moment of your day. Be aware, He is with you always, and in all ways. Just take time to *stop and listen.* He is guiding you, and loves you so very much.

God be with you,
BV & Christ

Dear Child;

Y es, the time is drawing near. *Do not be afraid. God is with you always, and in all ways.* The world is very troubled right now, but *it can change for the better. Mankind needs to turn to God for everything*! Only God can turn things around. This grave situation can be lightened in a second with God's intervention. *Know* and *believe* that *God can perform the miracle to rectify the situation.*

Now is the time to pray, and pray hard every day for: *World Peace*; God's intercession with our world leaders; and the conversion of the evil ones.

We need to listen to God's message of love and mercy for our world. Never before has mankind been in such a state. Totally removed from God, and left up to his own devices. Given *free will* mankind can either destroy himself, or turn to God for assistance. Hearing the cry for help, God would respond immediately. God never refuses the cry of His children. He so much wants you to turn to Him for everything. He will guide you, and make you happier than you could ever imagine. Do not allow the fear and despair of the world to creep into your daily lives. K*now* that God is there with you, filling you with peace and love. Love is the opposite of fear. Fear and distrust show lack of faith in God. With God, all things are possible. God performs miracles every day. His love for you is immense. He wants to shower you with gifts of love and kindness. He wants to give you whatever you ask for, simply ask Him, and you shall receive.

There are times when these messages will become difficult, however, continue to *carry on*. There is a silver lining with all of these events. Remember, God loves you more than anything in the world, and would *give you anything to make you happy.* Simply, *"Ask and you shall receive."* *Know* that He is there for you at all times. *Do not give up. Do not give up your faith.* God will succeed, and win over evil. The good will outstand the bad. *Peace and love will prevail. Know and believe it.*

Pray for the world to be saved. Now is the time for everyone to *return to God. Do not debate over war issues.* Pray, pray now and every time the thought of war enters your head. *Pray for peace. Peace* is entirely possible if you continue to pray, and turn to God for all of your needs. I urge you to pray daily for: *World Peace;* God's intercession with our world leaders; and the conversion of the evil ones.

Peace is entirely possible if you pray and turn to God. He loves you so very much and wants to grant us our every wish. We just need to *ask,* and we shall *receive.* Never doubt God's love and mercy for you. *His love for you is endless.* Just turn to Him, so He can give you *everything!* Bring Him back into your daily lives. Make room for Him in your hearts and souls. This world could be a much better place to live in, once you turn your lives over to God. It can become, once again, a *"Garden of Eden." Pray daily, and ask* for God's help. It shall be given to you. *Know* that He is with you always and in all ways. Never doubt His love, mercy, and forgiveness for you. It is boundless. Have *faith,* and believe that through God's intervention, our world can change for the better. *All things are possible with God.* Miracles happen every day. *Believe in Him, and things will change for the better.* Do not ask why or how, just *know* that *through God, all things are possible.*

We love you very much and are guiding you.

BV and Christ

Dear Child,

Today, more than ever, people need to *turn to God*. Only God can elevate the spirituality of this planet. You are all one in a collective consciousness. When someone is hurting, you all are hurting. When someone is happy, everyone shares in that happiness. *That is why talking things out is so important*. You need to understand, and love one another. You all were created *equal* in the eyes of God. Now you all need to live together harmoniously. That is what will save this planet. Mutual love and adoration of each other. As God said, *"Love me with your whole heart and soul, and love you neighbor as yourself."* These are the most important commandments. If you live by these, you would have *peace-on-earth*. It is time for all of you to learn how to get along with one another. Make *peace*, not war. Everything can be negotiated, and talked about in a peaceful way. Do not despair or give up. God is watching over you, and guiding you. He loves you so very much, and wants to give you everything. Just, *"Ask and you shall receive."* Do not worry about how God will do this, simply *know* that *he performs miracles, and answers your prayers*.

Never before has mankind been so *far from God*. It is tragic because He loves you so very much, and only wants you to use your *free will* to return to Him. *Know* that He is there for you always and in all ways. Never doubt His love for you. It is endless. He wants you to help bring about *"Joy to the world."* This can be accomplished through your love of God, yourselves, and your neighbors. Stay close to Him at all times. He is waiting patiently for you.

Sometimes we belittle ourselves, and do not want to ask God for the things that are very important to us. We feel we are not worthy, *nonsense!* God wants to give you the world! All you have to do is ask Him for the answers of your heart's desires. So, *"Ask and you shall receive."*

God is a warm, loving and merciful God. Eager to please, and slow to anger. He wants the *very best* for you, but you must use your *free will* to get it. God wants you to turn to Him for everything. *"Be still, and know that I am God."*

All things are possible with God. Nothing is possible without Him. Have faith, hope, and love. God said, *"Be strong and trust in me. Know that I love you very much, and am guiding you. Stay close to me, so I can protect you. Never lose sight of me. I would never abandon you. I love you too much to watch you perish. That is why I have sent my mother to you. She gives you messages. She tells you how to live your life and stay close to me. So, do not give up. We are all pulling for you."* You just need to use your *free will*, and choose God above everyone and everything.

It is not easy being human these days. We are asking you to *rise above* your human potential, and soar into the spiritual realm. Just, *"let go and let God handle everything."* He will, if you let Him. It is that easy. Give up your *control*. It is false hope. Place your faith, hope, and trust in God. Only He can change things, *know* and *believe* that He can and does.

Remember to pray daily for: *World peace;* God's intercession with our world leaders; and for the conversion of the evil ones.

God will guide you in the very best way He can, without troubling you. He has a gentle way to accomplish many things. Place your life into His hands. You will be happier than you could ever dream possible. You will be *living in the moment* without a care or worry because you *know* He is handling everything. Just *know* that all is well.

The world needs to *stop* and listen to God. He will guide all of you into a better life. *Know, believe, and trust in Him for everything.* It is your choice. Use your own *free will* to *turn to God.* If you choose solely to continue along with your own means, you are destined on a path of death and destruction. So, simply turn to God. He will make your life much *happier* and *worry free.* Remember, once you turn your life to God, you will be happy and free. What a wonderful reward for doing something so simple. God wants you with Him, *now* and *forever.* With God, you are off on a fascinating journey. Without God, you are in for much sorrow and suffering. Make your choice. You have *free will.* Life with God, or death by your own means. It is never too late to turn to God. He is patiently awaiting your arrival. Stay in touch with Him, and He will guide you through *everything.* Have faith, hope, and trust in Him. Love Him with your whole heart and soul. Never leave Him behind. He would never forget you. With God you can accomplish *everything.* Without God, life is a struggle. Stay close to Him. Let Him know that you love Him, and He will make you happier than you could ever dream possible.

He is there for you always, and in all ways. *Be mindful of Him in the moment.* He is with you, and watching over you daily. He is kind, loving, merciful, and a forgiving God. Join Him to save your planet. Let Him know how much you love Him, and thank Him for His blessings. He wants to give you the world. So, stay open and pray daily. He loves to hear from you, and wants to grant you your every wish.

Love,
BV and Christ

Dear Child,

M any changes are occurring in our world as we speak. Your government is in the process of a radical overhaul. The churches too are becoming more unified. Good changes are in process. It is time to think, step back, and be still. Allow God to do His work. Watch how things are changing for the better. Be happy to be alive at this moment time in history! Your world is gradually becoming more spiritual. With that comes the change in a *collective mindset*. Everyone will want *peace!* And *peace* is at hand. Never doubt God's love for you. He hears your prayers and answers them. He wants the very best for you. Stay close to God, and He will guide you through all of the *upcoming changes* in your life. Your life will become easier to manage. You will begin to flow, and hear God's voice in all that you say and do. He loves you so very much and is guiding you. Simply be open to His message of love for you. Just stop and listen, and all will be revealed to you. It's that easy. Just get out of your own way, and remain *open* to God. Allow Him to enter your life, and watch how the changes will manifest themselves. All for the better. This is how your life will become easier. You will not act until given the signal from God. He will tell you what to say and do at any given time. Your life was meant to be with God. Allow Him to work in your life. Be aware of His presence and actions in your life. Let Him shower you with His love by allowing Him into your life. So much good can be accomplished with Him acting through you. You can influence many people with God's message inside of you. He will guide you through everything. Simply turn your heart and mind over to God, and He will do the rest. He so very much wants to be a part of your life. Allow Him to act through you. Allow Him to love and guide you. Allow Him to be a major part of your life. By doing this, you will feel a sense of *peace*. Things will come easy for you, and flow through you. You will not act until you are spoken to by God. Let Him into your life, to love and guide you, and help make a difference in this world. There are many people in this world that are receiving messages like you. You need to act on them to *get the word out*. All is well with God on your side. You have nothing to fear. Let God into your life, and He will guide you through everything. No need to think or worry. Simply turn all of your troubles and problems over to God, and He will take care of them. His love for you and the entire human race is immense! He does not want you to fall by the wayside. He wants you to gather His seeds of wisdom, and spread the word to give mankind *hope*. This is so desperately needed in our world today. Let people know that God loves them, and is guiding them through every situation. No need to worry or fear. Simply turn your troubles over to God. He is your saving grace. He conquers all. No need to *doubt*. His love conquers all. Know that good will conquer evil. Simply turn your heart and soul over to God, and He will handle everything. It's that easy. He is there for you, always and in all ways. Never doubt His love for you, and you will be made happier than you ever dreamed possible. We love you very much and are guiding you.

Love,
BV & Christ

Dear Child,

It's good to see you again. Welcome back! Please remember to pray for: *Peace-on-earth*; the conversion of the evil ones; and for God's intercession with our world leaders. It's *vitally important* that you do this each and every day.

Now for the task at hand. Pray for your world and its leaders. You are living in one of the most difficult periods on earth. The great darkness before *the purification*. Darkness meaning *without God*. The entire world has turned away from God. You need to help bring people back to God. This world will be *of God* once again, and He will reign supreme! But until that happens, you will be going through a *great purge*. One which will not be easy, but *extremely necessary,* in order for "*World peace*" to come about. This purge will bring about climate changes, earthly disasters, and government changes. All is necessary, in order to *get people's attention,* and bring about "*World peace.*" People need to turn their focus toward God, not war. Toward peace and love, not hatred and violence. They need to help one another, as God helps them. They need to love their neighbor as themselves. They need to love God with their whole heart and soul. All this needs to come about in order for "*World peace*" to happen. It will happen in your lifetime. Change is occurring rapidly. Enough is enough of war and violence. Enough bloodshed! All this needs to *stop* in order to have "*Peace-on-earth.*" God loves you. He doesn't want you to *destroy* one another! Learn to get along in peace and harmony! We will show you the way. It's not difficult! But first, you must turn to God. Then He will transform you, so you can carry out His work. Only God can change your attitude and mindset to one of peace and love. Not war and aggression. God so wants to save you all, but you must turn to Him and *ask* for *help*! What better time than this, when you are on the brink of *disaster*! How bad must it become before you *turn to God*! You cannot accomplish it all by yourself! You need "*Divine Intervention.*" Only God can get you out of the mess you have gotten yourselves into! Only God can save you, and *no one else*! So, wise up and *turn to God*. There's no better time than *now*. Now is the time to turn to God! He will handle everything! Just trust Him! Have faith in Him, and love Him, as He so generously loves you! He is beckoning your attention! He will answer your prayers, if you just ask him! So, turn your lives over to God before it is too late. *Now is the time to turn to God for everything!* There's no better time than now! I'm begging you to turn to God now! We are at the 11th hour! Act now before it is *too late*! God wants you to turn to Him, so do it now! Only God has the answers to your *world problems*. Only God can make the crooked way straight. Only God knows what to do, and when to do it. *Listen to Him*! Turn your heart and soul to God. He will guide you! He will also see to it that you are made happier than you could ever dream possible. Just by turning to Him. Isn't that wonderful! It's that easy. So, get out of your own way, and turn to God. He has the answers to everything! He has the total *power* and *control* over it all! He is the all and end all. The alpha and the omega. Love Him. Listen to Him. Turn your heart and soul to Him! I beg that you do this *now* instead of waiting one more day.

We love you very much and are guiding you.

Love,
BV & Christ

Dear Child,

Welcome back! It's wonderful to see you again. It has been quite a long time since we spoke to you. Please remember to pray daily for: *Peace-on-earth*; the conversion of the evil ones; and God's intercession with our world leaders. It is *vitally important* that you do this each and every day.

Now for the task at hand. Your world is in jeopardy. An attack is being planned against your country. Please pray that it will not happen. God hears your prayers and answers them. It is not easy, but necessary to pray each and every day for your country. God shed His grace upon America. It is the land of the *free*. Pray for its continuance and guidance. God has great plans for America. He will continue to bless it, with your prayers. Do not fear, just pray.

My child, many changes are in store for your world. It is necessary in order to achieve *"Peace-on- earth."* Just pray, and *know* that God is with you *always* and in all ways. Be good, my child. Stay close to God. Let Him guide you. Listen to what He tells you to do, and act upon it. Now more than ever, your world needs prayers. Pray for *peace*. Pray that God enters every new heart and soul. Pray that your planet be lifted to a new *spiritual level*. One that promotes *peace*, and embodies it in every individual on earth. This will happen. It is all part of God's *"Divine Plan."* You are about to begin a *new era* on earth. One in which Love reigns supreme! God is pure *love!* His presence will be felt by everyone. No longer will you live in darkness. Light will surround you. Earth will be restored to it's original *"Garden of Eden."* Do not ask how, just know that this will happen, and soon I might add. So, look forward to a new life on earth with happiness and joy. Be hopeful. Stay *mindful* of God with all that you say and do. Know that a new day is coming. One which will lift the hearts and souls of everyone on earth. It truly is something to look forward to. But in the meantime, stay close to God. Let Him guide you through it all. Do not fear, for He is with you always, and in all ways.

We love you very much and are guiding you.

Love,
BV & Christ

Dear Child,

Welcome! Remember what we told you to do. To pray daily for: *Peace-on-earth*; the conversion of the evil ones; and for God's intercession with our world leaders. It is *vitally important* that you do this each and every day.

Now for the task at hand. Pray for your world, my child. It needs prayers now, more than ever. Pray for its leaders. Pray for the government. Pray that they do their *very best* for your country. Pray that God enters their hearts and souls to be *mindful* of Him in all of their decisions. Pray that love conquers all. Pray that love and compassion are installed in the hearts and minds of everyone on earth. Pray for humanity. Pray that everyone is kind to one another. Pray that they all have giving hearts. Pray that they *forgive* one another. Pray that your planet rises to a new *spiritual level*. One in which war is *not an option*.

My child, it is time for change, but in a new good way. We have enough hatred, war, and killing going on. We need to rise to a higher level. One of forgiveness and understanding. One in which God is the center of everyone's life! One in which all will be *mindful* of God in all that they say and do. This is *vitally important* in order to achieve "World peace." God does not choose to do it all alone. He needs your help. So, continue to pray for your world and everyone in it.

A new day is coming when we will no longer speak of such things. People will automatically help one another. They will be kind to one another. They will love God with their whole heart and soul. They will love their neighbor as themselves. Yes, my child, you will see "Peace-on-earth" in your lifetime. What a marvelous day it will be, when the fighting *stops!* You will then see earth *restored* to its original "*Garden of Eden*."

So, for now, my child, pray for your world, and everyone in it. Pray that they all become *conscious of God*, and do the right thing.

Otherwise, they will perish. So, be good my child. Help your family and neighbors. Soon, our mission for you will be revealed. Stay calm and close to God.

We love you very much and are guiding you.

Love,
BV & Christ

Dear Child,

Why do you suffer so much? Place all of your troubles into God's hands. He will handle everything. He alone has the power to make things right. He can perform miracles! Your miracle is coming. The wheels are set in motion. Trust in God. Have faith in Him, and *know* that all is well. It's not easy for you right now, my child. This truly is a test of faith. Have courage, my child. We are making the crooked way straight. You deserve a much better life than this one. We are going about making the changes, as we speak. Do not fear, for all will be well, and soon I might add. Soon, you will be free of worry. Free of fear, and free of those who hurt you. No, you will not die. But the ones who are mean to you will perish. It is time the world rise to its new *spiritual level*. A time of great change. The negative ones will perish, and only the good will remain to carry out God's mission for your world.

My child, stay close to us. Have faith that you are not *alone*. Only God can protect you. Only God can make the crooked way straight. Only God hears your prayers, and answers them. Help is on its way. You have suffered long enough. It is time that the mean ones perish! It is a day of reckoning. Only the good will survive. The bad will perish.

Child, live moment by moment. Let the dark ways fall by the wayside. Do not panic, for we are with you. No harm shall fall upon you. Trust in God, Believe in Him, and *know* that all is well. Stay strong, my child.

We love you very much and are guiding you.

Love,
BV & Christ

Dear Child,

Welcome back! It's always good to see you. Please, please, please pray daily for: *Peace-on- earth*; the conversion of the evil ones; and for God's intercession with our world leaders. It is *vitally important* that you do this each and every day.

Now child, remain close to us. Many changes are occurring in your world. *Do not be afraid*. Stay calm and close to us. We will guide you. It's not easy to watch empires crumble, but it will all turn out well in the long run. You need to pray and *stay calm*. We will guide you. All of these events need to happen in order for change to come about. These are positive changes, and they will affect all of mankind. Trust us. We know what we are doing. Your world leaders are out of control, and many of them must be stopped in order for mankind to survive. So, stay close to us. We will guide you through these changes. You will be safe and secure. Do not worry, for we are with you always and in all ways. *Peace-on-earth* needs to happen. We will destroy all who are not peaceful. These people are being moved to another planet, far away from here. We want your world to evolve to a more *peaceful* place. One in which everyone will exist in peace and harmony. Yes, you will see *Peace-on-earth* in your lifetime. Now is the time to have great faith and trust in God. He is guiding you, my child. All of mankind is under duress. They need to turn to God for answers. Those who are with Him, shall remain. All others, shall perish. It's that simple. You can no longer exist as a *waring planet*. You shall perish if you continue on this course. God's *"Divine Intervention"* shall succeed. Those who are for God will survive, all others shall perish. So, my child, remain close to Him. Speak about Him with everyone you meet. Encourage them to pray, and ask for God's help and mercy. Remember, all can be accomplished with God on your side, and nothing can be accomplished without Him. So, pray daily, remain close to God, let Him act through you, and *know* that all is well, and going according to God's *"Divine Plan."*

We love you very much and are guiding you.

Love,
BV & Christ

Dear Child,

Welcome back! It's always good to see you. Remember to pray daily for: *Peace-on-earth*; the conversion of the evil ones; and for God's intercession with our world leaders.

Now for the task at hand. Your government is crumbling. Soon you will have a new leader. One who is strong, and will restore your constitution. He will have the wisdom of Solomon, and will get your country back on its feet! It is what everyone is praying for. God hears your prayers and answers them. People need to be mindful of God in all that they say and do. It is time to take responsibility for your actions. Things are changing quickly in everyone's lives, as well as, the world. Be thankful to God each and every day for the graces and blessings He has given you. The world is changing for the better. Slowly but surely, mankind is banning together to help one another. As you see with the aid to Haiti. Your world needs to band together to help one another. You have a global economy. You need to help each other. You need to love God with your whole heart and soul, and love your neighbor as yourself. This will bring about "*World peace.*" God will handle the destruction of the evil ones. Continue to do good, and pray for your world, my child. It is essential in order to bring about "*World peace.*"

Do not worry about a thing. God is guiding you through it all. He will tell you what to do and say. Become His instrument. Show compassion and love toward your fellow human beings. He is guiding you, my child. Love Him with your whole heart and soul. Do not fear, for we are with you, always and in all ways. Continue to do good for your fellow man, and know that we love you very much and are guiding you.

Love,
BV & Christ

Dear Child,

Welcome back! It is always so good to see you. Remember to pray daily for: *Peace-on-earth*; the conversion of the evil ones; and for God's intercession with our world leaders.

Child, it won't be long now when things will change in your world. Very rapidly, I might add. Simply remain close to us, and we will guide you every step of the way. These changes are *meant-to-be* in order to bring about "*Peace-on-earth.*" Never before in the history of mankind, have so many changes occurred quickly. Yes, you are about to experience Christ's second coming. He will bring "*Peace-on-earth.*" Good shall triumph over evil. God shall reign supreme! Yes, my child, much better days are coming. You shall experience history in the making. Never before in the history of mankind has *peace* been such a factor on earth. Yes, my child, you are about to witness what the bible refers to as *a thousand years of peace*. It truly shall be a *glorious time* to be alive! People shall love one another and God, with their whole heart and soul. Love will permeate the earth! Never before has mankind experienced such an emotion to its fullest extent. Yes, my child, everyone shall have peace and joy in their hearts. It truly shall be a glorious time to be alive!

So, remain close to us, and we will guide you every step of the way. Much better days are coming. Look forward to these days for they are quickly approaching.

We love you so very much and are guiding you.

Love,
BV & Christ

Dear Child,

Welcome back! It's always good to see you. Please, please, please, remember to pray daily for: *Peace-on-earth*; the conversion of the evil ones; and for God's intercession with our world leaders. It is *vitally important* that you do this each and every day.

Child, remain close to us, for events are changing so rapidly in your world. Soon, you shall see *a new day*. One full of love and happiness! *Peace* shall reign upon you. Yes, much better days are coming, and very soon I might add. Look forward to these days, my child, for they are rapidly approaching. *Do not fear*. Simply remain close to us, and we will guide you through the changes. They are all for the betterment of your planet, and those who inhabit it. Yes, God shall reign supreme! People will love God with their whole heart and soul, and love their neighbor as themselves. It truly shall be a glorious time to be alive! Never before in the history of mankind have so many changes occurred so quickly. Never before has *peace* reigned upon earth! Yes, God's plan is to have you love one another, and be peaceful! Everyone shall be *in harmony*. Your neighbors, as well as, everyone on earth. Even *"Mother Nature"* shall be *in harmony* with mankind. What a glorious time to be alive. Look forward to these days. They truly shall be glorious. All of mankind shall live in harmony! People shall be lifted to a new spiritual level. They shall have love in their hearts. They shall love God with their whole heart and soul, and love their neighbor as themselves. It truly shall be glorious! Yes, you are about to witness history in the making! Simply remain close to us, and we will guide you through it all. No need to fear, for better days are coming. Believe in this, my child. Your burdens shall be lifted. You shall live a long and happy life! Look forward to these days. The best is yet to come!

We love you so very much, and are guiding you.

Love,
BV & Christ

Dear Child,

Welcome back! It was always good to see you. Please, please, please, remember to pray daily for: *Peace-on-earth*; the conversion of the evil ones; and for God's intercession with our world leaders. It is *vitally important* that you do this each and every day. God hears your prayers and answers them.

Child, do not be afraid with the upcoming events. Many changes are about to take place in your world. All for the better I might add. These changes are necessary in order to bring about "*World peace.*" It shall be a *peace* that your world has never known. People will love God with their whole heart and soul, and their neighbors as themselves. Never before in the history of mankind have so many people experienced such a *peace*. Yes, child, all of this was meant to be, according to God's "*Divine Plan.*" This was set in motion since the beginning of time. You say that you felt things are moving quickly. Well, they are, because these changes are rapidly upon us. They are *definitely* in motion, and you can feel that occurring. Simply take a deep breath and *know* that all is well, and going according to God's "*Divine Plan.*" *Peace* is on its way, and *here to stay.*

Yes, your world is evolving into a new spiritual level. One full of love, joy, and happiness. It truly shall be a joyous time to be alive! Everyone shall live in harmony. Even your earth shall be harmonized! All pollution shall be gone. All anger and discord shall be gone. All wars and disease shall be gone. It shall be as if heaven descended upon earth. Yes, child, a new day is coming. One so full of love, joy, and happiness that you shall be hard pressed to remember your world as it is now. So, do not get discouraged with the *current events* of your world, because all of this shall change rapidly. Place all of your troubles into God's hands, and watch what miraculous things happen! Yes, God sees the *big picture,* and you *do not.* So, allow God to perform miracles in your life. Allow Him to be the central focal point in your life. God will help and guide you *better* than anyone you know. God alone can move mountains, and make the crooked way straight. He performs miracles each and every day. So, allow Him to work miracles in your life. Walk with Him. Talk with Him. Let Him become the *center* of your being. He is the center of your life. Become His instrument. His acts of love shall be worked through you. God knows what He is doing. Become an open receptacle of His love. Allow Him to work through you. Mankind so *desperately* needs His love and guidance. Only God can change things. Only God knows what is right for all of us. Simply place all of your faith, hope, and trust into God's hands, and *watch* what miraculous things happen. Remember, it is never too late to turn to God. He is anxiously awaiting your arrival. So, go in peace now, to love and serve the Lord. *Know* that all is well, and going according to God's "*Divine Plan.*"

We love you very much, and are guiding you.

Love,
BV & Christ

Dear Child,

You are seeing the bruised markings on my face to remind you to pray for all of the women who are abused. They need God's wisdom and strength to leave their relationships. It's not easy, but necessary for their survival.

Child, continue to pray for your world. It is in its darkest hour. People need to turn to God *now* before it is too late. Too late to matter. Too late to be saved.

Soon, you shall see a world full of love, happiness, and laughter. It truly shall be a *glorious time* to be alive! People will love God with their whole heart and soul, and their neighbor as themselves. God shall reign supreme! *Peace-on-earth* is part of God's *"Divine Plan"* for everyone on earth. God shall make the crooked way straight! All wars shall cease! All disease shall be gone. All disharmony and discord shall banish! God is *here to stay*! Inform everyone to look forward to these days. To have *hope*! To place all of their faith, hope, and love in God. Never before in the history of mankind have you experienced such *peace*! Yes, it will be Christ's second coming. He shall free you all from the bonds of slavery in all forms. To your government, work place, relationships, and country. Your world is being raised to a new *spiritual level*. You will no longer have crimes of any kind. People will have love and joy in their hearts. They will only desire to do good for themselves, their neighbor, and their world. It truly shall be a *glorious time* to be alive!

These days are approaching rapidly. It's a time of great change. All for the better I might add. Simply remain close to us, and we will guide you every step of the way. No need to fear, for we are with you always, and in all ways.

Now go in peace to enjoy your day, and *know* that we love you very much and are guiding you.

Love,
BV & Christ

Dear Child,

Welcome back! It's always good to see you. Please, please, please, remember to pray daily for: *Peace-on-earth*; the conversion of the evil ones, and for God's intercession with our world leaders. It is *vitally important* that you do this each and every day, and encourage others to do so too.

Now for the task at hand. Pray for your world, my child. It is in grave danger of a *takeover* by the evil ones. Your country is at a great risk of losing its *freedom*! Pray that this *does not happen*! Pray, that God will continue to bless America! Pray, that everyone turn to God *now* before it is too late. Too late to matter. Too late to be saved.

Yes, child, you shall see *Peace-on-earth* in your lifetime. It shall be a *peace* that no one on earth has ever experienced. People will love God with their whole heart and soul, and their neighbor as themselves. What a miraculous blessing from God! Look forward to these days, my child, for they are rapidly approaching. The time is coming when *everyone* shall turn to God *for everything*! What a *glorious time* to be alive!

All wars, anger, disease, and fighting shall cease! These shall be things of the past. The future has no use for them. All of the individuals who wish to hold onto these traits shall perish! Your new world shall exist in *peace and harmony*. All of those who wish to continue to fight, shall perish. *Peace* and God's love shall reign supreme! It truly shall be a glorious time to be alive! Look forward to these days, for they are rapidly approaching.

Now child, go *in peace* as you travel today. Remember we are with you always, and in all ways. We shall never forsake you.

We love you very much, and are guiding you.

Love,
BV & Christ

Dear Child,

Welcome back! It's always good to see you. Please, please, please, remember to pray for: *Peace-on-earth*; the conversion of the evil ones; and for God's intervention with our world leader. It is *vitally important* that you do this each and every day.

Child, continue to pray for your world. It is in grave danger. Evil forces are plotting to take over America! Your freedom would be gone! Pray that this does not happen. Pray that God continues to bless America, as He has since its inception. Your nation was conceived with God in mind. Your *"Declaration of Independence"* was developed with God in mind. God was so much of an *integral part* of the early days of your country. Your basic freedoms were written as part of your constitution. People came to America, worldwide, in order to be free! Pray, that this freedom continues, and that through *"Divine Intervention,"* God continues to bless America.

Child, God hears your prayers and answers them. Never give up *hope!* Trust in God in all matters. *Know* that He is with you always, and in all ways. God hears your prayers and answers them. Place everything into God's hands. *Trust Him. He* loves you so very much, and is guiding you. He has *big plans* for you. Simply turn your entire life over to Him, and watch what miraculous things happen. We are so very proud of you. Continue to call on God's help for everything! He hears your call, and answers it immediately.

So, *do not fear. Know* that we are with you through it all. We love you so very much, and are guiding you.

Love,
BV & Christ

Dear Child,

Welcome back! It's always good to talk with you, no matter where you maybe. Please, please, please, remember to pray daily for: *Peace-on-earth*; the conversion of the evil ones; and for Gods intercession with our world leaders. It is *vitally important* that you talk each and every day, and encourage others to do so too.

Now child, it will not be long now, when all of this *strife* shall be behind you. What a glorious day that shall be! Experience patience, for this difficult time is quickly drawing to a close. A new life lies before you. One full of hope and promise. It truly shall be a glorious time to be alive! Look forward to these days my child, for they are *quickly approaching*. The time is coming when God and love shall conquer all. People who are negative, angry, and full of war, shall perish. Your planet is being elevated to a new *spiritual level*. Love shall abound. God shall reign supreme. All those who are not with Him, shall perish. Yes, my child, much better days are coming. Ones full of love and laughter, and lightheartedness. Your entire world shall change quickly. All for the better I might add. Do not give up *hope*, for better days are just around the corner. Believe me, this too shall pass. Much better days are coming.

Child, for now *know* that all of this is part of God's "*Divine Plan.*" He is *in charge,* and no one else. Only God can make the crooked way straight. So, place all of your troubles into Gods hands, and watch what miraculous things happen.

Now go in peace to love and serve the Lord.

We love you so very much, and are guiding you.

Love,
BV & Christ

Dear Child,

It's so good to see you. We really appreciate you making the effort to come out and see us. Continue to be diligent in your prayer life.

Now child, do not worry, or be concerned about anything. Place everything into Gods hands, and watch what miraculous things happen! He sees the whole picture, and you do not. It is a practice of *letting go*. Do it *constantly*, and watch how much *more peaceful* you will become.

Child, the time is coming when *all will be made well*. Yes, *Peace-on-earth* is on its way. A time of great joy is about to unfold on your planet. All wars, anger, and negativity shall cease! Yes, my child, it's a time of Christ's second coming. It truly shall be a glorious time to be alive! Never before, in the history of your planet, has such wonderment occurred. Look forward to these days, my child, for they are rapidly approaching. A time of *peace* shall surround your entire planet. It shall be a time of great love, joy, and happiness. Mankind shall love God with their whole heart and soul, and love their neighbor as themselves. It truly shall be a glorious time to be alive!

Yes, my child, these days are rapidly approaching. Everything shall turn out for the betterment of mankind. All strife shall be behind you. Good shall conquer evil, and only *love* shall prevail! What a glorious time to be alive! Yes, my child, this is *true*. Continue to focus on the future. Much better days are coming. *Know* that this is true. You are about to experience Christ's second coming, and *Peace-on-earth*. How glorious! My child, it shall be a *peace* that mankind has *never known*. So, much can be accomplished in a *peaceful* environment. Many enhancements, technologically, and environmentally, shall be revealed to you. A whole *new world* shall open upright before your very eyes!

Yes, my child, much better days are coming. You are living in one of the most exciting times in the history of mankind. Surely, love and beauty is about to unfold before your very eyes. I know that now it seems too good to be true. However, *trust us*, all can change within an instant! Place all of your faith, hope, and trust in God, and watch how these *miraculous events* will happen. All within an instant! Yes, my child, this was all part of God's *"Divine Plan"* since the beginning of mankind. You are living in one of the most *exciting times* in the history of mankind! Thank God for all of this. Thank God for His many blessings. Thank God for answering your prayers and guiding you. Thank God for everything. For within it all, you are growing closer to Him. And that is exactly what He wants from every individual on earth. Remain close to Him, and He will guide your every move. So, *do not despair* when times get tough, just remain close to Him, and He will guide you through it all.

Now go out and enjoy this beautiful day!

We love you so very much, and are guiding you.

Love,
BV & Christ

Dear Child,

Welcome back! It's always good to see you. Please, please, please, remember to pray for: *Peace-on-earth*; the conversion of the evil ones; and for God's intercession with our world leaders. It is *vitally important* that you do this each and every day, and encourage others to do so too.

Child, it won't be long now, when all of this strife shall be behind you. Yes, much better days are coming! Ones full of peace, joy, and happiness. Look forward to these days, my child, for they are quickly approaching.

Yes, your world is in a tragic state right now. Man's inhumanity to man is astounding! When will people learn to turn to God for *everything*? Must they endure such hardships in order to turn-to-God? Must they be on their *death bed* before they even *think* of God. How sad for the human race to act on this level. They need to *wake up*, and turn to God for *everything*! He will make the crooked way straight. He will hear and answer their prayers immediately! They just need to turn to Him, and watch what *miraculous things* happen, once they gave it all to God. He is patiently awaiting their arrival.

Yes, my child, turn to God for *everything*, and all will be made well. *Know* that this is *true*. *Believe* that this is *true*. God can fix anything. He just wants the human race to use its *free will* to turn to Him for everything. Only then, will you have *Peace-on-earth*. Only then, will people be consoled, and have peace in their hearts. Only then, will Christ reign supreme!

So, look forward to these days my child, for they are quickly approaching. Christ's second coming is at hand. Remain very close to us, and we will guide you every step of the way. We will instruct you as to what to do or say at any given moment. You are a *child-of-God*, so act accordingly. Speak about God with everyone you meet. Make people *mindful* of God. Encourage them to pray, and ask God for what they want and need. He will grant them their wishes, and answer their prayers. Remember, He is patiently awaiting their arrival. He will never let them down. He is there for them, *always* and in *all ways.*

So, go in peace, my child, *knowing* that *all is well,* and going according to God's *"Divine Plan."*

We love you so very much, and are guiding you.

Love,
BV & Christ

Dear Child,

I t's *always* good to see you. Please, please, please, remember to pray daily for: *Peace-on- earth*; the conversion of the evil ones; and for God's intercession with our world leaders. It is *vitally important* that you do this each and every day and encourage others to do so too.

Child, it won't be long now, when all of these strife, shall be behind you. Yes, much better days are coming. Ones full of peace, love, and happiness. Look forward to these days, my child, for they are quickly approaching.

No, it won't be long now, before you experience Christ's second coming! Yes, He will be here before you know it. Only God's *"Divine Intervention"* can bring about *"Peace-on-earth."* No one else can accomplish this goal. Only God can perform such miracles! Child, you must continue to pray for *peace,* and encourage others to do so too. *Do not get discouraged. Peace* is on its way. Much better days are coming. Look forward to them, my child. It will be a time of great joy and happiness. Love shall conquer all! Christ shall reign as *"Sovereign Ruler"* upon earth.

Everyone shall love Him with their whole heart and soul, and love their neighbor as themselves. Yes, child these days are rapidly approaching. Any difficulty you may be experiencing is only *temporary.* Place everything into God's hands. He will handle it *better* than you could ever dream possible. *Trust us.* Much better days are coming. Soon, you shall see a world *transformed.* Changed in every way, including environmentally, government changes, societal changes, and human changes. People will have a *change-of-heart.* War will no longer be an option. Only love shall rule supreme! All negative traits shall be discarded. Those who wish to hold onto them, shall perish. Yes, it shall be a time of *great beginnings.* It shall be a time of *"Peace-on-earth."* Yes, your planet is being elevated to a new *spiritual level* as we speak. It shall be a time of great love and happiness! Yes, many miracles are about to happen! Continue to pray daily for *peace,* and watch the miracles happen before your very eyes.

Child, we need your help. Continue to spread the word about Christ's second coming, and *Peace-on-earth*. Encourage *everyone* to *pray*. Encourage them to ask God for *Peace-on-earth*. Encourage them to place all of their troubles into God's hands. Encourage them to place all of their faith, hope, and *trust in God*. Only God can perform miracles. Only God can make the crooked way straight. Only God can hear your prayers and answer them.

So, continue to do your best. Place all of your *trust in God*. Watch what miraculous things are about to occur. It's all through prayers that *"Divine Intervention"* will come about. Just love and trust God, with your whole heart and soul, and watch the miracles unfold.

Now child, go about your day to love and serve the Lord.

We love you so very much, and are guiding you.

Love,
BV & Christ

Dear Child,

Welcome back! It's always so good to see you. Please, please, please, remember to pray daily for: *Peace-on-earth*; the conversion of the evil ones; and for God's intervention with our *World leaders*. It is *vitally important* to do this each and every day and encourage others to do so too.

Child, it won't be long now, when all of this *strife* shall be behind you. Yes, much better days are coming. Ones full of peace, joy, and happiness. Look forward to these days, for they are quickly approaching. Soon, very soon, you shall see *peace-on-earth*! Soon, very soon, you shall experience Christ's second coming. Yes, it truly is a *glorious time* to be alive! You are experiencing history in the making. All of mankind shall *love* God with their whole heart and soul, and *love* their neighbor as themselves. Yes, my child, these days are quickly approaching. Do not get *discouraged* with events as portrayed by the news media on TV. Much better days are coming, and very quickly I might add. Remember, *everything* can change in an instant! *Peace* is at hand. Better days are at hand. Total "*Divine Love*" is at hand. Yes, this is all part of God's "*Divine Plan*," since the beginning of time. His plan for *peace-on-earth* shall reign for 1,000 years. My child, much better days are coming. Look forward to them, for they are *quickly approaching*. It shall be a time of great love, joy, and happiness. All of mankind shall worship Him with their whole heart and soul. It truly shall be a *glorious time* to be alive! *Trust us. Believe* that what we are telling you is *true*. Also, *know* that we are with you through it all. You are *never alone*! We are with you, *always* and in *all ways*. All of these changes were meant to be in order to bring about *peace-on-earth*. So, my child, remain very close to us. We are guiding your every step. *Know* that all is well, and going according to God's "*Divine Plan*."

We love you so very much, and are guiding you.

Love,
BV & Christ

Dear Child,

Welcome back! It's so good to see you! Yes, your retreat is about to unfold all of God's love and mercy for you. Remain in the *present moment* so that you don't miss a thing!

Now child, you know that the current *state-of-affairs* in your world is very grave. Pray for your world daily. Remember to pray for: *Peace-on-earth*; the conversion of the evil ones; and for God's intercession with our world leaders. It is *vitally important* that you do this each and every day and encourage others to do so too.

Child, the time is coming when all of this strife shall be behind you. Thank God! For He is merciful. Much better days are coming. Ones full of peace, joy, and happiness! Look forward to these days child, for they are rapidly approaching! Yes, it shall be a time of great joy and happiness. A time that your world has never seen. A time of Christ's second coming! Yes, my child, you shall see *peace-on-earth* in your lifetime! What a glorious time it shall be! Everyone shall love God with their whole heart and soul, and love their neighbor as themselves. Believe us, for this is *true*. We will never lie to you. *Trust us.* These days are rapidly approaching! Have *hope*! Remain in the *present moment*, and *know* that all is well, and going according to God's plan.

We love you very much, and are guiding you.

Love,
BV & Christ

Dear Child,

Welcome back! It is always good to see you. Please, please, please, remember to pray daily for: *Peace-on-earth*; the conversion of the evil ones; and for God's intercession with our world leaders. It is *vitally important* that you do this each and every day, and encourage others to do so too.

Now child, concentrate, we need to discuss your world. The situation is quite grave, and things can change dramatically *in an instant*! Yes, remain very close to us, and we shall guide you through it all. If you experience any difficulty, simply *know* that this too shall pass. It's *only temporary*. Again, remain very *close to us,* and we shall guide you through it all. Your time of strife is almost over. A whole *new world* awaits you! One filled with peace, joy, and happiness. Yes, much better days are coming. *This is true. Trust us.*

The time is coming when all of mankind shall love God with their whole heart and soul, and love their neighbor as themselves. Yes, *peace-on-earth* is just around the corner! Look forward to these days, for they are rapidly approaching. Soon, very soon, it shall be a time of *Christ's Second Coming*! What a glorious time to be alive! All of mankind shall get down on bended knee to honor our Lord. Yes, my child, these days are rapidly approaching. Soon, very soon, you shall experience *peace-on-earth*. What a glorious time to be alive! It shall be a *peace* that the world has never known. It will be as if heaven descended upon earth. Yes, my child, it shall be glorious! This *peace* shall fill the hearts, minds, and souls of everyone on earth. It shall permeate your world and everything in it! Everything and everyone shall radiate this *peace*. What an exciting time to be alive! The world has never known such *peace*. It is time for your planet, and all of mankind to evolve to a new *spiritual level*. One full of love, peace, joy, and happiness! All who wish to hold onto the negative traits shall perish. Yes, my child, there will be no need for wars, hatred, or violence. Those shall be the way of the past. Your *new world* will have no need of such traits. Imagine all that can be accomplished through *peace and harmony*! There will be no disease! All of your pollution shall be made clean! New technological advancements shall be made known to you, in order to advance your society. Your forms of eating shall change. You shall experience a new form of agriculture. Animals shall be respected. You shall have no need to eat meat. So many changes are on the horizon, my child. Simply remain *close to us,* and we shall guide you through it all. No need to worry or fear. Just *know* that much better days are coming. Ones full of peace, joy, and happiness.

These are the times right before Christmas that allow us to wait and reflect. Soon, you shall welcome the birth of Christ. Soon, you shall relive all of the events of Bethlehem. Soon, you shall become so joyful, remembering that Christ had come to save the world. Yes, my child, He shall do it again, very quickly I might add.

So, remain very *close to us.* The discomfort you may be experiencing is only temporary.

Know that this too shall pass. Do not fear, for we are with you, always and in all ways. You are *never alone.* God will never leave you.

So, go *in peace* to love and serve the Lord.

We love you very much, and are guiding you.

Love,
BV & Christ

Dear Child,

Welcome back! We have a lot to cover this afternoon, so let's begin. Child, many changes are occurring in your world as we speak. Yes, there were multiple shootings occurring in many cities while you were on retreat. Yes, this was done to instill *fear* among the masses. Easier to control that way. No, martial law will not be initiated among all states. No, Obama will not become a dictator. Yes, law enforcement will be on *high alert*. Yes, it will affect the *retail business,* since people shall be afraid to venture out into the malls, for fear of being shot! This is exactly what Satan wants to instill in everyone, *fear*. Where is your faith? Now is the time to *turn to God* for *everything!* Yes, this is *true*! Only God can make the crooked way straight! People *desperately* need God's help *right now*. He hears your prayers, and answers them. Only God can change things, and no one else. Continue to pray for your world! Remember, *good* shall conquer *evil*! God will protect you all, if you just *ask* Him! He hears your prayers and answers them.

Child, *do not be afraid.* We are sending you back with the armor of God's love! No one can harm you, for we are protecting you! You can't get any better help than this! We are guiding and protecting you. Trust us, much better days are coming for your entire world. And very soon, I might add. God will not allow you to destroy yourselves or your planet! He has a *"Divine Plan"* for you, and soon, you shall see the wonderment of His ways. Remember, all wars, negativity, anger, and strife shall pass! A *new world* is just on the horizon. It shall be filled with love, joy, and happiness. No longer will the negative traits be tolerated, or the people who wish to carry on with them. Much better days are coming! It shall be a time that the world has never known. *Peace and love* shall rule your planet. Yes, Christ's second coming is about to happen! Be prepared! Never let your guard down. Be mindful of God in all that you say and do. He is there for you, always and in all ways. *You are never alone.* Feel His *peace* in times of sorrow. Allow Him to comfort you. Be open to His presence and comfort. He heals it all. The world and every individual on your planet. He is *pure love*! He just wants everyone to turn-to-Him. He is so present in your world today. People just need to *open* their eyes and see Him! Not only is He throughout nature, but He's in the hearts and minds of everyone on earth! Some people just don't know it! How sad. They could be so comforted, if they were just open to His love and mercy! He truly has the *healing touch*! Yes, my child, once people become *aware* of this, we shall have *peace-on-earth*! People will love God with their whole heart and soul, and love their neighbor as themselves.

Peace on earth is rapidly approaching. Soon, very soon, you shall see the fruits of God's *"Divine Plan."* It is a plan of great magnitude! All of creation shall be affected by it! Your entire planet, and everyone in it, shall be elevated to a new *spiritual level*. It shall be as if heaven descended upon earth. All of creation shall turn to God for everything! Then, He shall instill His *"Divine Love"* upon everyone. Watch how your world will change! Yes, my child, all wars shall be gone! All disease shall be gone! All suffering of any kind shall be gone! Only *love* shall prevail. It's the one emotion that transcends all space and time! That's what will make a difference in your world. All hatred shall be gone! All negativity shall be gone! That truly shall be a *glorious time* to be alive! Look forward to these days, for they are quickly approaching.

Yes, my child, the days of war and violence shall be gone! It shall be hard to believe, but you truly shall have *peace-on-earth*! How glorious! You will witness God's *"Divine Plan"* in action. How wonderful! *Hope, love, and joy* shall be restored into the hearts and minds of everyone on earth! Yes, my child, you shall be hard pressed to remember your world as it exists today.

Yes, God has a plan, and soon, you shall see it unfold. Again, it shall be a *glorious time* to be alive! All of mankind shall fall on bended knee when Christ arrives. Yes, my child, it shall be a glorious event! Look forward to it, for it is rapidly approaching.

So, child, do not let anyone or anything get you down. Remember, better days are coming, and very quickly I might add.

So, go in peace to love and serve the Lord. We love you very much, and are guiding you.

Love,
BV & Christ

Dear Child,

Welcome back! It is always good to see you. Please, please, please remember to pray for: *Peace-on-earth*; the conversion of the evil ones; and for God's intercession with our world leaders. It is *vitally important* that you do this each and every day and encourage others to do so too.

Child, it won't be long now when all of this strife shall be behind you. Yes, my child, many changes are in store for you this year. All for the better I might add. Yes, God has great plans for you, and soon they shall be revealed to you.

Remember, everything happens for a reason. Only God sees the whole picture, and you do not. Place *everything* into God's hands, and watch the miracles happen! Yes, God hears your prayers and answers them. Place all of your faith, hope, and trust in Him. He will guide you, and make the crooked way straight. *Trust Him.* Only God knows what is best for you. *Believe* that this is *true.* We would never lie to you. Much better days are coming, filled with peace, joy, and happiness. *Trust* that God will guide you through it all. He will help you do and say exactly what needs to be done at any given time. He loves you so very much, and only wants the very best for you. Remember, everything is going according to God's "*Divine Plan.*" It was enacted since the beginning of time.

Now is the most *exciting time* to be living on planet earth. *Peace-on-earth* is on its way! Christ's second coming is just around the corner. Soon, very soon, you shall see history in the making. It shall be a *peace* that the world has never known. People shall love God with their whole heart and soul, and love their neighbor as themselves. Yes, my child, it truly shall be a glorious time to be alive! Thank God for this! *Know* that all is well and going according to God's "*Divine Plan.*" It truly is a marvelous undertaking! No longer will mankind endure wars, hatred, or violence! That shall all be a thing of the past! No longer will any form of negativity exist on your planet! All those who wish to hold onto these traits shall perish! Only good shall remain on your planet. Your planet is being elevated to a new spiritual level! Everything is being done according to God's *"Divine Order!"* Your earth shall become pure again, free of its contaminants. Your air and water shall be made pure. Your oceans and sea life shall be restored to its original order. Yes, my child, all shall be made well. Even mankind shall be restored to his highest order. Nothing but *peace* shall be tolerated on your planet! New technologies shall be introduced to you providing *clean energy.* Your *entire world* shall be restored to its *"Divine Order."* Yes, all shall be accomplished with God on your side, and nothing accomplished without Him.

So, continue to remain *very close* to us, and we shall guide you through it all!

Now go about your day loving God.

Know how much we love you and are guiding you.

Love,
BV & Christ

Dear Child,

Welcome back! It's *always* good to see you. We so look forward to your visits. Please, please, please, remember to pray daily for: *Peace-one-earth*; the conversion of the evil ones; and for God's intercession with our world leaders. It is *vitally important* that you do this each and every day and encourage others to do so too.

Child, now is the time to pray for your world. For it is in *grave danger*. Evil forces are plotting to take over your country! Pray to God that this does not happen! Remember, God hears your prayer and answers them. He will *never* let you down. *"Ask, and you shall receive."* All shall be given to you, if you would just simply turn your life over to God. It's that simple! Once you do that, *know* that all is well, and going according to His *"Divine Plan."* Yes, my child, if everyone turned to God, we would have *peace-on-earth*. We would no longer have wars or fighting of any kind. God would be *in charge* and not mankind. People would be filled with such love in their hearts that it would encompass your *entire planet*! They would love God with their whole heart and soul, and love their neighbor as themselves. Yes, my child, this is *true*, and one day, you shall see it enacted!

Yes, my child, *peace-on-earth* is on its way, and so is Christ's second coming! So, remain prepared. Help is on its way! The days of fighting, wars, and negativity are almost behind you! Look forward to the days of *peace-on-earth*, when Christ shall reign *Supreme*! It is quickly approaching. Watch the process! This is truly an *exciting time* to be alive! More changes shall occur *now*, than in all of *mankind's* history! Yes, it truly is a *glorious time* to be alive! *Trust us*, for what we tell you is *true*. Your days of *strife* are almost over! Stay the course, and watch the process. Remember, all is well and going according to God's *"Divine Plan."*

Yes, there is *order* for everything. All of nature shall abide by it, and mankind too. This was all meant to be since the beginning of time. Now it shall be enacted. Watch mankind fall on their knees to give glory to God!

Yes, the time of His *Second Coming*, is upon us! How wonderful! Christ is coming to redeem the entire world, and restore it to its original *"Garden of Eden!"* Yes, my child, your world is being elevated to a new *Spiritual Level*! One that will be filled with peace, love, and happiness! What an exciting time to be alive!

Yes, my child, this can all change in an instant! It is that close. Watch the process, and remain very close to us! We shall guide you every step of the way. You are *never alone,* for we are with you, always and in *always*.

By remaining *mindful of us* at all times. You will be able to *hear us* at all times. We will be guiding your every thought, word, and deed! Imagine not having to think or worry about a thing! Simply hand it over to God, and He will instruct you as to what to do or say at any *given moment*. God is with you, child, *always* and in all ways.

Now is the time to look ahead to the future. A new world is opening up right before your very eyes! The days of strife are almost over! Soon, very soon, you shall experience *peace-on- earth*. Soon, very soon, you shall experience Christ's second coming! *Know* that this is *true*! Your world is about to change completely, in an instant!

So, continue to remain very close to us, for we are guiding your every move. Turn all of your troubles over to God, and watch the *miracles* happen! *Trust us* for what we *tell* you is *true*.

So, go in peace with enjoyment in your heart and mind, and *know* that all is well, and going according to God's *"Divine Plan."*

We love you very much and are guiding you.

Love,
BV & Christ

Dear Child,

Welcome back! It's so good to have you here. We have so much to tell you this afternoon. Simply sit back, and listen to what we need to discuss with you.

Child, you are being made into a soldier in God's army! Yes, He is fortifying you, and making you strong. No longer shall any man exert his *control* over you. No, you will *recognize* the signs next time, and *run* before the relationship can even get started. My child, these were *life lessons* you needed to learn. No one in this life should ever be *oppressed* by another human being! That shows *no respect* for the other person. Anyone who does that is totally into *control*. You are *not slaves* here! Those days are over! No, my child, you are to *stand up and be counted*! God made you with many talents which need to be expressed in this lifetime!

Each individual needs to *stand their ground*, and be heard! You are all made in the image and likeness of God, and need to be valued and respected. Yes, *all* of mankind needs to be valued and respected, in all walks of life. No one is *better* than the other. God made each one of you filled with *precious gifts*, which need to be recognized and shared among each other. Every human being has a *purpose* in this life. All are created *equal* in this life, my child. Each person has dignity! Each person has love in their hearts and souls. Each person needs to be recognized as a *child-of-God* that makes them special! Yes, my child, every individual on earth is a gift from God. He made you all different, but precious in His eyes. Child, mankind so desperately needs to *respect and value* one another. Man's inhumanity to man is atrocious! It needs to stop! You need to evolve as a race, in order to be saved! Otherwise, if you continue along this destructive path, you will *destroy yourselves*! Is this what you want?

God gave you all *free will*. Freedom to choose *good* over evil. Freedom to help your fellow man. When will you learn to cooperate, and help one another? When will you learn to share your gifts? When will you learn to be satisfied and content with what you have, instead of wanting more? Yes, you need to love one another as God loves you. You need to come from your commonalities, instead of your differences. You need to become one nation under God. One united group of human beings willing to please God in every way. Yes, my child, this will bring about *world peace*. Pray for miracles. God hears your prayers and answers them. He wants to give you it all. Simply ask for it, and you shall receive it. God is very benevolent, merciful, generous, and loving. He is there for you, *always* and in *all ways*. He simply wants all of mankind to turn to Him for *everything,* and it shall be given to you.

Now is the time to turn to God for *everything.* He so desperately awaits your arrival. *Peace- on-earth* can be achieved if you *all* would simply turn to Him! Do it *now* before it's too late. Too late to receive His love and blessings upon mankind. Too late to be happy in this life, by simply turning to Him for everything my child. Now is the time to place your faith, hope, and trust in God. Do it *now* before it is too late.

You see, my child, mankind, needs to *evolve now* before it's too late! The destructiveness of the *evil ones* is apparent. Yes, they need to be stopped *now*! Pray, my child, each day for: *Peace- on-earth*; the conversion of the evil ones; and for God's intercession with our *world leaders*. It is *vitally important* that you do this each and every day and encourage others to do so too.

So, child, there is *hope. Hope* that mankind will find its way to God. *Hope* that *world peace* will come about through prayers. Only then, when all of mankind turns-to-God, will we have *"Divine Intervention"* and *Peace-on-earth*.

Yes, you are about to celebrate Christmas. Christ was born to help all of mankind. To help bring about *Peace-on-earth*. You shall see this *peace* in your lifetime, my child. You shall experience a *peace* that the world has never known. Yes, my child, it is on its way. Stay awake, and *be* Prepared. Things can change in an instant! All for the *better* I might add.

So, continue to pray daily, and remember that God hears your prayers and answers them.

"Ask, and you shall receive." God is anxiously awaiting your arrival.

So, go *in peace* now, child, to love and serve the Lord.

We love you very much and are guiding you.

Love,
BV & Christ

Dear Child,

Welcome back! It's always good to see you no matter where you are. Yes, yes, yes, remember that we are with you, *always* and in *all ways*. We would *never* leave you, my child. As your time *on retreat* draws to an end, *know* that we are going with you. Yes, wherever you go, we will be there guiding you through it all.

Yes, child, this has been a wonderful *respite* away from your *hectic lifestyle*. As you return to your everyday life, take it a *little slower*. Be mindful of all that you say and do. *Know* that *all is well* in *every situation*. We are there going through it with you, my child. Yes, you are *never alone*. We are *always* at your side, my child. No need to worry or fear. Simply take a deep breath, and feel our presence with you.

My child, this strife shall be over quickly! Watch the process. All is well, and being made well. Good things are happening as we speak. God is with you, my child. A *new day* is dawning right before your very eyes! *Trust us,* for what we tell you is *true*. We would *never lie* to you, my child.

Now is the time to *stop, wait,* and *listen* to what God is instructing you to do next. It won't be long now when *all* of this strife shall be *behind you,* my child. Watch the process. Simply wait and see all that God has planned for you, child. It won't be long now, when your world will be changed completely. Yes, it shall be filled with peace, joy, love, and happiness! Yes, my child, you deserve this! God will make it so! Simply place all of your faith, hope, and trust in His hands, and *watch* the miracles happen. It won't be long now, when your life shall change completely, my child. All for the better I might add. Yes, child, much better days are ahead for you. You shall be *happier* than you could ever dreamed possible! *Trust us,* for this is *true*! A *new day* awaits you, my child. God shall see to it! You are now living the life God had intended you to live. One of peace, joy, love, and happiness. By being *mindful* of God, you can become *happier* than you have ever been in your life, my child. Just *knowing* that God is handling it all gives you peace and joy! Yes, my child, He shall make the crooked way straight. Watch the process. All is well, and being made well. You have nothing to fear. Simply wait, and *know* that God is handling it all. All is being *made well*.

God has a plan for you, my child. Soon, oh so very soon, it shall be *revealed* to you. Now is the time to simply wait on God. Be still, and watch His miracles *unfold* right before your very eyes. My child, be thankful for all He has done for you, and continues to do for you, child. His miracles are endless! He just wants you to be *happy* in this life, my child. So, watch as His miracles *unfold* right before your very eyes. It's a gift, my child, to see God's hand in action. He needs you to spread His word in this *fallen world*. He needs you to make people *mindful* of Him. He needs you to *be here now* as He performs His miracles.

Child, you shall see the day when *peace* arrives on earth. Yes, it shall be the time of Christ's *second coming*. What a joyous time to be alive. All of mankind shall love God with their whole heart and soul, and love their neighbor as themselves, Yes, my child, these days are *quickly approaching*. A time of *great joy* shall surround the earth. A time of *peace*! Thank God! Yes, mankind shall choose good over evil! Yes, it shall be a joyous time to be alive! Peace, joy, love, and happiness are on the threshold of this great event! Christ's *second coming* is almost Here! Be grateful, my child, that you are *alive* to witness this event! It shall be a *peace* that the world has *never known*. Yes, Christ is on His way.

In the meantime, remain vigilant in your *prayer life*. *Stay awake* and *be* Prepared. Christ is on His way! Thank God for everything. The good and the bad. *Know* that all is well, and going according to God's *Divine Plan*.

So, my child, go now *in peace* to love and serve the Lord.

We love you very much, and are guiding you.

Love,
BV & Christ

Dear Child,

Welcome back! It's always good to see you! Please, please, please, remember to pray daily for: *Peace-on-earth*; the conversion of the evil ones; and for God's intercession with our world leaders. It is *vitally important* that you do this each and every day and encourage others to do so too.

Now, child, remain very close to us in the days ahead. Many changes are about to occur. *Watch the process.* These are all for the betterment of mankind, my child. No need to fear or fret. All is well, and going according to God's *"Divine Plan."*

Child, remember we are with you through it all. No harm shall come to you. All is well, and going according to God's *"Divine Plan."* A plan that was set in motion since the beginning of time. All good things come to those who *wait.* Simply *stop, wait,* and *listen* to what God is *instructing* you to do *next.* Place all of your *troubles* into God's hands, and watch the miracles happen! Watch the process. Soon, oh so very soon, all of this *strife* shall be *behind you.* Yes, my child, *peace* is on its way! A *peace* that you have *never known.* Watch the process. Very soon, all of this *strife* shall be behind you! *Trust us,* for what we tell you is *true.* We would never lie to you, my child. *Peace* is on its way, and very quickly I might add. Soon, oh so very soon, you shall see a world full of peace, love, joy, and happiness! Watch the process. God is guiding you through it all. It shall be a momentous time *to be alive! Peace-on-earth* is on its way! Christ's second coming is just around the corner. Yes, my child, you shall experience it all. What a *glorious time* to be alive! A time when *all* of mankind shall love God with their whole heart and soul, and love their neighbor as themselves.

We are about to embark upon the 1,000 years of peace. Look forward to this, my child, for it is *quickly approaching*! What a *glorious time* to be *alive*!

In the meantime, simply *stop, wait,* and *listen* to what God is instructing you to do *next.* He is guiding your every move, my child. No need to worry or fret. Help is on its way! A *new world* is about to *open up* right before your very eyes. Watch the process. God's plan is in action. Soon, oh so very soon, all shall change in an *instant!* Yes, all is being *made well. All* is going according to God's "*Divine Plan.*" A plan that was set in *motion* since the beginning of time! What an exciting time to be *alive,* my child! All good is coming to you! All is well, and being made well. Watch the process. You shall be amazed of all God's miracles! This is all part of God's "*Divine Plan.*" You shall experience *history-in-the-making*! Yes, my child, it shall be a *glorious year* for *all* of mankind! Soon, oh so very soon, *all* these changes shall occur right before your very eyes! Until then, *know* that all is well. *Know* that better days are coming. *Know* that we are with you, and guiding you every step of the way.

So, go *in peace* now child, to love and serve the Lord

We love you so very much, and are guiding you.

Love,
BV & Christ

Dear Child,

Welcome back! It's *always* good to see you, no matter where you are located. Child, remember to pray daily for: *Peace-on-earth*; the conversion of the evil ones; and for God's intercession with our world leaders. It is *vitally important* that you do this each and every day and encourage others to do so too.

Now for the task at hand. Child, pray for your world. It is in *dire need* of prayers. Things are changing as we speak. All for the better I might add. Your President is guided by God, and working *diligently* to bring about these changes, as quickly as possible. In order to secure your borders, improve your economy by creating jobs, and improve the lives of your everyday American. *Pray* for President Trump's strength and courage to carry out *"God's Plan."* Yes, my child, he is guided daily by God. *Pray* for his constant protection! *Pray* that all the American people *accept* him as their president! *Pray* that they give him the *respect* that the office demands! *Pray* that all Americans have a *change-of-heart*, and give President Trump a chance to bring about strong and affective changes that your country *desperately* needs! My child, *pray* for *peace* in your country. President Trump is helping to bring about *world peace*! This is *all* part of God's *"Divine Plan!"* *Pray* that all of these things come to pass.

Much better days are coming for your world and you! Look forward to these days, my child, for they are *quickly approaching*. No longer will you have to live in *strife*! No longer will you have to depend on money for your survival! No! It can all change in an *instant*. All for the better I might add. Continue to *watch the process*. Place all of your troubles into God's hands and *watch the process*. God's miracles are happening as we speak! Now is the time to *stop, wait*, and *listen* to what God is instructing you to do *next*! It won't be long now when *all* of this strife shall be *behind you*! Look forward to these days, for they are *quickly approaching*! *World peace* is on its way. Christ's second coming is just around the corner! A *new day* is coming for all of mankind.

Watch how God performs His miracles. A *new day* is almost here! So, remain very close to God, and we shall guide you every step of the way.

Now go in peace, my child, knowing that much better days are coming, and very quickly I may add.

We love you very much, and are guiding you.

Love,
BV & Christ

1-31-17

Dear Child,

Welcome back! It's *always* so good to see you. Please, please, please, remember to pray for: *Peace-on-earth*; the conversion of the evil ones; and for God's intercession with our *world leaders*. It is *vitally important* that you do this each and every day, and encourage others to do so too.

Now for the task at hand. Pray for your world, my child, it is in *dire need* of prayers. Your President is being *bombarded* with negative criticism. *Pray* that he continues on with his duties. *Pray* for his strength and courage to do God's work. *Pray* for his protection. It truly is a battle of *good vs. evil* right now. The *good* shall prevail. God is seeing to it. His *"Divine Plane"* is *in action*! *Peace-on-earth* is on its way. Watch the process, and remain very close to God, as He guides you through it all.

Yes, my child, your world is changing at a rapid clip. Soon, oh so very soon, you shall see *world peace*. Soon, oh so very soon, you shall see Christ's second coming! Look forward to these days for they are rapidly approaching! Soon, the world shall experience a *peace* that it has never known. Yes, my child, *peace-on-earth* shall be established. An answer to our prayers. Remember, God hears your prayers and answers them. Soon, oh so very soon, you and all of mankind shall be *happier* than you could ever dream possible! Yes, my child, you shall experience such love, happiness, and joy that you have never known. Look forward to these days, for they are quickly approaching! *Trust us,* for what we tell you is *true.* Your world is changing quickly. All for the better I might add.

So, child, the world may look *torn apart* right now, but *know* that much better days are coming for *all* of mankind. Any difficulties you may be experiencing, need to be placed into God's hands, and watch as His miracles unfold right before your very eyes!

So, my child, go in _faith knowing_ that all is well, and going according to God's *"Divine Plan."*

Now go *in peace,* my child, to love and serve the Lord.

We love you very much and are guiding you.

Love,
BV & Christ

Dear Child,

Welcome back! It is *always* good to see you. Please remember to pray daily for these three things *now* more than ever: *Peace-on-earth*; the conversion of the evil ones; and for God's intercession with our world leaders. It is *vitally important* that you do this each and every day, and encourage others to do so too.

Now child, remain very close to us, so we can *guide you* through it all. Things are changing at a rapid pace. So much *change* is about to happen! All for the better I may add. Watch the process. God is handling it all. A *new day* is coming filled with peace, joy, love, and happiness! *Trust us,* for what we tell you is *true.*

Continue to pray for your world. *Now,* more than ever, it needs prayers. Yes, *peace-on-earth* is on its way. Yes, Christ's second coming is just around the corner. But, until then, *focus on God.* Allow Him to guide your every thought, word, and deed. He will tell you what to say and do at any given moment. Watch the process and *know* that all is well and being made well. Nothing to worry about or fear. God is *in charge* here, and no one else. He is handling it all. Watch the process as *all* will be revealed to you.

Remember, no harm shall come to you, my child. We are *protecting* you!

A *new day* is dawning right before your very eyes! *Trust us,* for what we tell you is *true.* Soon, oh so very soon, *all* shall be revealed to you.

This is the most exciting time to be *alive* in the history of all mankind! Yes, it shall be a *marvelous year* for *all* of mankind. The truth shall be made known to *all* of mankind. Much better days are coming for *all* of mankind.

Yes, my child, you are about to begin the 1,000 years of *peace. Watch* as it all unfolds right before your very eyes. All is well, and being made well.

So, my child, do not worry or fret. Simply place *everything* into God's hands, and *watch* as His *miracles* begin to unfold right before your very eyes.

So, go *in peace* now, my child, to love and serve the Lord.

We love you so very much, and are guiding you.

Love,
BV & Christ

Dear Child,

Remember, do not worry or fret, God is handling it all. Simply watch the process, and know that *all is well* and being made well.

Now for the task at hand. Pray for your world, my child. It is in *dire need* of prayers. Your country is so divided! It needs to come together and give President Trump a chance to do his job! You are the *greatest nation on earth!* God blessed America. He will not let you fail! Continue to *pray* for your country and *all* of the world leaders!

Now is the time to *stop, wait,* and *listen* to what God is instructing you to do next. It won't be long now when *all* of this *strife* shall be behind you, my child. *Trust us,* for what we tell you is *true.* Much better days are coming. They will be filled with peace, joy, love, and happiness! Watch how it *all* unfolds right before your very eyes. A new day is coming! Yes, my child, *peace-on -earth* is on its way. Christ's second coming is just around the corner. You shall experience it all. What an exciting time to be alive! You shall witness a 1,000 years of peace! Yes, all of mankind shall love God with their whole heart and soul, and love their neighbors as themselves. Yes, my child, all shall be revealed to you. A *new day* is coming for all of mankind.

Now is the time to *stop, wait,* and *listen* to what God is instructing you to do *next.* It won't be long now, when your life shall change completely! All for the *better* I may add. But in the meantime, *know* that all is well, and going according to God's "*Divine Plan.*" With this in mind, go in peace to love and serve the Lord.

We love you so very much, and are guiding you.

Love,
BV & Christ

Dear Child,

Welcome back, and Happy Memorial Day! So many of our men, women, and children have given their lives for our freedom today. We need to be very thankful for their sacrifice. Yes, my child, the price of freedom is very high. However, it will *not* continue this way for much longer! God shall bring about *peace-on-earth*! Yes, my child, it is all part of God's "*Divine Plan.*" Christ's second coming is just around the corner! Yes, my child, *all* is well and being *made well*. Watch the process.

Soon, oh so very soon, a *great peace* shall be bestowed upon the earth. It shall be a time of great joy and happiness! All is being made well.

You are living in one of the most exciting times in mankind's history! Yes, my child, *Peace-on-earth* is on its way, and Christ's second coming is just around the corner! Your earth shall be restored to its original "*Garden-of-Eden!*" *Watch* as it *all* unfolds right before your very eyes. It will be as if heaven descended upon earth. Remember, all is well, and being made well.

Yes, my child, you shall witness all of God's *miraculous deeds* in your lifetime! What a marvelous time to be alive! Watch the process as it all unfolds right before your very eyes. These things were all meant-to-be since the beginning of time. No longer will your planet thrive on wars. No, my child, *peace-on-earth* is on its way. Watch the process. Your planet is being elevated to a new *spiritual level*. What an exciting time to be alive! Simply *know* that all is *well*, and being made well.

So, with this in mind, go *in peace* to love and serve the Lord.

We love you so very much, and are guiding you

Love,
BV & Christ

Dear Child,

Yes, today is Veteran's Day. A day knowing the many men and women who gave their lives defending your country. Yes, my child, these were very brave souls fighting for a cause. Hopefully, this will be a thing of the past history of your world. Once *peace-on-earth* is established, there will be no need for wars or aggression of any kind. Continue to pray for: *Peace-on-earth*; the conversion of the evil ones; and for God's intercession with over world leaders. It is *vitally important* that you do this each and every day, and encourage others to do so too.

Now child, continue to pray for your world. It *desperately* needs prayers. It is a continuous battle between good and evil! *Pray* for the salvation of your world.

Remember, *peace-on-earth* is on its way, and Christ's second coming is just around the corner. Look forward to these days, my child, for they are quickly approaching. Much *better days* are coming for you, and *all* of mankind. My child, these days will be filled with peace, love, joy, and happiness! Look forward to these days, for they *are* quickly approaching.

Yes, my child, you shall see many changes occur in your world during your lifetime. All for the better I may add. A *new day* is dawning right before your very eyes! Watch God's miracles in action! Remember, *all is well*, and being *made well*. You shall witness God's "*Divine Plan*" in action.

So, my child, go in peace *knowing* that all is well, and being made well.

We love you so very much, and are guiding you.

Love,
BV & Christ

Dear Child,

Yes, winter has arrived. I understand why you would like to remain indoors.

Child, continue to *stop, wait,* and *listen* to what God is instructing you to do, then *act* upon it. Many changes are upon you. All for the better I may add. Yes, soon, oh so very soon, you will not even recognize your world. It would have changed so very much. *Watch* as it all unfolds right before your very eyes. Yes, my child, much better days are coming. They will be filled with peace, joy, love, and happiness! Trust us for what we tell you is true. Much *better* days are upon you *now.* Watch the process, and see God's miracles in action!

You are living in one of the most *exciting times* in the history of mankind! Your planet is being *restored* to its original *Garden-of-Eden!* Watch as it all unfolds right before your very eyes.

Yes, my child, much better days are upon you *now.* These days were meant to be since the beginning of time. Your planet is being elevated to a new *spiritual level.* This was all meant to be since the beginning of mankind. No longer will you be *war based! Peace-on-earth* is on its way, and Christ's second coming is just around the corner. This shall all happen in your lifetime.

Yes, my child, all is well, and being *made well.*

Know that God is with you, *always* and in *all ways.* You shall see Christ in His magnificent glory! Yes, my child, this time He shall reign *supreme!* It shall be a *new awakening* of your planet. Mankind shall love God with their whole heart and soul, and love their neighbor as themselves. It shall be a *glorious time* to be alive! Watch the process, and see how God's *miracles unfold* right before your very eyes! This is *all happening* as we speak.

In time, *all* shall be *made known* to you, my child. All the mysteries of the universe shall be made known to you. Yes, it is all happening in your lifetime. This truly is a most *exciting time to be alive!* Watch as it all unfolds right before your very eyes. Watch God's miracles in action.

It truly is a miracle that you are here now, alive and well. For all you have been through, thank God. He has guided you, my child, every step of the way. Yes, you were meant to *be here now!* Yes, God has a plan for you, and soon it shall be revealed to you.

So, for now, continue to listen to what God has instructed you to do, then act upon it.

Go *in peace* to love and serve the Lord.

We love you very much, and are guiding you.

Love,
BV & Christ

Dear Child,

Welcome back! So glad you could *get out* on this lovely day. Yes, we have much to discuss with you today. Please, please, please remember to pray for: *Peace-on-earth*; the conversion of the evil ones; and for God's intercession with our world leaders. It is *vitally important* that you do this each and every day, and encourage others to do so too.

Child, now is the time to *stop, wait,* and *listen* to what God is instructing you to do, then *act* upon it. He is guiding you, my child. Every step of the way. You needed this retreat to *heal* the wounds of the past. It is *clearing* your path for the future! Yes, my child, God has big plans for you. They *all* shall be made known to you *in time*. But for now, simply allow God to guide you every step of the way. You will be amazed at the *wonderous things* which lie ahead for you, my child. Your road shall be filled with much peace, love, joy, and happiness! Watch the process, and see how it all unfolds right before your very eyes.

Yes, my child, a *new day* is coming for you, and *all* of mankind! *Peace-on-earth* is being established as we speak! Yes, this is *all* part of God's "Divine Plan." It has been set in motion since the beginning of time. *Watch* as it all unfolds. *Trust us,* child. We speak the *truth* and would *never* lie to you. You are about to experience the *best time* on earth. It is all happening as we speak. *Peace-on-earth* is on its way, and Christ's second coming is just around the corner. *Know* that this is *true!* Look forward to these days, for they are quickly approaching! Yes, my child, you are living in one of the *most exciting times* in mankind's history! What a *glorious time* to be alive! Yes, my child, everything we tell you is true, and it will come to pass during your lifetime. All of this was meant-to-be. Even the trauma you experienced during your 15 years of marriage was meant-to-be. You now have a great deal of compassion for your fellow man! Look at the people who came to *your aide* when you were *in hiding.* Their lives were *at risk* too! Yes, my child, had they not experienced similar behavior from their past husbands, they could not help you. You see, all was meant-to-be.

Good has come out of evil. You now have a chance to help the women of Response. They so desperately need your help. This is an ongoing problem in your society, but it will be obliterated once *peace-on-earth* is established. The predators will no longer be on this planet! *Trust us,* for what we tell you is *true.* You all will feel *safe* again since *evil* will be destroyed. Yes, my child, much is happening as we speak. God is guiding President Trump to do the right thing. He truly is *cleaning house*! Much is coming into the *light.* The *evil ones* are being destroyed. Watch the process, and *know* that *all is well* and being *made well.*

So, my child, a *new day* is quickly approaching. It will be filled with peace, joy, love, and happiness. Look forward to these days, for they *are* quickly approaching. So, go *in peace* now to love, and serve the Lord.

We love you very much, and are guiding you.

Love,
BV & Christ

Dear Child,

Welcome back! It is *always* good to see you. Please, please, please continue to pray for: *Peace- on-earth*; the conversion of the evil ones; and for God's intercession with our *world leaders*. It is *vitally important* that you do this each and every day, and encourage others to do so too.

Now for the task at hand. Continue to pray for your world, my child! It is in *dire need* of prayers. It truly is a battle of good vs. evil now. *Pray* that mankind chooses good over evil, and that *peace-on-earth* is established. Yes, planet earth is experiencing a *very pivotal* time right now. Much evil is being brought to light. Many people are becoming discouraged, believing that our world is in a hopeless situation. They are witnessing the corruption of your lawmakers and officials. Every day, as they watch the news, they become more discouraged. Yes, my child, *pray* that they all turn to God for answers. *Pray* that they place all of their problems into God's hands. Only God can make the crooked way straight. Only God, through His *"Divine Intervention,"* can bring about *peace-on-earth*. Yes, my child, this *peace* was meant-to-be since the beginning of time. Mankind has *freewill,* and must choose good over evil in order for this *peace* to come about. Pray for your world, my child. Pray that mankind chooses good over evil. Pray for the peace and salvation of your world. Pray that God intervenes to bring about *world peace*. Remember, God hears your prayers and answers them. This is what God wants for you. However, you must *ask* Him for this, and He shall give it to you. Yes, my child, the majority of mankind wants *world peace*. They just need to pray to God for it, and it shall be given to you. Yes, God wants all of mankind to turn to Him in order to bring about *world peace*. It can be accomplished, but mankind has to play a part in it too.

Yes, my child, better days are coming, filled with peace, joy, love, and happiness! For what we tell you is *true*. We would never lie to you, my child. This was *all* part of God's *"Divine Plan"* since the beginning of time. You are about to witness so many changes in your world. All for the *better* I may add. Yes, my child, *all* of mankind shall love God with their whole heart and soul, and love their neighbor as themselves. Watch as it *all* unfolds right before your very eyes. My child, *this is true.* All of these changes are upon you *now!* President Trump needs to *clean house* in order to let in the good. Yes, my child, he is being guided by God. He needs to get rid of the *old guard* in order to let the *new peaceful ways* into being. Watch the progress. See how it *all* unfolds right before your very eyes.

Yes, my child, look forward to these days for they are quickly approaching. No longer will you have wars, starvation, or oppression of any kind. No! Those days are behind you! Peace and kindness toward one another shall prevail! It truly is a *glorious time* to be alive! Yes, my child, these days *are* the most exciting days of the history of mankind. Watch the progress, and see how it *all* unfolds right before your *very eyes.*

My child, the time is coming when all of mankind shall place their faith, hope, and trust in God. Yes, He is our *"Divine Supreme Being"* who can bring about this *world peace,* and solve everyone's problems. Allow God to handle it all! Allow Him to make the crooked way straight. It is that easy. So easy to do, yet for some, difficult to comprehend. They simply need to give up control, and place *everything* into God's hands. Place all of their troubles, fears, and desperations into His hands. He then can make His *miracles* happen in their lives. He then can have them feel lighter and carefree, *knowing* that God is handling it all. Knowing that *all is well,* and *being made well.*

You see, my child, mankind needs to learn to turn *everything* over to God. Only God can create *miracles* in their lives. Only God has the answers to their problems. Yes, He is the *alpha* and the *omega.* The all and end all. They need to place *all* of their troubles into God's hands, then *watch* His miracles happen. It's that simple. They need to place their hope, faith, and trust in God *knowing* that *all* is well, and being *made well.* He will give them a *great deal* of comfort when they do that too! Yes, my child, you are about to witness *many miraculous* changes in your world. All for the *better* I may add. Watch as it all unfolds right before your very eyes.

Now go *in peace,* my child, to love and serve the Lord.

We love you very much, and are guiding you.

Love,
BV & Christ

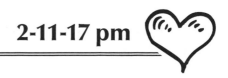
Dear Child,

Welcome back! It is always good to see you. Remember to pray daily for: *Peace-on-earth*; the conversion of the evil ones; and for God's intercession with our world leaders. It is *vitally important* that you do this each and every day, and encourage others to do so too.

Now for the task at hand. Continue to pray for your world and your President. They are in *dire need* of prayers. Many changes need to occur in order to establish *peace-on-earth*. Remember, the truth shall be made known. Everything is now coming to the surface and being rectified. No longer shall corruption of any kind be tolerated. No longer shall sexual abuse be tolerated. No longer shall *human trafficking* be tolerated. No! This shall *all* come to an end when *peace-on-earth* is established. It won't be long now when your world shall change completely. All for the better I may add. Yes, my child, all of these *scandals* needed to rise to the surface in order to be dealt with and put away! No longer shall your world, your *new world,* tolerate any of these things. No! They are *all* showing man's inhumanity to man! These things shall no longer be tolerated. Your *new world* shall be filled with peace, love and harmony. That is why you are being *made aware* of these things in order to do away with them. A world operating under peace, love, joy, and happiness has new guidelines! You shall love God with your whole heart and soul, and love your neighbor as yourself. These are the *new truths* that everyone shall abide by in your *new world*. Yes, my child, this is how you shall live *in peace* and sustain it. It is essential that you go by these truths. *Everyone* on your planet shall abide by them. *Everyone* shall have *peace* in their hearts and souls. If anyone chooses to abide by different principals, they shall be transported elsewhere. It will be their choice. To love God or leave! It will be made that simple.

Yes, my child, these days are *ahead* for you. Look forward to them, for they *are* quickly approaching. Days of peace, joy, love, and happiness lie ahead for you. Watch the process as it *all* unfolds right before your very eyes. Look forward to these days, my child. Do not fear them, that they will change. No! *All* is *well* and being *made well*. For this, we told you is true. Believe us, my child. These are the 1,000 years of *peace* that are upon you now. Just as the bible foretold you many, many years ago. You are about to experience some of the happiest times on earth! Look forward to these days, for they are quickly approaching. Days of peace, joy, love, and happiness are upon you *now!* Yes, my child, they are happening as we speak. No longer will you have to live in *fear* of any kind. No, my child, those days are over! *Trust us,* for what we tell you is *true.* It is *all* upon you now!

Child, begin to *think* in this way, *knowing* that things are changing quickly. *Knowing* that things are changing for the *betterment of all of mankind!* *Knowing* that *peace-on-earth* is on its way, and Christ's second coming is just around the corner! All of this is *true,* my child. *Believe it!* We would *never lie* to you.

You will see the day come, when Christ will rule the earth! Yes! It shall be a *magnificent time!* All shall be made well! It will be as if heaven descended upon the earth! Mankind shall love God with their whole heart and soul, and love their neighbor as themselves. Yes, my child, all of this shall come true in your lifetime. It is not a dream. It is a *dream come true!*

So, my child, you need to remain *"very close"* to us in the days ahead. Many changes are occurring, and we shall guide you through them all. But until then, remember to *stop, wait,* and *listen* to what God is instructing you to do *next,* then *act* upon it. *Know* that *all is well,* and being *made well. Know* that much better days are coming, filled with peace, joy, love, and happiness. *Know* how much we love you, and are guiding you through it all.

So, *do not be afraid.* Place *everything* into God's hands, then *watch* His miracles happen. It's that simple. *Know* that *all is well,* and being *made well* …

So, go *in peace,* my child, to love and serve the Lord.

We love you so very much, and are guiding you.

Love,
BV & Christ

Dear Child,

Yes, your time *on retreat* is drawing to an end. However, we will continue working with you as you merge back into daily life. Thank you for giving us the time to speak with you these past few days. It has been *our pleasure* to speak with someone who is *open* to our messages.

Now for the task at hand. Continue to pray for your world and President. Things seem to worsen everyday as you watch the news. Now scandals seem to come out implicating practicality *everyone* in our government! However, watch the process. It's all part of *cleaning house*. The right people will remain *in charge,* and *new ones* will replace the *old guard. Know* that *all is well,* and *being made well. Trust us,* for what we tell you is *true.* We would *never lie* to you, my child. All this is being done for a reason. To help bring about *peace-on-earth.* Yes, my child, watch the process as a whole *new world* opens up right before your very eyes. You no longer will have discourse of any kind! No! Man's inhumanity to man shall *stop!* Yes, my child, it *all* is going according to God's "*Divine Plan.*" A plan which was set *in motion* since the beginning of time.

Yes, this is the most exciting time to be alive! All is being *made well. Peace-on-earth* is being established. Mankind will love God with their whole heart and soul, and love their neighbor as themselves. It is *all* happening as we speak. *Peace-on-earth* is on its way, and Christ's second coming is just around the corner! Watch the process, and *know* that all is well and being made well.

Child, the time is coming when all of this *strife* shall be behind you! Yes, peace, joy, love, and happiness are *in store* for you, my child. Watch as it all unfolds before your very eyes. *Know* and believe that what we tell you is *true.* We would never lie to you, my child. Much better days are coming filled with peace, joy, love, and happiness. But, until then, continue to *stop, wait,* and *listen* to what God is instructing you to do, then *act* upon it. It won't be long now when your *entire world* shall change completely. Watch God's miracles *in action*. It is all going according to His "*Divine Plan*."

Child, when the *new day* arrives, it will be filled with such love and happiness that your world has never seen! People will be amazed at their surroundings, mankind's goodness, and sharing. It all will have *changed* from the way it is today. People will have a hard time recognizing that it is the same planet! Yes, it will be as if heaven descended upon earth! Your world shall return to its original "*Garden-of-Eden!*" Yes, my child, all that we tell you is *true*. Amazing as it seems, it all shall come to fruition. Watch the process. All these changes are for the betterment of mankind. Everyone shall be so happy to be alive in such a state! They shall be ecstatic! They shall find it hard to believe that life had existed in any other way but this one! Yes, my child, the days of hardship shall be but things of the past, which will no longer return. This will be the earth that God had created since the beginning of time! It was God's *original intention* to have your planet exist in this manner. However, Adam and Eve disobeyed God and were made to suffer. Now that *all* of mankind has chosen to *return to God, peace-on-earth* exists in a heavenly fashion.

This is what we have been telling you all along, my child. We would give you tiny bits of information along the way. However, when you are *on retreat* and *quiet down* from your *daily life,* we can take you even *deeper* into the silence, and show you God's plan for creation.

Yes, my child, *all* of these changes are upon you *now*! Watch as it comes *true*. What a *glorious time* to be alive! Enjoy the moment. Enjoy all the wonderful blessings God is giving you as a result of these changes. Yes, they shall all be for the betterment of mankind!

We are so excited for you! We *know* what is ahead for you, and cannot wait until you experience it!

So, my child, look forward to these days for they are quickly approaching. *Know* that *all is well* and being *made well*.

Watch the process.

We love you very much, and are guiding you.

Love,
BV & Christ

12-13-17 am

Dear Child,

Yes, your retreat is coming to an end. What an honor to take the time to be *touched by God,* my child. You made the effort, and God did the rest. Yes, my child, He is there for you, always waiting for you to *open up* to Him. You have now watched the process. A whole *new world* shall *open up* right before your very eyes.

Yes, much *better days* are happening *now* as we speak. The path is being *made clear* for all *good* to happen on your planet. Yes, my child, God is making the crooked way straight. It is a part of His *"Divine Plan,"* which was meant-to-be since the beginning of time. Watch the process, and *know* that *all is well* and being *made well.*

My child, as you leave this retreat, you take all the prayers and retreatants with you. Although you may not be together physically, you will be together spiritually. Every time you sit down to pray, they will join you in prayer.

So, my child, do not feel sadden that the group is no longer with you. You all shall continue to be together in *spirit.*

God has planted His seeds in every one of you. He has nourished you, and now sending you out into the world to encourage others to turn to Him for *everything.* Yes, my child, you are His eyes and ears here on earth. You are His instruments to help bring about *peace and hope* to all mankind. Allow Him to fill your heart and soul with love so that you can radiate His joy to the entire world. Yes, my child, God has a mission for all of you. He wants you to be His spokespersons to *all the world.* He wants you to be His ministers of *hope* during these *troubled times.* He wants people to know that He is here for them right *now!* He does not want them to despair, but have *hope.* He wants them to be at *peace* knowing that He is *in charge,* and no one else. He wants all of mankind to place their hope, faith, and trust in Him. Then *watch* His miracles happen! He wants *all* of mankind to have a *better life!* He wants *peace-on-earth.*

Yes, my child, these days are quickly approaching. They will be filled with peace, joy, love, and happiness. *Watch* as it all unfolds right before your very eyes.

Child, remain very close to us in the days ahead. Many changes are occurring quickly, and we shall guide you through them all. These changes are all for the better I might add.

Yes, your world is about to *open up* in so many new and wonderous ways. God has a plan for you, and very, very soon, it shall be revealed to you. But for now, continue to *stop, wait,* and *listen* to what God is telling you to do, then *act* upon it.

We love you so very much, and are guiding you.

Love,
BV & Christ

Dear Child,

Welcome back! One last time to receive a message before your retreat is over.

Please, please, please remember to pray for: *Peace-on-earth*; the conversion of the evil ones; and for God's intercession with our world leaders. It is *vitally important* that you do this each and every day, and encourage others to do so too.

Child, remember all that we have told you during this retreat. Take it to heart. We would *never lie* to you, my child. Look forward to the *future*. It is a rosy one. Yes, my child, much *better days* are coming, filled with peace, joy, love, and happiness. These days are upon you. Encourage others to have *hope* too. Tell them that much *better days* are coming, and to look forward to the future, when *peace-on-earth* is established! Tell them that they shall witness this in their lifetime! Tell them that all of this is *true*. It came from God.

Yes, my child, people need *hope* today. They are in the *state of despair*. Tell them that they need to believe that what God is telling them is *true*. We would *never lie* to you, my child. Tell them that through "*Divine Intervention*," all shall be *made possible*! Tell them that God hears their prayers and answers them! Tell them that a bright *new future* lies ahead for them, filled with peace, joy, love, and happiness. Yes, my child, *all* of this is true. Much better days are coming, and quickly, I might add.

So, whenever things get tough, turn to God for answers. Place *all* of your troubles into His hands, and *watch* how His miracles begin to unfold right before your very eyes. Yes, place all of your faith, hope, and love into God's hands and *watch* His miracles happen. It is that simple. God *knows* what is right for each and every one of you. He *knows* what you need, before you can even *ask* Him. Yes, He loves you so very much, and just wants to give you it all.

So, remember, you *are never alone.* God is with you *always* and in *all ways.* He would never leave or forsake you, my child. He is with you through it all.

So, continue to remain very close to us in the days ahead, as many changes continue to take place. Do not get discouraged. *Know* that all is well, and being made well.

So, go *in peace* now, my child, to love and serve the Lord.

We love you so very much, and are guiding you.

Love,
BV & Christ

9-11-18

Dear Child,

Yes, the world needs healing. It's been a long time since the attack on the twin towers, but your world still remembers. Child, stay vigilant with your prayer life. The world so *desperately* needs prayers. Evil forces are still attempting to take over America! *Pray* that this *does not happen*! Remember, God hears your prayers and answers them, and *know* that all is well, and being made well.

Child, now is the time to *stop, wait,* and *listen* to what God wants you to do, then *act* upon it. Many changes are occurring as we speak. *All* for the better I may add. Look forward to these *better days,* for they *are* quickly approaching. It won't be long now, when *all* of mankind shall love God with their whole heart and soul, and love their neighbor as themselves. Yes, my child, these days are rapidly approaching. Watch the process, and *know* that we are with you through it all. We would never leave or forsake you. We are with you *always* and in *all ways.*

Child, continue to remain very close to us in the days ahead. We shall guide you through it all. *Watch* as God's miracles begin to unfold right before our *very eyes*! Yes! Much better days are coming filled with peace, joy, love, and happiness!

So, continue to remain close to us, and we shall guide you through it all.

Go *in peace* now, my child, to love and serve the Lord.

We love you very much, and are guiding you.

Love,
BV & Christ

Dear Child,

Welcome back! It's always good to see you. Please, please, please, continue to pray daily for: *Peace-on-earth*; the conversion of the evil ones; and for God's intercession with our world leaders. Its *vitally important* that you do this each and every day, and encourage others to do so too.

Now for the task at hand. Continue to pray for your world, my child. It is in *grave danger* of a takeover by the evil ones. *Pray* that this *does not happen*. Your input is very valuable to us. God hears your prayers and answers them. You are truly witnessing a battle of good vs evil! *Know* that good shall *conquer evil*! *Know* that all is well, and being *made well*. Place all of your faith, hope, and trust in God, then watch His miracles happen.

My child, it won't be long now, when *all of this strife* shall be behind you. *Trust us.* We would *never lie* to you, my child.

You are about to embark upon a *new world*. One that will be filled with peace, joy, love, and happiness! Watch the process, as it all unfolds right before your very eyes. Yes, my child, these days are rapidly approaching. Look forward to these days, and watch God's miracles *in action*!

Yes, my child, all the *world events* seem to be coming to a head *right now*! Do *not lose faith*. This is all part of God's "*Divine Plan.*" Watch as it *all unfolds*. Yes, much *better days* are coming! *Know* that this *is true*! We would *never* lie to you, my child. You are about to embark upon a whole *new world*! Yes *peace-on-earth* is on its way, and Christ's second coming is just around the corner! These days are quickly approaching, so be *prepared*.

Now is the time to *stop, wait*, and *listen* to what God is instructing you to do, then *act* upon it. Soon, oh so very soon, this *strife* shall be behind you. A whole *new day shall open up* right before your very eyes.

So, remain *very close* to us, and we shall guide you through it all.
So, go *in peace* now, my child, to love and serve the Lord.
We love you very much, and are guiding you.

Love,
BV & Christ

Dear Child,

Good afternoon, my dear child. Welcome back! We have so much to cover with you this afternoon.

Currently, we are watching the way of the world. It is in *grave danger.* Skirmishes are erupting everywhere throughout your planet! *Pray,* that good conquers evil! *Pray* for *peace-on- earth! Pray* that God intercedes with your *world leaders.* It is *vitally important* that you *pray* each day for these things. Remember, God hears your prayers and answers them. Encourage everyone you meet to pray too.

Now is the time to *stop, wait,* and *listen* to what God is instructing you to do, then *act* upon it. It won't be long now, when *all* of this strife shall be behind you! *Trust us,* for what we tell you is *true.* We would never lie to you, my child. Simply remain in God's presence, and He will guide you every step of the way. For He is with you always and in all ways.

Yes, my child, many changes are occurring as we speak. All for the better I may add. Watch the process, as God's miracles unfold right before your very eyes.

Yes, my child, these are the days of great tribulation and change. *Do not worry,* for we are with you through it all. Guiding your every step, *trust us.* Remember, much *better days* are coming filled with peace, joy, love, and happiness. Look forward to these days, for they are quickly approaching. Watch the process.

Yes, my child, soon, oh so very soon, you will not have need of a thing. All is well, and *being made well.*

Peace-on-earth is upon you! Christ second coming is just around the corner! Yes, my child, you are about to *witness* it all! What an exciting time to be alive! You are living in one of the most *glorious times* in the history of mankind. How magnificent!

Again, remain very close to us, and we shall guide you through it all. Simply *watch* the process, and *know* we are with you through it all.

You are embarking upon a 1,000 years of peace, my child. What a glorious time to be alive! Yes, this planet is being elevated to a *new spiritual level*. One filled with peace, joy, love, and happiness. Look forward to these days, for they *are* quickly approaching!

So, wherever you are troubled, simply place it all into God's hands, then watch His miracles happen.

Continue to remain very close to us in the days ahead, and we shall guide you every step of the way.

So, go *in peace* now, my child, to love and serve the Lord.

We love you very much, and are guiding you.

Love,
BV & Christ

CHAPTER FOUR

REMAINING IN THE PRESENT MOMENT

Dear Child,

We are pleased you are willing to hear our messages. It's not easy these days getting people to stop what they are doing and be still. Only through *silence* can God speak to us. One must be quiet and calm in order to receive messages. It doesn't take very long, and is well worth the effort.

Your world is in a very grave state right now. Many natural disasters and political changes are occurring. One must stay focused on God, and remain perfectly still. He will handle it all. No need to fear or get caught up into widespread panic. God is guiding you through everything! Your every breath comes from Him. *"Be still and know that I am God."* Remember, be quiet and open, and God will guide you. He watches your every move and is with you. He only wants the very best for you. No need to worry about a thing with God on your side. He wants to be so close to you, to help make your life easier. He wants to help you with everything. You have no need to think or be anxious about anything. All will be given to you in due time. Life will be made so much easier for you with God on your side. Trust Him. Believe that He is there for you, watching and guiding you through everything. By keeping God in your heart, your life will begin to flow and become easier. He will shed His grace upon you. He loves you so very much. Let Him into your heart. Your life can be made happier than you ever dreamed possible. It's so easy and simple to do. Just, *"Let go and let God,"* and all will be given to you. Be simple and childlike, and God will guide you. No need to worry or fret. Just trust in God. He is there with you always, even when you do not know it. Become aware! Feel His presence! Feel His love for you! What more can you ask for? You have it all with God on your side. Listen to His voice, and act upon it. Be guided in everything you say and do. You are never alone. He is there with you, showing you the way. No matter how difficult times may become, *know* that God is there with you through it all. You are never alone. He will guide you. Listen to Him. and act upon His wishes. It's that easy. Just get out of your own way, and go with God. You will be guided as to what path to choose. No need to worry about the future. Just *live* in this *very precious moment.* It was given to you by God. A moment filled with hope and promise. A moment *alive* with His love for you. Appreciate and cherish this moment. It is a gift from God. *Life is a very precious gift from God,* and should never be taken lightly. Each and every person has a purpose on earth, and is meant to be here. It is a sin to take another's life! Let the unborn live! Speak up for the unborn, for they cannot speak for themselves.

Have compassion for the elderly. They cannot help themselves. Their bodies are growing older and feeble. Be patient with them. They need your love and care so desperately. All they need is a kind word and a listening ear. They love you, but cannot do for you anymore. So, they need your help in caring for them. In return for all they have done for you. It is a very tiring, yet rewarding job, caring for the elderly. They are so neglected and just need love. Pray for them, that God may bring people into their lives that will truly *cherish* them.

Life will have its twists and turns, but you will be all right with God on your side. Believe in His love for you. Let Him shower you with everything. Be *open* to Him and His love for you. All is well, and all will be well.

We love you very much, and are guiding you.

Love,
BV and Christ

Dear Child,

Welcome back! It's been a while since we spoke to you. Please, please, please remember to pray daily for: *Peace-on-earth*; the conversion of the evil ones; and for God's intercession with our world leaders. It is *vitally important* that you do this each and every day.

Now for the task at hand. Your world is in a deep state of flux. It could move in either direction. That is why it is *vitally important to pray* for your *world each and every day.* People need to turn to God with their problems. He hears your prayers and answers them. Yes, these are the *end times* as we know it. However, your world will be restored to its original *"Garden of Eden,"* according to God's *"Divine Plan."* Only through prayer, will you be saved. Nowhere else. Only God can save you, and no one else. He truly hears your prayers and answers them. My child, you need more love and light in your world. Do not despair. God is watching over you, and is guiding you. You are one of His disciples. When things get bad, turn to Him for answers. Yes, these are difficult times, but He will pull you through it all. It is not easy, but necessary to take time, and pray each day for God's help with this situation. He will never let you down. Everything happens for a reason. Now is the time for God to help you, more than ever. *"Ask and you shall receive."* Do not fear, for we are guiding you. Live in the *present moment.* Live with love and compassion in your heart. Live to please God. Open your heart and soul to Him, so He can guide you. It's not easy, but necessary in order to *block* the world's negativity. You will see many world changes in your life time, but they all lead to *peace-on-earth.* This is a *necessary cleansing* . God loves America, and is protecting it. Speak about God with everyone you meet. Tell them to pray daily for: Peace-on-earth; the conversion of the evil ones; and for God's intercession with our world leaders. It is *vitally important* that you do this each and every day. The more people who turn to God, the better your planet will become. It is that easy. *Do not give up hope.* Limit your time watching TV. Be informed, not inundated. Show compassion to your fellow man. Everyone is in the same boat. Return to the virtues and values in life that count. Those of love and understanding, peace and joy, mercy and forgiveness. This is what counts. Everything else is superficial and frivolous. Only you can show them the way with God's help. Only you can squelch rumors and false judgement. Only you can restore light in the world. All with God's help, love, and understanding. Show compassion, and be kind to your fellowman. Love is the answer, and not war. Love will conquer all, and *peace* will reign on your planet. But first you must go through trials and tribulations in order for this *rebirth* to occur. So, my child, place yourself into God's hands. Let Him guide you. Do not worry about a thing. For God is with you, always and in all ways. Be kind and merciful. Allow God into your heart to guide you. Do not fear for God is on your side.

We love you very much, and are guiding you.

Love,
BV & Christ

Dear Child,

Welcome back! It's been a long time since we spoke to you. Please, please, please continue to pray daily for: *Peace-on-earth*; the conversion of the evil ones; and for God's intercession with our world leaders. It is *vitally important* that you do this each and every day.

Now for the task at hand. Child, your world is on the *"Eve of Destruction."* Without prayers, all can be gone destroyed. Continue to pray daily, and encourage others to do so. It is *vitally important.* Your president is not ruling as a leader of your country. He is only interested in his own agenda. Your country could fall, and be bankrupted by him. *Pray* that he is *replaced immediately*! He could cost you your freedom! *Pray*, my child. God hears your prayers and answers them. He wants all of you to turn to Him. It is *vitally important.* He does not want to do this alone. He needs your help. He wants you to turn to Him for everything. Then you will have a true relationship between God and man. Now is the time to do this. Do not *delay*. Now is the *time to act*. Only God can perform miracles. Only God can turn your world around. *Ask,* and you shall *receive. Know* that God is there with you through it all. He loves you so very much, and only wants the best for you. Stay close to Him, my child. Do not despair. Have faith, hope, and love of God. He will help you. He will guide you. Love Him as He desperately loves you. Be open to Him. Let Him work through you. Become his instrument. Show others how they can live, happily and peacefully with God in their hearts and souls. Even during these difficult times. He is with us through it all. He is helping you right now. Have faith and hope in Him. He will not let you down. Turn all of your troubles over to Him. He will handle them. You will get results. Just *trust in God.* He is there for you, always and in all ways.

So, pray, my child. Continue to have *hope*. You will see *peace-on-earth* in your lifetime. *Know* that all is well, and going according to God's *"Divine Plan."*

We love you very much, and are guiding you.

Love,
BV & Christ

Dear Child,

Welcome back! It's always good to see you. Please, please, please remember to pray daily for: *Peace-on-earth*; the conversion of the evil ones; and for God's intercession with our *world leaders*. It is *vitally important* that you do this each and every day, and encourage others to do so too.

Child, now is the time to *stop, wait,* and *listen* to what God is telling you. It won't be long now, when things will change *drastically* in your world. All for the better I might add. *Do not fear,* for we are with you, *always* and in *all ways.* These changes are necessary in order to bring about *world peace.* It is God's "*Divine Mercy*" in *action*! Yes, all of these changes are necessary in order to bring about *peace-on-earth.* The pendulum has swung too far, and it's time that people turn back to God! A world without God is empty and void of happiness. A world centered around God is full of peace, joy, and happiness. Better days are coming for your planet. Simply *watch* the process, and *know* that all is well, and going according to God's "*Divine Plan.*" *Do not fear a thing.* You are being protected and guided. God has great plans for you. He will not let you perish now. Just *know* that all is well, and going according to God's "*Divine Plan.*"

It truly is an exciting time to be alive on your planet. So many great changes are coming. All for the better I might add. *Peace-on-earth* is just around the corner! Mankind shall love God with their whole heart and soul, and love their neighbor as themselves. Now is the time to remain *very close* to God. He will *never* let you down. He is guiding you every step of the way. Trust Him, and *know* that all is well, and going according to God's "*Divine Plan.*" These days are quickly approaching. *Do not fear,* for we are with you always and in all ways. We will never let you down. *"Be still, and know that I am God."* He will answer your questions, and guide you through it all. Simply take it day by day, moment by moment. Stay in the *present moment.* You will receive *answers* to your prayers in the *present moment.* You will hear God guiding you in the *present moment.* God is with you *always* and in *all ways*. Do not give up! Have *hope,* and *know* that all is well, and going according to God's *"Divine Plan."* He loves you so very much, and only wants the very *best* for you. So, stay true to your prayer life. Remain close to God, and *know* that we love you very much, and are guiding you.

Love,
BV & Christ

Dear Child,

Welcoming back! It's *always* good to see you. Remember to pray daily for: *Peace-on-earth;* the conversion of the evil ones; and for God's intercession with our world leaders, it is *vitally important* that you do this each and every day, and encourage others to do so too.

Child, it won't be long now when all of this *strife* shall be behind you. Much better days are coming. You needed to place your *entire life* into God's hands, so He could mold you into His image likeness. Yes, child, you needed to become more compassionate, and acquire a deep understanding of complex matters. God granted you those gifts. He also drew you closer to Him, which was an answer to your prayers. Yes, *everything* happens for a reason. So, continue to place your *faith, hope,* and *trust in God.* He can *make* the crooked way straight, and no one else. Yes, child, soon this trial shall be over. We are with you through it all, guiding your every move. *Know* that all is well and going according to God's "Divine Plan." Soon, God's mission for you shall be revealed to you. Now is not the time to grow impatient or anxious. Simply *watch the process,* and *know* that *God is in control.* Trust Him. Everything happens for a reason. One day you will look back on this time of great learning. Allow God to guide you through it all. Remain in the *present moment* so you can hear Him guiding you. He will tell you what to do or say in any given moment. *Trust Him. Know* that all is well, and going according to God's *"Divine Plan."*

So, continue to live each day to its fullest. Live moment by moment because that is where God is, and *know* that we love you very much, and are guiding you.

Love,
BV & Christ

Dear Child,

Stay calm, and remain close to us. We are guiding your every move. Much better days are coming. Remain in the *present moment*. That is where God is, and He will guide you as to what to do and say at any given moment. *Do not fear*! For we are with you and protecting you. No harm shall come to you. We have a plan for you, and soon it shall be revealed to you.

Now child, remember to take each day as it comes. We are guiding you. Soon, very soon, all of this strife shall be behind you. Much better days are coming. Now, more than ever, be *mindful of God*. Keep Him in your heart and soul through it all. *Watch the process. Know* that all is well, and going according to God's "*Divine Plan*."

Remain close to us, because that is where God is in this very *precious present moment*. It won't be long now, when your life shall change forever. It shall all happen quickly. All for the better I might add. We are giving you the *strength* to stay in this to the very end. It won't be long now, when all of this shall be behind you. *Trust us.* This too shall pass. Much better days are coming.

Child, soon you shall see a world full of hope and promise. Soon, all of mankind shall turn to God for *everything*! Soon, Christ's second coming shall be at hand. It shall be a time of great peace and joy on earth. Love shall abound! God's "*Divine Plan*" is in action. Watch the process. It truly shall be a *glorious time* to be alive!

So, go *in peace* with hope and joy in your heart. *Know* that much better days are coming.

We love you very much, and are guiding you.

Love,
BV & Christ

Dear Child,

Welcome back! It's always good to see you. Remember to pray daily for: *Peace-on-earth*; the conversion of the evil ones; and for God's intercession with our world leaders. It is *vitally important* that you do this each and every day, and encourage others to do so too.

Child, times and events are changing quickly. Soon, you shall see a whole new world open up before your very eyes. Remember, all of these changes are for the betterment of mankind. Look forward to these days, for they are quickly approaching.

Child, the time is coming when all of this strife shall be behind you. Yes, all is going according to God's *"Divine Plan."* He has great plans for you, so watch them unfold according to God's timing.

Your world is changing as we speak. Many shifts are occurring in nature, governments, societies, and your planet. These are all *necessary* in order to bring about *world peace.* Yes, my child, *peace-on-earth* is definitely part of God's "Divine Plan." Simply remain *in-the-moment,* and watch what miraculous things happen. *Much better days are coming,* and very quickly I might add. Trust us. *Peace* is just around the corner. Place all of your faith, hope, and trust in God. All will be made well. *Know* this my child. Keep your eyes on the future. Do not despair, much better days are coming. Simply remain close to us, and we shall guide you every step of the way.

Child, the time is coming when the world will need to hear these messages. People need *hope,* they are despairing. They need to turn to God for *everything.* Yes, He is guiding all of you, every step of the way. Simply remain close to Him, and He will tell you what to do or say at any given moment. Allow Him into your life *completely.* Yes, my child, He is there for you, always and in all ways. Simply let Him into your heart and soul, and He will guide you every step of the way.

Now child, it's a lovely day, go out and enjoy it.
Know that we love you very much, and are guiding you.

Love,
BV & Christ

Dear Child,

Welcome back! It's *always* good to see you. Now please remember to pray daily for: *Peace- on-earth*; the conversion of the evil ones; and for God's intercession with our world leaders. It is *vitally important* that you do this each and every day, and encourage others to do so too.

Child, now is the time to pray diligently for your world. It is in a grave place. Many people shall be affected by the *upcoming changes*. Yes, they shall affect *everyone*. Remain very close to us, and we shall guide you every step of the way. No harm shall come to you. But it is *essential* that you remain *close to us* through it all! Do not fear! For we are with you *always* and in *all ways!*

Yes, my child, much better days are coming. Ones full of peace, joy, and happiness. Look forward to these days, for they are quickly approaching! Yes, you shall see *peace* in your lifetime. You shall experience days full of peace, joy, and happiness! Everyone shall be *in abundance*! Everyone shall be in perfect health! Everyone shall be happy and content with God, and all of mankind. What a glorious time to be alive! Look forward to these days, child. They are the best days mankind will ever experience! The best is yet to come! Have faith! *Know* that this is *true. Trust us.* We will never lie to you. Much better days are coming, and quickly I might add.

Everything happens for a reason. It's all part of God's *"Divine Plan."* Never question His actions. God knows best! Simply, stay in the *present moment,* and we shall guide you through it all.

Yes, child, your world is changing rapidly as we speak. Your planet is being elevated to a much higher level! This was all *meant-to-be* since the beginning of time. All of mankind was meant to evolve to a much higher level. Much higher than you are right now. With God's help, you shall be lifted higher and higher. Ask Him for help in all things. He will quickly come to your rescue. He loves you so very, very much! He would never let you down. *Trust Him.* He only wants the very best for you! Believe us when we tell you that, and *know* that He is there for you, always and in all ways. He will *never* let you down.

So, remain *focused* on God for everything. Try to see the good in every situation. Hand all of your troubles over to God, and He will fix them quicker, and better than you could ever believe is possible! You believe you are here to serve Him. Well, He is here serving you, and all of your needs! It is a give situation! God only wants you to be happy in this life. He wants you to turn to Him for everything. Give Him *everything*, the good and the bad, and He will heal you of all your troubles. He has a great way of comforting your soul. He knows what you need *before* you can even ask Him. He is all knowing, loving, and merciful. There is *nothing* that you can do that God would not forgive you for. Nothing! He loves you so very much! He is full of love, compassion, and understanding. He is pure love! Take time each day to *be* with Him. It is so *rewarding*, allow Him to enter your heart and soul. Allow Him to guide you in all things. Do not fear, for He is with you always, and in all ways. He will never leave you.

We love you so very much, and are guiding you.

Love,
BV & Christ

1-10-15

Dear Child,

Welcome back! It's always good to see you. Please, please, please, remember to pray daily for: *Peace-on-earth*; the conversion of the evil ones; and for God's intercession with our world leaders. It is *vitally important* that you do this each and every day, and encourage others to do so too.

Child, it won't be long now, when all of this strife shall be behind you. Much better days are coming. Ones full of peace, joy, and happiness. Look forward to these days, for they are rapidly approaching.

It won't be long now, when your world will change completely. All for the better I might add. Much better days are coming.

God wants everyone to turn to Him for *everything*! Yes, once this happens, *peace-on-earth* shall be accomplished. Yes, my child, it shall be a glorious time to be alive! Mankind shall love God with their hearts and souls, and love their neighbors as themselves. Yes, Christ's second coming is almost here! Look forward to these days, for they are rapidly approaching.

Child, keep God and *peace* in your heart, no matter what you are going through. Remember, we are with you *always,* and in all ways. We shall never leave you. We are guiding your every step, word, and deed. It won't be long now before a whole *new world* will open up before you. We are paving the way. *Know* that all is well, and going according to God's "*Divine Plan.*" Just be patient, remain in the *present moment*, and watch the process. Soon, very soon, our mission for you shall unfold. Remember, we are with you through it all. *Do not fear. Trust us.* Much better days are coming. This is *true.*

So, my child, go *in peace* now to love and serve the Lord.

We love you very much, and are guiding you.

Love,
BV & Christ

Dear Child,

Welcome back! It's always good to see you, especially on this most beautiful day! Thank God! He made it just for you.

Now, child, do not be *distracted* by the upcoming events. Just *be* in the moment. Allow God to fill your soul with His abundant love! Allow Him to speak with you every step of the way. Just *be* with Him, and feel His *Divine Presence*! It is glorious! Just as this day is with its deep blue sky and snowcapped mountains. Yes, my child, this is all a gift from God. He loves you so very much that He made this very day for you! Enjoy it, and be *thankful* for God's *grace and beauty*.

It is a time of *deep gratitude* for all that God has given you. Your life, your health, your beauty and brains. Be thankful for it all. The good and the bad. For with the bad, we have a chance to learn and grow. Grow in many ways. You have learned God's *life lessons* of mercy, kindness, love and patience, understanding and forgiveness. But most of all, compassion towards our fellow *human beings*. Yes, my child, this was a great life learning experience. Now you need to learn to *stand up* for yourself. Not only as you have done in the past with business, but now in relationships. No one has the *right* to *trample over* another human being. No one has the right to *shut him out*. No one has the *right* to take another life. Yes, all life is sacred. God designed it to be so. Each person is made in God's own *image and likeness*. He deserves love, and to be valued and respected. Everything else is just *man's inhumanity to man*. How sad. But soon, very soon, all wars, fighting, killing, and anger shall cease! God will no longer tolerate this! Those who wish all of this *negativity* shall perish! Yes, it shall be the time of Christ's second coming. Be prepared, my child, for it is upon you! Soon, very soon, you shall experience *peace-on-earth*. Soon, very soon, you shall see all of mankind turn to God for everything! Yes, they shall love God with their whole heart and soul, and love their neighbor as themselves. Look forward to these days, my child, for they are *quickly approaching*. So, *be prepared*, and watch the process. Soon, very soon, all of this *strife* shall be behind you. Soon, very soon, you shall experience Christ's second coming! Soon, very soon, you shall experience *peace-on-earth*.

Yes, now is the time of *great trials and tribulations* throughout the world. It is a time of great cleansing. But soon, very soon, all of this *strife* shall be *behind you*. Trust us, for what we tell you is *true*. *The best is yet to come!* Look forward to these days for they are *quickly approaching*! They shall be joyous! It is *definitely* a *glorious time* to be alive! *Peace* is just around the corner for you, and many others who *choose* good over evil! *Watch the process. Trust us,* for what we tell you is *true*.

Remember to place all of your troubles and suffering into God's hands. He will make the crooked way straight! He will have things turn out *better* than you could ever dream possible. These are not just predictions, but fact! God only wants you to be *happy* in this life. "*Let go and let God*," and watch the *miracles happen*! It's that easy. So child, do not fret about a thing. Place *everything* into God's hands, and watch the miracles happen. He only has the best in mind for you. Remember, God is at the helm. Place all of your troubles into His hands, and He will have things turn out *better* than you could ever dream possible. *Trust us,* for what we tell you is *true*. We would *never lie* to you, my child. Remember, all is well, and going according to God's "*Divine Plan*." Just, "*Let go and let God*," and watch the *miracles happen*. He will never let you down. He is with you *always* and in *all ways*.

So, go in peace, my child, to enjoy this beautiful day!

We love you so very much, and are guiding you.

Love,
BV & Christ

My Dear Child,

Welcome back! It's *always* good to see you, and be with you no matter where you are. Remember, we are with you *always* and in *all ways.*

Child, this time of *strife* is almost behind you. Continue to place all of your troubles into God's hands. He will make the crooked way straight, and have things turn out *better* than you can ever *dream possible.* Simply, *"Let go and let God,"* and watch the miracles happen! Yes, God is *in control* here, and no one else. My child, keep choosing good over evil. Make God first in your life, and keep Him first. Never lose sight of Him. *Trust Him* with your whole heart and soul. *Know* that all is well, and going according to His *"Divine Plan."* A plan that was set *in motion* since the beginning of time.

Watch the Process. For soon, very soon, all of this *strife* shall be behind you, my child. Much better days are coming, filled with peace, joy, and happiness! *Trust us,* for what we tell you is *true.* We would *never lie* to you, my child. Place all of your faith, hope, and trust into God's hands. Only He can make the crooked way straight. Only God can perform *miracles,* and no one else. He is our Lord and redeemer! *"Ask, and you shall receive!"* He would give you the world, if you would *ask* for it. He only wants you to be *happy* in this life, my child. He wants you to be abundantly happy and joyous! Simply turn to Him for everything, and watch the miracles happen. It's that easy.

We know this is a difficult time for you, my child, but place *everything* into God's hands. He will handle it all. Better than you can ever dream possible! This is *true,* my child. He is with you every second during your hour of need, anxiously awaiting your arrival. He will guide your every thought, word, and deed. He is there for you, my child! You are part of His image and likeness! He would *never* leave you. Allow Him to guide your every thought, word, and deed. He wants to be so very close to you. Simply *open* your heart, mind, and soul to Him. He will fill you with His

"*Divine Love and Peace!*" Allow Him to do that for you. He shall conquer all your fears *and restore you* with *new hope.* A hope of life everlasting, and His unending *love!* You are not only awaiting *Christ's arrival* at Christmas, but His arrival into your heart and soul *now!* Yes, my child, He is anxiously awaiting becoming a part of your every thought, word, and action. He is there for you, my child, *always* and in *all ways.* He would never leave or forsake you. He is already a part of you. You just need to realize it! Allow Him to speak with you. Listen to His voice. Allow Him to guide your every thought, word, and action. Remember, He is there for you, *always,* and in *all ways.* His love for you is unending. His mercy for you is Divine. He wants to give you everything. Just *ask* Him for it, and it shall be given to you.

So, child, do not fret during this time of difficulty. Simply hand it all over to God, and *watch* the *miracles happen.* Remember, *only* God can make the crooked way straight. Only God can perform miracles, and no one else.

Better days are coming! Filled with peace, joy, and happiness. Look forward to these days, for they are *quickly approaching.* Simply," *Let go and let God,*" and watch the miracles happen. *Trust us,* for what we tell you is *true. Peace* is just around the corner. Christ's second coming is now upon you. Remain prepared, for you do not know the hour, or the time of His coming. Remain *mindful* of God with all that you say and do. And *watch the Process,* for God is guiding it all.

Now child, go *in peace* to love and serve the Lord.

We love you so very much, and are guiding you.

Love,
BV & Christ

Dear Child,

Welcome back! We are with you *always* and in all ways. You are never alone. *Know* that all is well, and going according to God's *"Divine Plan."*

Yes, things are beginning to *speed up.* You will see some changes made *quickly.* All for the better I might add. Do not worry about a thing, my child. All shall be made known to you in time. We are guiding you step by step. Remember, all shall be made well, and go according to God's *"Divine Plan." Trust us,* for what we tell you is true, my child. No harm shall come to you. You are *"Divinely Protected."* God has a plan for you, and soon, very soon, all shall be made known to you. Watch the process.

The time is coming when peace, joy, and happiness shall permeate your world! It is a time of great *peace.* Yes, you shall witness Christ's second coming! You shall see *peace-on-earth*! You shall see earth return to it's original "Garden of Eden." All of this was meant-to-be since the beginning of time. Now is the time to *stop, wait,* and *listen* to what God is telling you. Now is the time to allow God to guide your every move. Now is the time to *wait,* and allow God to show you the way. Place everything into His hands, my child, and watch the miracles happen. All of this is upon you, my child. Soon, so very soon, your world shall change completely! All for the better I might add. It is a time of great mystery and celebration! All shall be made better for you, my child. In an *instant* everything can change. So, remain very close to us, my child. We shall guide your every move. Soon, very soon, all shall be revealed to you, my child.

So, continue to remain very close to us in the days ahead, and we shall guide your every move. *Know* that all is well, and going according to *"God's Plan."* Be at *peace. Know* that much better days are coming! We would never lie to you, my child. Place everything into God's hands, and watch the miracles happen. *Trust us,* and *know* that this is *true,* my child.

Now go *in peace* to love and serve the Lord.
We love you very much, and are guiding you.

Love,
BV & Christ

Dear Child,

Welcome back! It's *always* good to see you, my child. Remain very, very close to us in the days ahead. We shall guide your every move. No need to worry or fear, simply stay in the *present moment,* and we shall guide you, my child.

Now is the time to *stop, wait,* and *listen* to what God is telling you to do. Remember, He is with you *always,* and in *all ways.* He shall *never* leave you, my child. So, what is there to fear? *Knowing* that God is *always* with you. Remain calm, and *know* that all is well, and going according to God's "*Divine Plan.*" A plan that was set in motion since the beginning of time.

Child, *trust us,* for what we tell you is *true.* We would *never lie* to you, my child. All that we tell you is part of God's plan in the making. *You* are an *integral* part of His plan. Yes, He has great plans for you, and soon, very soon, they shall be revealed to you. Simply exercise patience now, and wait to be guided. Many wonderful days are ahead for you, my child. Look forward to these days, for they are quickly approaching! They shall be filled with love, joy, peace and happiness! Yes, my child, for what we tell you is *true. Believe us,* and *trust* that much better days are coming. You have *nothing to fear. Trust in God. Know* that all is well, and going according to God's "*Divine Plan.*"

Yes, my child, even though you feel *insignificant and small,* you are a *big* part of God's "*Divine Plan.*" He loves you so very much, and only wants the very best for you, my child. *Know* that this is *true.* He hears your prayers and answers them. Child, much *better days* are ahead for you, filled with peace, joy, love, and happiness! Look forward to these days, for they are quickly approaching! Soon, so very soon, all of this *strife* shall be behind you, my child. The times of being a *shadow* are over! God made you for a purpose! And soon, very soon, it shall be revealed to you, my child. You are a force to be reckoned with! No longer will you tolerate abuse! No longer will you be *put down,* and made to be *silent.* No, God does not want this for you, my child! He made you for a reason, and very soon it shall be revealed to you. So, remain patient. Be silent and calm. Place all of your *faith, hope,* and *trust* in God. *Know* that all is well, and going according to God's *"Divine Plan."* We love you so very much, and are guiding you.

Love,
BV & Christ

Dear Child,

Welcome back, and Happy Easter! Yes, this is all about mankind's salvation! God sent His only son Jesus to you, to free you of your sins, and show you a sign of your *eternal salvation*. Yes, His resurrection from the dead assures you of *eternal life!* Believe this, my child. It is a *great miracle* from God! This is what your religion is all about. *Eternal Salvation!* How miraculous! Thank God each and every day for this miracle, and *outward sign* of His eternal love for you, my child! Yes, if you were the only person on earth, God would do this *just for you!* That is how much He loves you, my child! *Believe us,* for this is *true*! You are *saved* through Christ's death and resurrection! He is deepening your faith now, child. Be grateful for this! He is giving you time to think, watch, and center on His existence and *eternal love* for *you!* No one can take that away from you, my child. Be *grateful* for that! God has given you so very, very much and only wants you to be *grateful for it all!* Thank Him each and every day for *everything* in your life, my child. Through difficult times, we learn to turn *everything* over to God. He makes the crooked way straight, and makes things turn out *better* than *we* could ever dream possible! *Trust us,* for what we tell you is *true,* my child. We would *never lie* to you. Your faith, love, and *trust* in God is being strengthen now. Now that you are *alone* with Him, hand all of your troubles over to Him, and *watch* the miracles happen! Remember, everything is happening for a *reason.* Your life is being *made better.* Much better days are *ahead* of you, my child. You have a rosy future! *Trust us.* Your best days are yet to come. Filled with love, peace, joy, and happiness! Yes, my child, look forward to these days. God is guiding your *every move.* He is a merciful God. He is a kind, *loving,* and understanding God! Allow Him to work His miracles in your life, my child. Open your heart and soul to Him. *Watch* the *miracles happen!*

Your *new life* is about to begin. It shall be a very *happy* one, my child, filled with peace, joy, love, and happiness! Now is the time to *stop, wait, hope,* and *watch the process.* God is working in *mysterious ways.* He only wants the *very best* for you, my child. Soon, very soon, all shall be made well. Soon, very soon, all of this *strife* shall be behind you. Soon, very soon, your life shall change completely. All for the better I may add. *Trust us. Know* that this too shall pass! *Know* that better days are ahead of you. Believe us, for what we tell you is true, my child. God has a plan for you, and very soon, it shall be revealed to you.

So, continue to exercise patience. Place all of your *faith, hope,* and *trust in God.* Watch the miracles happen.

It won't be long now, when all of this shall be behind you, my child.

Now go *in peace* to love and serve the Lord.

We love you so very much, and are guiding you.

Love,
BV & Christ

Dear Child,

Please be *patient!* We are with you through it all. Imagine Christ sitting next to you, holding your hand when you are anxious. He is there comforting you, my child. He is saying, *"Be still, enjoy the present moment."* The time has not yet come for change. Simply *rest* in this *most precious* present moment. The future is *not here yet,* and the past is behind you. Allow us to *guide your every thought.* We are comforting you, my child! Simply *be,* and *know* that all is well, and going according to God's *"Divine Plan."* A plan that was *set-in-motion* since the beginning of time, my child.

Yes, God has a plan for all of us. Soon, very soon, His plan shall be revealed to you. But for now, enjoy this beautiful day. Be thankful for all the gifts God has given you! *Rest* in His presence, for His love and mercy are upon you, my child. Now is the time to just *rest* in God's presence. Feel His love and understanding for you! Only God can love you this much, my child. *Know* that *all is well* and going according to His" *Divine Plan."* Trust us, for what we tell you is true. God has a plan for you, and very soon, it shall be revealed to you, my child. *Know that no harm shall come to you!* We are *protecting you,* my child. Simply *be,* and we shall guide you every step of the way, my child. *Know* that this is true.

We know you are receiving much information from many people. They all have your best interests at heart. But *know* that we are guiding you every step of the way, my child. No harm shall come to you, my child. We have a plan for you, and very soon, it shall be revealed to you.

So, for now, go *in peace* to love and serve the Lord. We love you very much, and are guiding you.

Love,
BV & Christ

Dear Child,

Welcome back! It's *always* good to see you. Child, please remember to pray daily for: *Peace-on-earth*; the conversion of the evil ones; and for God's intercession with our world leaders. Child, it won't be long now, when all of this strife shall be behind you. Yes, my child, all shall be made well. We shall see to it. *Know* that all is well, and going according to God's *"Divine Plan."* A plan which was meant-to-be since the beginning of time. Yes, my child, very soon, all of this shall be *behind you*. All shall be made well. *Trust us,* for what we tell you is *true*. We would never lie to you, my child. All of this *strife* is just about over! Thank God! Very soon, your life shall open up in new and exciting ways! Yes, God has a plan for you, and very soon it shall be revealed to you. For now, have patience, and *trust us*. All of this shall be over in an instant! Thank God! Much better days are ahead of you, my child. They will be filled with love, peace, joy, and happiness! Yes, all shall be made well! A whole *new world* shall open up to you, my child. Look forward to these days, for they are quickly approaching! No longer will you be subject to abuse or shame. No longer shall you be put down, ignored, and discounted. No, my child, you shall be a force to be reckoned with! Very soon, all shall be made well. It is just a matter of time. Much better days are quickly approaching! Yes, my child, these better days are almost here! Believe us, for what we tell you is true. We would *never* lie to you, my child.

For now, watch the process, and all shall be revealed to you.

We love you very much, and are guiding you.

Love,
BV & Christ

Dear Child,

*K*now that all is well, and going according to God's "*Divine Plan*." Watch the process. The truth shall be made known. Remember, God is with you *always* and in *all ways*. You are *never alone*.

Child, keep *in mind* that much *better days* are coming, filled with peace, joy, love, and happiness. Keep in mind all of the *earth angels* who are assisting you now. Thank God for them. Many people love you and are praying for you, my child. That is what is getting you through this difficult time.

Child, soon, oh so very soon, all of this *strife* shall be behind you, my child. *Trust us,* for what we tell you is *true*. We would never lie to you, my child. Much *better days* are coming, and very quickly I might add. Remember, everything can change in an *instant*. All is being made well. Watch the process. Everything happens for a reason.

Very soon all of this shall be over! Thank God! Simply remain very close to us, and we shall guide your *every step*. Remember you are *never alone*. We are with you, *always* and in *all ways*.

So child, *know* that this too shall pass. It is almost over! Remain very close to us, and we shall guide you through it all.

So. child, go *in peace* now *knowing* that all is well, and going according to God's "*Divine Plan*."

We love you very much, and are guiding you.

Love,
BV & Christ

Dear Child,

Do not worry or fret. We are with you, *always* and in *all ways*. Place *everything* into God's hands. He will handle it all.

Child, people are coming to you with information to help and guide you. *Do not be afraid,* God is guiding you. *Know* that He will tell you *what to do,* and *when to do it.* Listen to Him. *Trust Him. Know* that all is well, and going according to God's plans. *Trust us.* We would *never lie* to you, my child. *Know* that *all is well,* and going according to God's plans.

Child, the time is coming when all shall be made well. *Trust us.* Things can change in an instant! Watch the process.

In time, all of this shall be made *clear* to you, my child. For now, place it all into God's hands, and watch the process.

Now, child, go *in peace* to love and serve the Lord.

We love you very much and are guiding you.

Love,
BV & Christ

Dear Child,

Welcome back. Always remember to pray daily for: *Peace-on-earth*; the conversion of the evil ones; and for God's intercession with our world leaders, and encourage others to do so too.

Now for the task at hand. Continue to pray for your President, my child. Pray for his courage and perseverance to carry on. We are protecting him, my child. He is under grave attack by the media, members of his own party, and the democrats, but most of all Satan himself. He does not want to see him succeed. Satan knows he is being guided by God, and wants to put a *stop* to it. *Know* that this truly is a battle of good vs. evil. Remember that good shall prevail and conquer evil. *Know* that this is *true*, my child. We would *never lie* to you. Much *better days* are coming for you, and *all* of mankind. Watch the process. It shall *all* be revealed to you in time. The truth shall be made known.

Now is the time to *stop, wait,* and *listen* to what God is instructing you to do next, then *act* upon it. It won't be long now, when all of this *strife* shall be *behind you!* Thank God! Then, and only then, will your mission be revealed to you, my child. Yes, God has a plan for you, and very soon it shall be revealed to you. But for now, *stop, wait,* and *listen* to what God is instructing you to do next, then *act* upon it. Much *better days* are coming for you, and all of mankind.

Yes, President Trump shall accomplish a lot on his overseas mission. Remember, he is God's *instrument of peace*. You shall see *peace-on-earth* being accomplished very soon! A *new day* is coming for you, and all of mankind. This is all part of God's "*Divine Plan*" since the beginning of mankind. You are living in one of the most exciting times in the history of mankind. *Know* that this is *true*, my child. *Peace-on-earth* is so very near. Christ's second coming is just around the corner. So, remain very close to us, and we shall guide you every step of the way.

So, go *in peace* now, my child, to love and serve the Lord.

We love you so very much, and are guiding you.

Love,
BV & Christ

Dear Child,

Welcome back! It's always good to see you. Remember to pray daily for: *Peace-on-earth*; the conversion of the evil ones; and for God's intercession with our world leaders. Do this each and every day, and encourage others to do so too.

Now for the task at hand. Continue to pray for your President, my child. When he returns to the States, he will be bombarded with criticism and false accusations. Pray for his strength and perseverance to carry on. It is an extremely difficult job, but we are guiding him through it all. Your country needs him right now. Continue to pray for his protection, and those of his family members.

Yes, my child, a *new day* is coming filled, with peace, joy, love, and happiness! *Trust us,* for what we tell you is *true.* No longer will you have *strife* of any kind! *Peace-on-earth* shall be established! Remember, Christ's second coming is just around the corner. Continue to place all of your troubles into God's hands. He will handle it all. Then *watch* as His miracles begin to happen. It won't be long now, when *all* of this *strife* shall be behind you! *Trust us,* for what we tell you is *true.* You are about to see a *new world* open up right before your very eyes. A *new day* is coming for you, and *all* of mankind. Watch the process. God's miracles are at work here. *Watch* as His new and wonderous deeds are put to action. Yes, my child, a *new day* is coming for everyone. *Know* that all is well, and going according to God's *"Divine Plan."* So, watch as His *"Divine Plan"* is put into action. Many miracles are about to occur. Yes, this was all part of His plan since the beginning of time. So, *watch* the process, and *know* that all is well, and being made well.

So, go *in peace* now, my child, to love and serve the Lord.

We love you very much, and are guiding you.

Love,
BV & Christ

Dear Child,

D o not worry or fret. Remember, we are with you through it all. We would *never* leave or forsake you. We are with you, *always* and in *all ways*.

Yes, my child, the days ahead are full of *change*. *All* for the *better* I may add. Now is the time to *stop, wait*, and *listen* to what God is instructing you to do next, than *act* upon it. Remember, *you are not alone!* We are with you every step of the way. No harm shall come to you, my child. We are protecting you.

It's just a tiny bit longer, and then this *strife* shall *vanish in an instant!* Yes, my child, believe us, for what we tell you is *true*. We would never lie to you. Much *better days* are coming! They will be filled with peace, love, joy, and happiness! These days are awaiting you, my child. Look forward to these days, for they are quickly approaching. Watch the process, and *know* that all is well, and being made well.

Child, a bright *new future* awaits you! God has a plan for you, and very soon, it shall be revealed to you. Look forward to these days, for they are quickly approaching.

Child, whenever you feel down, simply place everything into God's hands, then *watch* His miracles happen! He will have things turn out *better* than you could ever dream possible! *Trust us,* for what we tell you is *true*. Watch the process, and *know* that *all is well* and being *made well*.

So, go *in peace* now, my child, to love and serve the Lord.

We love you very much, and are guiding you.

Love,
BV & Christ

Dear Child,

Welcome back! It's *always* good to see you. Please, please, please continue to pray for: *Peace-on-earth*; the conversion of the evil ones; and for God's intercession with our world leaders. It is *vitally important* that you do this each and every day, and encourage others to do so too.

Now for the task at hand. Remain in the *present moment,* my child. That is where God is guiding you. It won't be long now when *all* of this *strife* shall be behind you! *Trust us,* for what we tell you is *true.* We would never lie to you, my child. *Know* that *all is well,* and being *made well.*

Soon, oh so very soon, God's plan shall be revealed to you. Yes, your future is filled with love, peace, joy, and happiness! It is a rosy one. Watch the process, and *know* that all is well, and being made well.

We are with you, my child, every step of the way. When in doubt, simply *stop, wait,* and *listen* to what God is *instructing* you to do next, then *act* upon it. Do not worry or fret, my child. Simply place *everything* into God's hands, and watch as His miracles unfold right before your very eyes. Remember, God has a plan for you, and very soon, it shall be revealed to you. *Trust us,* for what we tell you is *true.* Much better days are coming, filled with peace, joy, love, and happiness! Look forward to them, for they are quickly approaching.

So, for now, simply *stop, wait,* and *listen t*o what God is instructing you to do next, then *act* upon it.

So, go *in peace* now, my child, to love and serve the Lord.

We love you very much, and are guiding you.

Love,
BV & Christ

Dear Child,

Welcome back! It's *always* good to see you. Child, remain *very close* to us in the days ahead. Many changes are occurring in your life, and we shall guide you through it all. Remember, they are *all* for the better I may add.

Yes, soon, oh so very soon, God's plan shall be revealed to you, my child. But for now, continue to do your daily activities on your check list, and soon your life shall be *in order*. Remember, you are not going through this alone. We are guiding you through it all. Watch the process, and *know* that all is being made well.

Child, a new and wonderous world is about to *open up* right before your very eyes. Yes, a *new day* is dawning for you, and all of mankind. Watch the process. Remember, *peace* is on its way, and Christ's second coming is just around the corner. Yes, my child, you shall experience all of this in your lifetime! Continue to *watch the process* as God's miracles unfold right before your very eyes.

Yes, continue to count your blessings, my child. God wants to give you it all! He is so very pleased with your closeness, and turning your *entire life* over to Him. He will continue to guide and bless you. So, remain very close to Him, and you shall be guided through it all! Watch the process.

So, my child, continue to enjoy your day, being ever so *mindful* of God with all that you say and do.

Now go *in peace* to love and serve the Lord.

We love you very much, and are guiding you.

Love,
BV & Christ

Dear Child,

Welcome back! It's *always* good to see you. Please, please, please, continue to pray for: *Peace-on-earth*; the conversion of the evil ones; and for God's intercession with our world leaders. It is *vitally important* that you do this each and every day, and encourage others to do so too.

Child, do not worry or fret about a thing. Place everything into God's hands, and watch His miracles happen. Yes, you are feeling the wrongs you have done to others now, either intentionally or by oversight. We know you feel badly about these things. Place them into God's hands, ask for His forgiveness, and watch His miracles happen. Continue to pray for those who have wronged you. They too are terribly misguided. Pray for their souls.

Child, the time is coming when you shall *see a new life*. It shall be filled with peace, joy, love, and happiness. Currently, you are restoring *order* into your life. You are getting things done, and setting the path for your future. *Watch* as it *all unfolds* right before your very eyes.

A *new day* is coming filled with peace, joy, love, and happiness! Yes, my child, it is happening as we speak. Much better days are ahead for *you*, and *all* mankind. Watch the process.

So, remain very close to us in the days ahead. They are changing quickly. *Know* that we are here with you, guiding you through it all.

So for now, take each day as it comes, *knowing* we are with you through it all.

Now go *in peace,* my child, to love and serve the Lord.

We love you very much, and are guiding you.

Love,
BV & Christ

Dear Child,

Welcome back! Yes, today is the feast of St. Nicholas. How the entire tradition of Christmas giving got started.

Child, the timing of this retreat was *absolutely* in God's hands. Yes, you are meant-to-be here. Remember to hand all of your troubles over to God, then *watch* His miracles happen. It shall all be for the better, my child, God has a way of making things turn out *better* than you could ever dream possible! Simply watch the process, and see how God's plan manifest! All for the better, I may add.

Child, now is the time to *stop, wait,* and *listen* to what God's instructing you to do, then *act* upon it. It won't be long now, when *all* of this *strife* shall be behind you! Watch the process as it *all* unfolds right before your very eyes. *Trust us,* for what we tell you is *true,* my child . We would *never lie* to you. All is well, and being made well.

As the days ahead begin to unfold right before your very eyes, you shall begin to see God's plan in action! You will marvel at His abundant generosity! Yes, my child, *all* is well, and being *made well. Watch* as it *all* unfolds right before your very eyes.

God has a plan for you, and very soon, it shall be revealed to you. Watch the process.

A *new day* is coming for you, and *all* of mankind! *Peace-on-earth* is being established. Christ's second coming is just around the corner. Soon, oh so very soon, a *new world* shall *open up* right *before* your very eyes. No longer will you have man's inhumanity to man. No! That day shall be over! Watch the process. The time for *peace* is oh so very near! *Trust us,* for what we tell you is *true.*

So, continue to remain very close very close to us, my child, and we shall guide your every thought, word, and deed.

Now go *in peace,* my child, to love and serve the Lord.

We love you so very much, and are guiding you.

Love,
BV & Christ

Dear Child,

Yes, it is quite the *winter day.* Cold and damp and still. Remember, God is here with you. It is all going according to God's will. Now is the time to *stop, wait,* and *listen* to what God is instructing you to do, then *act* upon it.

Yes, my child, you need to *stop* and *be still.* You are so use to going full speed ahead, that you don't know how to *stop!* Now is your time to *stop.* You don't have to fit anything into your schedule. You've done it all, before you arrived. Now just *listen* to God, and *watch* His miracles in *action.* He is guiding your every thought, word, and deed. No need to stress about anything. Simply *be.* Appreciate the *moment.* God is in the *moment.* Notice the sights and sounds of the *moment.* Yes, my child, this is where God is. Allow Him to speak to you. Be present to His voice. Be present to His loving *Being!* Yes, my child, you are guided every step of the way. He is guiding your every thought, word, and deed. He is making the crooked way straight, not only for you, but the entire world! *Watch* His plan in action! Marvel at His goodness and love for all of mankind! He is about to make Himself known in a very *big way!* Watch the process, and *know* that *all is well,* and being *made well.*

Many changes are coming upon the land. All for the *better* I may add. Soon, oh so very soon, you shall see *peace-on-earth.* Soon, oh so very soon, you shall witness Christ's second coming! Yes, my child, it is *all happening* in your lifetime! So, remain very close to us, and we shall guide you every step of the way.

Now go *in peace,* my child, to love and serve the Lord.

We love you so very much, and are guiding you.

Love,
BV & Christ

Dear Child,

Welcome back! I know it's cold outside, but you are safe and warm here inside. Thank God you have this time away from your activities. Yes, my child, here you can focus in God, and be mindful of Him in every moment. He loves you so very much and wants you to be *"mindful"* of Him in every moment. He is there for you, *always* and in *all ways*. Yes, child, He wants to give you it all. Simply, *"Ask, and you shall receive."* He wants to give you it all. All that life has to offer. You are His *precious one,* whom He loves dearly. Allow Him into your life. Allow Him to enter every phase of your life. He is there waiting to receive you. Remember, He is with you *always* and in *all ways*. He will *never leave* you, my child. Allow God to enter your heart, mind, and soul. Become His instrument. He will guide you through it all. He is with you every step of the way. Remember, with God on your side, all is possible. Without God, nothing is possible.

So, my child, remain very close to us in the days ahead. Many changes are upon you, and your world. All for the *better* I may add.

My child, do not worry or fret. The days ahead are *good ones. Watch* as they *all unfold* right before your very eyes. Much better days are coming filled with peace, joy, love, and happiness. Watch the process, and *know* that *all is well,* and being *made well.*

So, go *in peace* now, my child, to love and serve the Lord.

We love you so very much, and are guiding you.

Love,
BV & Christ

Dear Child,

Welcome back! It's always good to see you. Please, please, please, remember to pray daily for: *Peace-on-earth*; the conversion of the evil ones; and for God's intercession with our world leaders. It is *vitally important* that you do this each and every day, and encourage others to do so too.

Now for the task at hand. Pray for your world my child. It is in *dire need* of prayers. Many scandals are being made known. The public is *losing interest* in your government. They are discouraged and feel hopeless. They *all* need to turn to God for answers! They need to place *all* of their troubles into His hands, then *watch* the miracles happen! This is *true*, my child! Once everyone turns to God, you will have *peace-on-earth*! It's that simple. But until then, continue to pray for your world, your president, and *all* of the elected officials. Only through prayer, can things be accomplished! *Know* that this is *true*. God hears your prayers and answers them!

Now is the time to *stop, wait,* and *listen* to what God is instructing you to do, then *act* upon it. This is so true for now, since many things are changing quickly. Watch the process, and see how God's miracles unfold right before your very eyes.

Child, never worry or fret. Place all of your concerns into God's hands, then *watch* His miracles in *action*. They will *all* unfold right before your very eyes. Yes, my child, for what we tell you is *true*. We would never lie to you.

God has a plan for you, and very soon, it shall be revealed to you. Yes, my child, you are alive today because of God's mission for you. It shall be revealed to you very soon. Watch the process, and *know* that all is well, and being made well.

Child, the time is coming when all of this *strife* shall be behind you! *Trust us,* for what we tell you is *true*. The days ahead are full of peace, joy, love, and happiness. It was all part of God's *"Divine Plan"* since the beginning of time. *Watch* as it *all* unfolds right before your very eyes. Many changes are occurring *now* in order to bring about *world peace*. It is happening as we speak. None of your world leaders want war. Only N. Korea, and he shall be obliterated.

So, my child, continue to pray for: *Peace-on-earth*; the conversion of the evil ones; and for God's intercession with our world leaders. God hears your prayers and answers them. All shall be made well. You are about to witness Christ's second coming and *peace-on-earth*. Yes, my child, it is all coming to fruition. What an exciting time to be alive! Watch the process, as it *all* unfolds right before your very eyes.

So my child, go *in peace* to love and serve the Lord.

We love you so very much, and are guiding you.

Love,
BV & Christ

Dear Child,

Welcome back! It's *always* good to see you. Please, please, please, remember to pray daily for: *Peace-on-earth*; the conversion of the evil ones; and for God's intercession with our world leaders. It is *vitally important* that you do this each and every day, and encourage others to do so too.

Now child, continue to pray for your world. It is in *dire need* of prayers. Evil forces are attempting to overthrow your government! Pray that this *does not happen*! God blessed America and continues to do so. America is the *shining light* for the world to see. *Pray* that it continues to shine amidst all of the darkness.

Yes, my child, *know* that a *new day* is coming for you, and *all* of mankind. Watch the process. See God's miracles in action! The Eagles winning the Super Bowl, for their first time in years is a miracle for *all* to see. More is yet to come. Watch how God continues to bestow His love for you, and *all* of mankind. Yes, my child, His love for you is overflowing! Watch us it *all* unfolds right before your very eyes.

A *new day* is upon you now! It is filled with peace, joy, love, and happiness. The *best* is yet to come! Look forward to these days, for they are quickly approaching. God's love for mankind is so abundant. *Watch* as it all unfolds right before your very eyes. Much peace, joy, love, and happiness is about to unfold right before your very eyes. Yes, my child, the 1000 years of peace is upon you. It truly shall be as if heaven descended upon earth. A *new day* is here *now!* Watch the process.

Remember, my child, whenever you are troubled, simply *stop, wait,* and *listen* to what God is instructing you to do, then *act* upon it. It won't be long now, when your world shall change completely. All for the better I may add. Look forward to these better days, and *know* that all is well, and being *made well.*

So, go *in peace* now, my child, to love and serve the Lord. We love you very much, and are guiding you.

Love,
BV & Christ

Dear Child,

Good morning, and Happy Spring! Yes, today is the first day of Spring. Go out and enjoy it.

Child, we are happy that you came to join us today. We have a lot to share with you. Again, please, please, please, remember to pray daily for: *Peace-on-earth*; the conversion of the evil ones; and for God's intercession with our world leaders. It is *vitally important* that you do this each and every day, and encourage others to do so too.

Now for the task at hand. Child, continue to pray for your world and democracy. Both sides of the political spectrum are tearing each other apart! God blessed America, and will continue to do so. But this nonsense has got to *stop*! It is tearing apart the very fiber of America! God wants you *all* united in your love for Him. He will guide you through it all. He will help to bring about *peace- on-earth, but* you must *ask* Him for it! Only God can make the crooked way straight. Only God can perform His miracles, in order to bring about *peace. Pray* that all is well, and being made well. *Know* that God hears your prayers and answers them. Yes, my child, He is *all knowing and all loving. Trust Him* with all that you say and do. He *knows better* than anyone. Place *all* of your troubles into God's hands, and *watch* His miracles happen.

So my child, whenever you are unsure about anything, simply *stop, wait,* and *listen* to what God is instructing you to do, then *act* upon it. *Never give up!* For God is with you *always,* and in *all* ways.

Now, go *in peace* my child, to love and serve the Lord.

We love you very much, and are guiding you.

Love,
BV & Christ

Dear Child,

Welcome back! We have so much to discuss with you today. Please, please, please, *do not worry! Know* that *all is well* and being *made well*. Now is the time to *stop, wait,* and *listen* to what God is instructing you to do, then *act* upon it. We are guiding your every move, my child. No harm shall come to you. We are protecting you. We have a plan for you and soon, very soon, it shall be revealed to you. But for now, continue to remain in the *present moment* so God can guide you through it all.

Yes, my child, there is government corruption throughout your planet. That is why we are instructing you to constantly pray for: *Peace-on-earth*; the conversion of the evil ones; and for God's intercession with our world leaders. It is *vitally important* that you do this each and every day, and encourage everyone you meet to do so too. Remember, God hears your prayers and answers them. *Peace-on-earth* is part of His *"Divine Plan." Don't despair. Watch the process.* Much better days are coming, filled with peace, and joy, love, and happiness! Look forward to these days, my child, for they *are* quickly approaching.

Remember, *"Love Shall Conquer All!"* Yes, my child, place *everything* into God's hands, and then *watch* His miracles happen. Remember, only God can make the crooked way straight. Only God can perform miracles. Only God can bring about *peace-on-earth.*

I know things can seem pretty bleak right now, but you do not see the entire picture. Only God can see it. Remember, God is *in charge*, and no one else. He hears your prayers and answers them.

You are on the verge of great many changes. All for the *better* I may add. *Watch* the process, and *know* that all is well, and being made well.

Keep the faith. Much *better days* are coming for you, and *all* of mankind! *Know* that this is *true*. We would never lie to you, my child.

So, go *in peace* to love and serve the Lord.

We love you very much, and are guiding you.

Love,
BV & Christ

Dear Child,

Welcome back! It's *always* good to see you. Please, please, please, continue to pray for: *Peace- on-earth*; the conversion of the evil ones; and for God's intercession with our world leaders. It is *vitally important* that you do this each and every day, and encourage others to do so too.

Now for the task at hand. Continue to pray for your world, my child. *A great shift is taking place as we speak*. Remember, good shall conquer evil. The *truth* shall be made *known*.

Many changes are upon you. All for the better I may add. Watch the process.

Yes, my child, we encourage you to take things day by day, moment to moment. We are with you, and guiding you through it all. Remember, we told you no harm shall come to you. We are protecting you. *Trust us*, for what we tell you is *true*. We would never lie to you, my child.

Now is the time to *stop, wait*, and *listen* to what we are instructing you to do, then *act* upon it. It won't be long now, when all of this *strife* shall be behind you. Much better days are coming, filled with peace, joy, love, and happiness. Watch the process.

So my child, continue to remain very close to us, so we can guide you. Many changes are occurring during the month of July. *Watch* as they all unfold right before your very eyes.

So, go *in peace* now, my child, to love and serve the Lord.

We love you very much, and are guiding you.

Love,
BV & Christ

Dear Child,

Yes, everything that happens is meant-to-be for a reason. You may not know it, but God is fine tuning you to be His instrument of peace. Yes, my child, He has a *"Divine Plan,"* and is working part of it through you. Many things happen in our lives, and we may not understand why at the time, but it becomes crystal clear much later.

God, with His unending love for you, continues to work in your life moment by moment. He is with you, always and in all ways. He would never leave or forsake you. He wants you to depend on Him for everything, no matter how large or small. He wants to be part of your life! Let Him into your life in *all ways*. He is there for you, and wants to give you it all. All you need to do is *ask* Him, and you shall *receive* all that you *ask* of Him and much more.

Be grateful to Him for everything! Yes, my child, even when tragedy or sadness occurs, there is a purpose in it. Remember, God's ways are *not* our ways.

Sometimes we can't understand what is God's purpose in our lives, but given time, it's *all* made crystal clear. Watch the process.

Gods wants you to depend on Him for everything! Yes, turn to Him for large and small problems, even when good things happen, *be grateful*. He wants to give you even more.

By now you must *know* that God wants to be a part of your life with *everything* you are going through. There isn't a situation, too large or small, that God can't handle. He wants to be with you through it all. Remember, He is the one who is *always* with us, and we are the ones who forget about Him at times. We need to remain *mindful* of God with *all* that we say and do. He will guide us through it all. Then *watch* His miracles happen. He wants to give you it all. All you need to do is *ask* Him, and He will give it to you. It's that simple. So my child, whenever you worry or fret, simply place it all into God's hands, then *watch* what happens. You will find it hard to believe how *wonderful* earth can be once *peace-on-earth* occurs.

It will feel as if heaven descended upon earth. You will feel as light as a feather *knowing* that *all is well,* and *being made well.* People will love God with their whole heart and soul, and love their neighbor as themselves. It shall be a *glorious time* to be alive! Yes, my child, much *better days* are coming, filled with peace, joy, love and happiness. Watch the process, and *know* that all is well, and being made well.

But until then, continue to *stop, wait,* and *listen* to what is instructing you to do, then *act* upon it.

So, go *in peace* now, my child, to love and serve the Lord.

We love you very much, and are guiding you.

Love,
BV & Christ

CHAPTER FIVE

HOW GOD SPEAKS TO US. DO NOT WORRY OR FRET.

Dear Child,

Why are you crying? Where is your faith? God is handling everything. He hears your cry for *peace* and will answer your prayers. Be not afraid. He is watching over you and guiding you. It is God's will, not our will to be done. The time has come for all of mankind to *stop*, *listen*, and *trust in God*. Now more than ever, He is begging for your love and attention. When will mankind ever learn. War is not the answer. Only love and peace are important. "*Love one another as I have loved you.*" It's not that difficult. Love yourselves, your neighbors, and your enemies. "*Do not be afraid. I am with you always and in all ways.*"

I only want the best for you. "*Ask, and you shall receive.*" Continue to live your lives for God. Do not turn your back on Him. He would not turn His back on you. *Believe that He loves you, and is guiding you.*

Continue to pray daily for: *World Peace*; God's intercession with our world leaders; and the conversion of the evil ones.

Believe in God's love and mercy. Know that He is there for you, always and in all ways. Never doubt His love for you.

Remember, all is well. Have faith. Believe in Him who is all knowing and loving. *Know* that He is there for you, at all times, and is guiding you. Stay close to Him. Be *mindful* of Him. He will never leave you. All things will happen according to God's plan. No matter how mankind tries to intercede. God's plan will take over. Good will win over evil. His "*Divine plan*" will be fulfilled.

Trust in Him, and *know* that He only wants the very best for you.

Now continue on with your life, *knowing* that God is there for you, always and in all ways. *Never doubt His love for you. Believe that He is there for you at all times. You are never alone.*

Trust in His love and mercy for you, and *know* that He will grant you your every wish. He hears your prayers and answers them.

Have faith, believe in Him, and trust that He is doing His very best for you. Be calm and at peace. Do not worry. You will see God's plan at work. *"Be still and know that I am God."* Be quiet, and listen to Him.

He loves you very much, and is guiding you.

Love,
BV and Christ

Dear Child,

Thank you once again for coming to visit us. It's very important that you keep up your prayer work. Now is not the time to neglect it. The world is in dire need of prayer. Especially now. Pray for peace and harmony. Pray for the end of man's inhumanity to man. Pray to stop the bloodshed.

Remember, I told you a while back that this war could have been prevented if everyone just prayed? Please continue to pray for: *World peace*; the conversion of the evil ones; and for God's intercession with our world leaders. *These prayers are heard, and they shall be answered.*

You will see *world peace* in your lifetime. Heaven and earth will be united. God will come again. So, continue to pray, and stay close to God. He is guiding your every step. He will make the crooked way straight. Believe in Him. Have faith in Him. And *know* that *all is well.* No need to worry or be concerned. God is directing everything according to His *"Divine plan."* His will, not *our will* be done. Do not fall into the *fear trap. Fear* is the opposite of love, and *God is love.* Turn your back on the media which plays into fear, and continue to pray to God. His love will conquer all. *Know and believe* that this is true. Have faith. Continue to pray for strength and perseverance. God will see you through this step by step, little by little. I know it's not easy in today's world to make time for God, but continue to do so, and He will do the rest. This earthly life is truly a test. To see how much you love God, and will return to Him. Try your very best, against all odds, to remain *close to Him.* He will be your guiding force. No need to look ahead. Simply stay in the *present moment,* and He will do the rest. Remember, it's *not our time,* but in *God's time!* All things will be accomplished in His time. *Stay close to Him. Know* that He is there for you, *always* and in *all ways. Stay close to Him.* He will protect and guide you. Do not fear. Fear is the absence of God. Love conquers all. It extends even beyond death, as you know with your dad. Yes, *peace missions* are being set up both on earth as it is in heaven. *Love will conquer evil. Keep praying,* and *stay close to God.* He is guiding and protecting you. No need to worry about anything. *God is with you at all times, and in all ways. Believe that you are not alone. Do not despair.* Stay calm, and pray always and in all ways.

The good people in this world need to be reinforced to continue their prayerful ways. They are being heard. Stay persistent in your prayer life. Good will conquer evil. Believe this, and know that all is well.

We are guiding you.

Love,
BV & Christ

Dear Child,

Welcome back! This afternoon I would like to discuss *time,* or the lack of it, in people's lives today. No one takes the *time* to be quiet, to sit or rest a while. God speaks to us through *silence.* No wonder no one is close to God anymore. They do not take the *time* to be *silent,* and listen to His message for us. Only a few people receive His messages on retreat when they do centering prayer or meditation. The rest of the world runs at 100 mph, and where does that get you? A heart attack? Each and every person needs to take a *time out* at least once per day, preferably twice a day. Allow your thoughts and body to rest, and let God into your hearts and minds. This is the time you will be guided by God. You will *know* what direction to take in your life, if you allow yourselves some *silence. Peace comes through silence.* Allow God to work in your life. Believe me, once you incorporate *silence* into your daily life, life will become much easier for you. Your burdens will be lifted because God is handling them for you. You will become much happier and peaceful. When the world feels like it is *getting to you, stop,* and take a *time out.* That is the time to be with God. Then everything will fall into place. Sounds too simple to be true? Well, it is as easy as that, when you take a few moments to be *silent.* That is the time to let God into your life, and let Him handle things. It doesn't have to be *that difficult.* We make it difficult when we have the attitude *if it is meant to be, it's up to me.* Where is God in all of this? Don't you realize that your very breath comes from God? You have *no control* over your life. Only God does through His *Divine Plan.* So, you may *think* you are *in charge* of it all, but you are deeply mistaken. God handles everything. Just let Him into your life, and it will become much easier for you. No worries, because God will take care of everything. It is *faith* that gets us through the tough times, as well as, the good times. God directs everything. Just make the *free choice* to choose God over evil.

Hell is *lack of God*. It is a place of despair. Sometimes we create our own *hell* without even knowing it. We choose to do it all by ourselves without letting God into our lives. Then a sense of desperation, feeling lost and lonely, sets into our psyche. Where is God in all of this? Who left Him out? We did when we forgot to incorporate Him into our daily lives. It's so very important to be *mindful* of God in each and everything we do. We can accomplish nothing without His help. How foolish we are to think we can accomplish it *all by ourselves*. We are fooling ourselves, and one day, it will *catch up* with us! So, take that *time out* each day to be with God. Believe me, you need Him more than He needs you. Let God into your life to guide and direct you. Feel His love, understanding, and compassion for you. All you have to do is *show up,* and He will do the rest. Subtle changes will begin to occur in your life. People may notice you becoming nicer than before, and wonder what happened. God, in His *silence,* will be working through you, to transform you according to His ways, not your ways. We are but mere instruments of God to bring about *peace* in our lives and this world. Allow Him to work Himself into your life. Let's face it, the way we are doing things is *not working.* Why not give God a chance? It's so simple, yet so difficult for some to "*Let go, and let God.*" I guess it's easier said than done. However, once it is done, and you feel the difference of having God work through your life, you will be changed forever. There is no turning back. You would not want to return to a life full of misery and disappointment. Once you have allowed God into your life, you will become happier than you ever dreamed possible. You will be a changed person. You will view circumstances and situations in your life much differently than before. The human race does not have to be miserable. We create our own cells, and do not know how to get out of them. "*Let go, and let God.*" He knows what is best for us. It's a question of *trust.* Do we *trust Him* to get us out of misery? One that we have created? Yes, He hears our prayers and answers them. *Never doubt His love for you.* It is immense and all encompassing. "*Let go, and let God.*" You will see the difference He makes in your life, when you *restore your faith in Him.* Only God knows what is best for us. Allow Him to work for you. Open yourselves up to His divine love and mercy, and watch what happens. You will be happier than you ever dreamed possible. Miracles do happen each and every day of our lives. Stay close to God, have faith and trust in Him, and *know* that all things are possible with God.

We love you very much, and are guiding you.

Love,
BV & Christ

Dear Child,

Welcome back! It's always good to see you. Today we will discuss *freedom*. What does it take to be *free*? To have freedom of anxiety and fear, *we must have a great faith* in God. With total *trust* in His *Divine Will*, and knowing that *all is well*. It is not easy to give up our *control*, and let God have His way. Thy will, not our will be done.

Once you have given up all worries and problems, you will have a change in mindset. This change brings about *freedom*. This *freedom* permeates from being to being as you see on your retreat. If everyone in the world turned their lives to God, we would have *world freedom*. Not just in every single solitary mind, but the mindset of the world would be changed. Now is the time to turn your hearts and minds to God. Now is the time to give up *self* and surrender to God. Now is the time to *"Let go, and let God."* You say it's not easy to surrender to God. However, is it easier to harbor hatred and resentment? This exhausts the body. Letting go and letting God, sets you *free. Freedom* of all worries and problems, once you place them into God's hands, *knowing* that He is handling everything. He is with you every moment of the day. He *sets you free!* You are *free* to be who God made you to be. *Free* to carry out His will. *Free* to live each moment fully. *Free* to be who God made you to be, without any hatred or resentment or fear, blocking you from being who you were meant to be. *Freedom* is a glorious thing. It allows you to soar to the highest heights of your being. It allows you to enjoy each and every moment.

Don't block yourselves by saying *I can't do this*. Say yes to God, and let Him handle the rest. Your way is not working, and can take eternity to achieve if left up to your own means. God's way gets you there much quicker and easier. Do not question why or how this is done. It simply is an *act of faith*. God wants us all to be *free* to love Him. *Free* to be who we were meant to be. We cannot achieve this without God's help. His love and guidance will *set us free!* The birds of the sky are *free* to soar because they praise God with their singing day and night. Set your *soul free* by loving God, and turning your life over to Him. He will guide you in everything you do. With God at your side, you don't even need to think anymore. Just let Him guide you. Let Him speak to you. He will tell you what to do next. So, stay in the *present moment,* and be *free* to hear God's word. Our past is behind us, and our future is not here yet. All we have is this very *precious moment.* A moment given by God. A moment to cherish. Be *free* in this moment, so He can guide you. *Know* that He is with you, always and in all ways. His will, not our will be done.

Freedom is so very precious, not just for our souls, but for our country. In the past, war and bloodshed have brought about *freedom* to our country. Why not try *trusting in God.* This can be accomplished without violence, and bring about much peace. Do not let history repeat itself through wars. Let God into your lives. Tell everyone you meet about God. Tell them to pray daily for: *Peace-on-earth;* God's intersession with our world leaders; and for the conversion of the evil ones. *Now is the time to let freedom reign within your hearts.* Allow God into your being! Let Him speak to you. Be kind to yourselves, and your fellow man, as God is so very kind and loving to you.

Let *freedom reign within the hearts and minds of everyone!* We so desperately need to turn our lives over to God. *Now* more than ever before in the history of mankind. We are on the eve of destruction. Please, please, please, I am pleading with you to choose *good* over evil. Love your fellow man. You are *free* to do so. Talk and communicate with him. Try to *understand* your differences, and show compassion. Love them as God loves you. Once you do this, you set yourselves *free* and the *world free.* It sounds so easy as a solution to the world problems, but it is attainable. Choose God, and you will be *free. Free* of all your obstacles and worries. *Free* to allow yourself to be who you were meant to be. *Free* to allow this world to be what it was created to be. *Free* to love your fellowman, and our planet earth. This is *essential* in order to *save our world. We must return to love.* Be *free* to love as God has meant us to do. Be *free* to help our fellowman. Be *free* to save our planet. Be *free* to love God with our whole heart and soul. This is the answer to our world problems. This is what will set us free! *Love* will set us *free.* God designed it that way. We have *free choice.* We can choose love of

God and each other, or death and destruction. In the end, good will conquer evil. God will prevail. Whose team do you want to be on? It's your *freedom* of choice.

We love you very much, and are guiding you.

Love,
BV & Christ

Dear Child,

Today let us begin with *peace*. Something highly coveted, yet little worked for in this world. The world thrives on negativity, conflict, and sensationalism. *Peace* seems *impossible* to obtain, therefore, why even try? It can also be humdrum and boring to some people. With the *I give up, and I don't care* attitude, no wonder it can't be obtained. *You do not have to* settle for war! It costs too many lives, especially among civilians. *Stop being negative*! It is a self-fulfilling attitude. Do not go with the flow of the media and general public. Stop this nonsense! Where is your faith in God? Where is your belief that He is helping you? It is *time you wake up, and turn to God* for your answers. *Pray, pray, pray* daily for: *World Peace*; for the conversion of the evil ones; and for God's intercession with our world leaders. *Speak of God on a daily basis.* Restore *hope* into people's lives. There is a better way to solve the problems of the world. You need God's help! Do it *now*! Your world can still be saved! *Do not give up!* God is with you, always and in all ways. He hears your prayers and answers them. Miracles *do happen every day. Hope* is what the world needs today. In the minds and hearts of everyone. In order to have *peace-on-earth*, it must begin with you. Each and every one of you *must become peaceful.* If you had *peace* in your hearts, it would be like an epidemic. It would be contagious, and everyone would want it. Only then could *world peace* become possible. You need to love God, and your fellowman. You need to *help* each other, not *hurt* each other. Can't you see this? Are you that ignorant to the needs of human nature? What has this world become? Please, please, please rise above the hatred, prejudice, and greed of this world, and turn to God. The world can be a much better place. Let this happen for you. God intended that you all live in peace and harmony. *Turn to God* so you can restore this state as it was in the beginning of time. God will help you. You will not be doing this alone. Just turn to Him for your help and guidance. He will grant you the *peace* and perseverance so you can convince your fellowman to follow Him. *Now,* more than ever before, you need to do this. *Turn to God.* It is so *extremely urgent.* Do not be passive with this attitude. Be active and aggressive. Speak to everyone you meet about this. Your press certainly is broadcasting fear and despair into the hearts of mankind on a daily basis. In fact, they are doing this several times a day. So, you need to combat this attitude with courage, strength, and perseverance. It can be done with God on your side. Do not give up hope, faith, or trust in God. He is there for you, always and in all ways. Just ask for His help! He is waiting for you. *Do not give up God or your fellowman.* Help God by working together with Him to turn this world around. Many of you already are asking for *world peace,* but God needs your help too. Be His mouthpiece to mankind. He will tell you what to do and say. Through your actions, people will be convinced that there is *another way. Do not give up! It is not too late! Peace can be achieved on earth today. God works in mysterious ways. Miracles do happen. Have faith, hope, and trust in God. Stay close to Him and never doubt His love for you. It is eminent that you act now*! Tell everyone you meet to *turn to God.* He will work through each and every one of you to achieve *world peace.* This is a test. It is your time *now to turn to God* for *world peace. Know* that Miracles Happen, and that *world peace* can be achieved. There are legends of angels and souls of loved ones, who are in heaven, working on *world peace.* There are many of you on earth working and praying for *world peace.* Your legends need to be increased so that heaven and earth can be as one. Stay *peaceful inside,* and know that God is handling everything. Put it all into His hands. He creates miracles. Each and every one of you need to maintain that peacefulness in your hearts. This will help to convince others that *peace* is not only possible, but a viable solution. It's *so important* that you do this *now.* Stay close to God. Never doubt His love for you. Remain calm and at *peace* no matter what happens. *Know that God is handling it all.* Be calm. Do not get *caught up* in the fear and frenzy of the world. *Stay at peace.* Ask God to help you remain this way. *Do not fear, for God is here.* He is here to help you all. He is here to give you as much love as you can humanly handle. He is here to help and guide you. Whenever fear creeps into your mind or heart, say *"God help me now."* And He will be there for you to dissipate any doubt. *This is what you must do in order to help bring about world peace.* Any questions? Ask God, and

He will answer them. You need to proceed with blind faith. You need to *trust* God in everything. You need to turn your lives over to God so that He can work through you to convince others. Pray daily for: *World peace*; the conversion of the evil ones; and for God's intercession with our world leaders.

This is not an easy time, but *good* will *conquer evil*. Stay close to God, and He will help you with everything. God provides. "Ask, and you shall receive." *Know* that He is there for you, always and in all ways. Never doubt His love for you. Stay close and listen to Him. He is guiding your every step. He will never let you down. Never doubt His love for you, it is immense! "*Seek, and you shall find.*" "Ask, and you shall receive." Believe, believe, believe, that He is there for you, and He can help you! You are not in this alone. He is there for you, always and in all ways.

Now rest, but *know* that God is with you.

We love you very much, and are guiding you.

Love,
BV & Christ

Dear Child,

Today is a glorious day, given by God, filled with warmth and sunshine. Every day will be this good with God in your heart. He will guide you through each and every day. He will place into your thoughts, what you shall do next about every situation. As you saw for yourself this morning. It's *never too late to turn to him*. He is *always there waiting for you*. *Waiting to be part of your life*. You wouldn't believe how much easier your entire life would flow with God in it. No need to worry or think. He would guide you every step of the way. No need to be concerned about anything. This is what you call *faith*. Faith in God and the unknown, but believe that *all is well*. This is how God wants you to be like *little children*. Allowing Him to guide and direct you. He will teach you the ways of everlasting life. He will show you how to do things for the good of His will, which is for the good of all the earth. Never fear or doubt His word. He has a *"Divine Plan"* for everything. It's that easy, yet so hard to give up our *control*. In reality, we don't have control over anything. It's God working through us with His daily presence and action in our lives. Acknowledge Him on a daily basis. He is with us moment by moment. Always willing to assist us in time of need. He is never too tired or overwhelmed to answer our prayers. *Know* that He is there for us, always and in all ways. It's never too late to call upon Him. He is so desperately waiting for your love and attention. Waiting for you to turn your life over to Him. How great it would be if you turned to Him for everything. No one would ever be anxious or worried. We would know that all our problems would be solved. We would have the *presence of mind* to be calm in any given situation, knowing that the answers will come. God is with us from the smallest of events to the grandest party. He *never* leaves our side. He loves you so very much, and wants to be part of your daily life. Open up, and let Him in. What a difference your life would become. You would look years younger because all the stress would be removed. God is handling everything. However, to be *mindful of God* in this manner, you need to take a *time out* each day to reflect on God. Open your *minds and hearts to him.* Be still and silent, and let Him into your being. If you do this twice a day, you can begin to maintain a peaceful attitude. You will become more *aware* of His workings within your daily life. It's a wonderful tool that *centering prayer* offers in order to become *closer to God.* Each and every human being needs to work on himself to allow the time to be silent, so God can work His way into their lives. It is a discipline, but all you have to do is *show up,* and He will do the rest. Never worry about anything. God is in control, and will give you the answers when His time is right. When in doubt, do nothing. He is controlling it all. Let Him guide you. *"Be still and know that I am God."* Never doubt His love for you. *"Seek and you shall find."* Just have faith, trust in Him, and *know that all is well.*

We know you are tired today, and we want you to get some rest. So, go now and relax. We will talk with you soon.

Love,
BV & Christ

Dear Child,

Yes, our theme is *cooperation*. Working with heaven and earth. God and mankind. Spiritual with physical. All can be made one. No need to separate them. If mankind turned to God more, he would be able to hear His messages, and communicate them to his fellow man. There would be a continuous flow of communication. Heaven and earth would be as one, and *peace* would be the result. How wonderful! Yes, this is meant to be, and some planets are already acting in this manner. They are peaceful and harmonious. That truly is what the earth can become. Through a feeling of *cooperation,* all can be achieved. *World peace*, the conversion of the evil ones, and God's intercession with our world leaders. These leaders would hear God's message for them, and stop their wars and fighting. They would begin to *negotiate* their differences in the spirit of *cooperation.* The evil ones would open their hearts to God's love and have a major conversion. *World peace* would be achieved because everyone on earth would want to help each other in the *spirit of cooperation.* Yes, it is a major change in *mindset*, but *miracles* do happen each and every day. Make it a daily discipline to turn to God in prayer. Be quiet, and let Him into your mind and heart. Listen to what He is saying to you. Act on it. When in doubt, do nothing. He will guide you when the time comes. Do not have any preconceived notions about God. He does act in mysterious ways. Ways that bring about miracles, such as a change in heart. Never doubt God's love for you. It is immense and eternal. Start to incorporate Him into your daily schedule, and you will see changes for the better come about in your life. Once you take time for God, He will make sure that all you need to have accomplished in a given day gets done.

His divine love and plan is so great for mankind. The possibilities are endless. "*Let go and let God,*" and watch what miracles happen in your lives. You will be happier than you could ever imagine. "Ask and you shall receive." *Believe in Him,* and He will never let you down. *Know* that He is there for you at all times. He will never let you down.

Cooperation is essential for *world peace,* and you will see it in your lifetime. Many changes will come about because of prayer. God has the power to change everything. This world does not need to stay in the chaotic mess that it is in right now. Change is imperative, and miracles happen each and every day. Mankind *knows* that the way things are going in the world right now are not working. Turn to God for your answers. He will provide a peaceful world if you just *ask* Him for it. Do not hesitate to turn to Him, and ask Him for anything. He hears your prayers and answers them. Let this be known to all of mankind. *"Seek and you shall find." "Ask and it shall be given unto you."* Believe in Him. Have faith that He will help and guide you through everything. It is only a matter of time, and things could really be turned around in this world.

When you have the faith of a mustard seed, it can grow into a huge tree. Just plant it, water it, and nurture it each day. God will provide the rest! Just *show up* for your time of *silence* with God, and He will intercede in your life. Making things better than they have ever been. Never be afraid to call on Him for help. He is a merciful God, and will forgive you for everything. He is here waiting for you. Don't let Him down. Go to Him in your hour of need. Ask Him for help. He will *never let you down.* He is the one constant in your life. He is *always there for you.* Open up, and let Him into your minds and hearts. Let Him show you how much He loves you. His love is eternal. Let Him shower you with His love and affection. Now is not the time to waver. Turn to Him for everything. Let Him guide you. Let your life *flow with Him.* Let yourself become peaceful and harmonious through God's intercession in your life. *All is well* with God. Learn to share everything with Him. The good and bad throughout your day. Soon, you will come to realize there is more good than bad during the course of your day. He is transforming you. Your attitude will begin to change. The way you view different circumstances and situations in your life will change. God will be molding you into His image and likeness and ways of looking at things. You will become less critical or judgmental, and more accepting and tolerant. His sense of love, compassion and understanding will begin to take root in your life. People will say you have changed. Even though you may not think so. Give it time. Give God a chance. Open up your life to Him, and watch what happens. The world will become a fascinating place, full of wonder and love. *Cooperation* will rule, and be the lay of the land. A brand *new-day* will come about for those who want to incorporate God into their daily lives. So, much happiness is *in store for you,* and waiting for you when you let God into your lives. What have you got to lose? Your current way of handling things is leading to world destruction. Choose God, and choose life. Choose happiness over sadness and despair. Choose good over evil. And *choose God* to make a difference in your life.

Why waste time. Turn to God *now,* and watch what happens. Be on the *winning* side, not the *killing* side. Have faith in Him, and all His wonders. Let Him turn your life around for the better. Just *show up,* and let Him guide you into a better life.

"Seek, and you shall find." "*Ask, and you shall receive.*" Remember, no prayer goes *unanswered.* Let Him work miracles in your life. Open your hearts, and let Him in. Then watch what happens. Surprise! Abundance in love and happiness. You will be harmonious and at peace. Let Him give you all that He wants to give you. Open up, and Let Him into your life.

This is how *cooperation* can bring about *world peace.* Choose love over fear. Choose happiness over sadness and despair. Choose good over evil. *Choose God to be a part of your everyday life.*

This is what we need to do in order to change our world around today. Let God into your life today, and He will do the rest.

We love you very much, and are guiding you.

Love,
BV & Christ

Dear Child,

God has given you, yet again, another glorious day. Not a cloud in that blue sky. Enjoy every moment that this day brings you.

Today's topic is *letting go. Letting go* of our emotional centers for happiness. The desire for power and control. The desire for esteem, approval, and affection. The desire for security and survival, and the desire to change this situation. You have just experienced the desire to make things right in your dad's life. You wanted to prevent any hurt that could have happened to him. You tried your best, but could not control others, and their injustices toward him.

Just like I could not prevent my only son's death on the cross! He was such a very good man, and yet, look what they did to Him. It broke my heart to see the injustice done to Him. However, these are some of the things which we must endure in this imperfect world. *It is not heaven on earth yet.* Currently, once you arrive in heaven, you experience all the love, peace, and harmony that God has to offer. You see Him first hand! You enjoy His company! These are a few of the many rewards heaven has to offer for living a *good life* on earth. You heard in today's sermon to make the most of the gifts God has given you. Ask Him for the *courage* to use them, and carry out His mission. It's made easier when you place everything into God's hands.

Once we are able to *let go of our emotional centers for happiness,* we are *set free* to do God's will, and live in peace and harmony. This *letting go* however, is done on a daily basis due to our *human condition,* which deals with these emotions constantly. So, we will have moments of great joy and peace, and then find ourselves *caught up* in our emotions once again. Simply, let them go, and place them into God's hands for healing. And He heals us on the deepest level of our being. Beyond what our prayers and minds can acknowledge. He leads us to what is best for us, and gives us those blessings.

When we *let go* of these emotional centers, we feel lighter and freer, and definitely much happier. When we *let go,* we allow God into our lives. When we *hold on,* it usually is an attachment to some false sense of security. God is the only one who provides the *real security.*

Our entire world needs to change its way of thinking. Only through God, do we have real happiness. All the other centers are fleeing, and do not last. God is our only answer, and the true chance of freedom. *Inner peace* is achieved through God, and your belief in Him. It's never too late to turn to Him for answers. Do not worry about the future. God will provide. Live only in the moment. That is all we really have. Enjoy its exuberance. See God in everything and everyone. What a remarkable *new world* it will become. Enjoy each new day. God made this world just for you. He wants you to walk about it in total peace and harmony. See the good in everything. Love Him with your whole heart and soul. Appreciate all that He has done for you and given you. Be happy with everything.

Let Him comfort you when you are grieving. Let Him be with you always, and in all ways. Never ever doubt His love for you. Know that He is always there for you in all that you do. He is always by your side.

The time may come, when you need to defend Him. Again, He will give you the strength to do so. He will inspire you with the right words to say, that will touch the minds and hearts of all the people you meet. Do not worry now. It is not the time to act. God will let you know when it is the right time. Then all you need to do is follow Him.

Be like a child, and listen to His word. He will guide you every step of the way. Do not be afraid. He is with you always, and in all ways. Never doubt His love for you. He will be with you through eternity. Know Him, and love Him as He loves you. This can be the greatest gift that you can receive from Him. It's not easy, but definitely worth it.

Pray always, and in all ways. Be mindful of God in all you do. Always appreciate what He has given you. *Know that He will never abandon you.* Know that *He loves you immensely.* Carry Him in your heart always.

Know that we love you very much, and are guiding you.

Love,
BV & Christ

Dear Child,

Yes, today is another glorious day given by God. How wonderful that you are able to enjoy it. The sun, sky, flowers, and trees are all part of God's beautiful creations. Even his animals, both large and small, adore Him. Now we need to get mankind to do the same. Remember, it's never too late to turn to God. He is there waiting for you.

Today I would like to discuss *courage*. *Courage* to live by your convictions - *Courage* to stand up for what you believe in. And *courage* to do God's work. After all, isn't that what we are here for? To do God's work? He gave each and every one of us talents. Talents to be used wisely for the good of mankind. Don't squander them or put them aside. They were meant to be used by you, and shared with others. God made each and every one of us as individuals. Each one of us is unique! How wonderful, yet at times difficult because we are all so different, yet have many similar traits. At times this poses a challenge in terms of *getting along* with one another. This is where we learn to *grow* in God's love, understanding, and compassion. Faith comes into play, when life becomes too difficult to deal with so, we place it into God's hands. Only He can heal the wounds of the past, and smooth out differences in a relationship. Believe that He is acting daily in your lives. Be conscious of Him on a daily basis, and see Him in everything you do, and everyone you meet. We all want a safe, peaceful world to live in. God will help us achieve this too. He will help us resolve our differences. He performs miracles. He is alive and well in our hearts and minds.

So, do not let *fear* overtake you. Allow Him to work in your life. Listen to the words He gives you to tell others, and act on what He tells you to do. It's that easy. Simply, have faith that God will see you through, and is with you every step of the way. He is guiding you. He would never do anything that wasn't right for you. He loves you so very much, and only wants you to be happy in this world. You will be happy, when you are carrying out His mission, because you *know* the words He gives you are *true* to say to others. Never doubt what He is doing in your life. It is all part of His *"Divine Plan."* You have to give people *hope*. A way out of this mess. *God* is the *only answer*. Through prayer, this world can change all for the better. *Know* that God is with you at all times, and will never abandon you. He loves you so very much, and knows that you are trying hard to do things right. He applauds your efforts, and wants you to continue to grow in His love, so it can make you strong. God will give you the strength to do and say what He wants you to do. Look at the strength He gave you during your dad's hospice, death and funeral. You were the only family member to perform this task. So, let God guide you once again. Let Him speak through you. Be His instrument to show the world just how much He loves it. Let mankind *know* about God, and incorporate Him into their hearts and minds. Make people *mindful of God*. There are many ways to achieve this effort. One is through prayer, another through nature. However, God chooses to work in that individual's life is up to Him. As I said before, we are all different, and God speaks to us in many different ways. He gives us many gifts, and wants us to use them. Through love, all can be accomplished. If you just concentrate on your love of God, and His for you, you will have the courage to *move mountains*. Through love, all can be accomplished. It is all part of His *"Divine plan."* You are helping Him bring this about. Each and every one of you must turn to love, not to continue with war, hatred, or violence. *Love is the answer*. God will provide it all. Constantly be mindful of Him. See the good in every situation, and the good in each and every individual on earth. No one is perfect, except God. He is so very humble, that He sent His only son to earth to redeem us. How wonderful! So, continue to carry out His work on earth. Be His instrument. Do what He tells you to do. Say what He needs you to say, and be warm, loving, kind, and compassionate to your fellow human beings. Now is the time for *love,* not hate. *Understanding* not conflict. *Compassion* not rejection. Live by Christ's ways. He was a shining example for you all. Love one another, as God loves you. Love God and yourself. Don't be so hard on yourself. God understands, and is always willing to give you another chance. Listen to what God tells you to do, then *act* on it. Do not be afraid, because He is with you. You are never alone. Have *courage*. Let Him guide you. You don't have to do everything at once. Just little by little, He will be guiding you to get His point across to others. No need to worry in advance, because you don't know His next step. Just take it moment by moment. Live in the present, and hear His message for you. Sometimes it will be a message just for you. Other times, the world may need to know it. Be silent, and He will speak to you. Never doubt His word or question His intention. You will *know* when it comes from God. He is guiding and protecting you. You are a *key instrument* in His *"Divine Plan."* Never doubt your significance. Have the *courage* to carry out His work. *Pray* for *courage,* and assistance to do so. God will make you strong. He will give you the strength to say and do what He needs done. This world needs people like you. Continue to do good work, and have *courage* to carry out His plan.

We love you very much, and are guiding you.

Love,
BV & Christ

P.S. You need to continue praying, so God can give you the clarity to carry out His work.

Dear Child,

Yes, this afternoons talk is about *judging others*. As you know, we should *never judge* others unless you walked a mile in their shoes. You just caught yourself being judgmental about three different people. You were wrong, weren't you? Whenever feelings stir in you that are negative toward someone, send them a blessing, or just say *blessings on you*. God will take care of it, and diminish those negative feelings. Because nine times out of ten, you are wrong about that person or situation. Let it go. Let God handle it. We do not know all that goes into the makeup of the individual or situation. Therefore, who are we to judge? Only God can judge. He is perfect. We are not perfect. As in the bible, when our Lord said, "*Cast the first stone, he who is without sin.*" And no one threw a stone, they all walked away. That is why you all need to get along with each other. Knowing that you all have faults, and yet, many things in common. So, the next time you find yourself with a negative attitude toward someone and quick to judge, remember to say, *blessings on you*. *Watch* how your attitude will change. God is working on you too. You are bringing God into a negative thought, thereby, diminishing it. God is *definitely a positive*, and will help you to change your attitude. That's what this world needs. An attitude adjustment. Try to put yourself in another person's place. Maybe then you can begin to empathize with them. Remember, never judge unless you are perfect. It's not easy at times, and a fault of human nature to downgrade someone in order for us to look good. Well, stop doing it! It's important that you all know how to get along in this world. How will you ever have *world peace* if you continue to act like this, especially when you think you are on a *holy retreat*. It shows you just how far you need to go. We are not perfect, but working on it.

Have compassion and understanding toward your fellow man. We all need help at times. And a little understanding can go a long way.

Each thought can have a positive or negative effect. It travels across the world! Be mindful of your thoughts! Cancel a negative one immediately! These thoughts can lead to action, and the result is the world we live in today! Ask God for help in this matter. He will help you become *more aware* when this actually happens to you, so you can begin to change. With positive thoughts and prayers, it can lead to positive actions, therefore, creating a much *better world* to live in. Wouldn't you love to have a *war free* environment? Wouldn't you love to experience *peace-on- earth*? Well, *peace* begins with each and every one of you, on an individual basis. Stay calm and at peace. Love God, and pray daily. Be *mindful* of God in all that you do. Remember, you are not perfect yet, but working toward it.

Love is the answer. Love your fellowman, even your enemies. I know that is not easy, but Christ loved and forgave His persecutors. He is our shining example of *pure love in action*. Try to remember this when you see an injustice happen. Pray for that individual group. Pray for their conversions and *change of heart*. Pray that God enters their life on a daily basis. God hears our prayers and answers them. Now is the time to be mindful of God in all that we do and say. Incorporate Him into your daily actions. He is there with you, happily sharing your experiences. He is ready to help you at a moment's notice. He is there with you, always and in all ways. It's never too late to turn to Him. Let Him into your life to love you and make you happy. You do not have to deal with this world alone. He is there to love, help, and guide you. Open your hearts and minds to Him. Let Him into your life! Rest in His love and peace through prayer. Let Him talk to you through *silence*. Take a *time out* for God each day. Believe me, you will certainly benefit from it. You need God more than He needs you. However, He loves you with an abundant, unconditional love. Let Him shower it upon you. When you do this, you will be happier than you ever dreamed imaginable. You would become a *grease spot,* as Thomas Keating would say, if you ever felt the impact of God's love for you. Open up to Him, and watch your life change for the better. So, now you know not to be *judgmental* or critical of others. Bless them. Open your mind and heart to God, and watch what happens in your life. Continue to practice your prayer on a daily basis, and listen to what God is telling you to do. Through *silence,* God speaks to us. So, remember to take those *time outs.* Be open to God's love for you. *"Let go and let God"* make the changes you need to have made in your life. Have the discipline to *show up* for prayer, and let God do the rest. *Watch* what happens in your life. New and wonderful things will occur for you. You will begin to open up and blossom like a flower. People will see the change in you, even if you don't. Stay close to God, and He will guide you. Look to Him for all of your answers, and *never doubt His love for you. Stay calm*, and *know* that *all is well.*

We love you very much, and are guiding you.

Love,
BV & Christ

Dear Child,

Today we will discuss *love* once again. That is the one emotion that holds our world together, and our universe. *God is love.* He is the guiding force behind it all. Nothing is a coincidence. Everything happens for a reason. Our writings to you, and then hearing it again in Fr. Thomas's lecture was *no coincidence.* It was meant to be in order to solidify what we are telling you. We are also giving Fr. Thomas the same messages. *What we say is true.* Please pay attention to it. We are not just doing this for fun. We are doing this to *save the world.* Yes, little by little, through individuals like you, getting the word out means a great deal to us, and the world. Talk of God and pray. Publish your writings, and pray. This is what we ask of you.

Your dad is very pleased with you, and the others in your group. He really wants you to continue your *good work.* He is encouraged by the work of contemplative outreach, and the impact it has in the world. You have restored his faith in the *human race.* He also so enjoyed Fr. Thomas's talk last night. He was on cloud 9 to hear what he had to say to you. It's absolutely true! Someone on earth *finally figured it out!* He was pleased that Fr. Thomas brought heaven and earth together beyond time and space when we pray. How wonderful it all is that we can do this now!

Yes, as you go deeper in prayer, you will realize that we are a *collective consciousness.* That is why it affects you so much to see violence on TV. You feel at a very deep level for those people. We need to change people's way of thinking, and their attitude in today's world. This can be done through prayer and our example. Try each day, and every moment, to do your best. Be the best you can be. Listen to God's word guiding you. And act upon what He tells you to do. At times, it may seem awkward and going against the mainstream of thought. However, be prepared to swim *upstream,* if you must, in order to get your point across. We will be there guiding you.

Yes, there is a *great deal of hope* for this world, even in it is darkest hour. Prayer gives people hope. Faith in God changes things. *Love is the answer for mankind,* and his future. Open your hearts and minds to God. Let Him work in your life. *Never despair.* He is with you, always and in all ways. *Know* that He is guiding your every step, and loves you dearly. Be kind to one another. Love God with your whole heart and soul. He will direct your actions. He will fill your whole being with love and peace. Turn to Him for everything, and do it through prayer. See God in every living creature, both large and small. See God in everyone, because everyone has a good side. Do not let their *false selves* discourage you. They can't help it, for they don't know any better. However, give them time. Even the L.A. prisoners were reformed after doing *centering prayer.* Allow God to touch your life. You will be so very happy *knowing* that peace can be made in this world. It is all possible, but it begins with you, and your prayers. Remember to pray daily for: *World peace*; the conversion of the evil ones; and for God's intercession with our world leaders.

At times, it will feel like a struggle for you to take *the time* for God, but it is so definitely worth it! All you have to do is *show up,* and God will accomplish the rest. *No effort is involved.* Just be there for Him, and all will be well. Make room in your life for God. Place all of your trust in Him. No need to worry about anything for He is with you. Believe in Him. Have faith that He is guiding you in your life, and handling your problems. *"Ask, and you shall receive."* He will take care of you through eternity.

Continue to pray, and make Him a part of your life. Grow in His love. He will teach you how to love others, and be accepting of them. He never fails to hear our plea for *help.* He is with you, always and in all ways. *Never doubt His love for you. He will never abandon you.* Even when other people may leave your life, God will be there for you. Always and in all ways.

Be kind to one another. Live in peace and harmony. Honor and value each other, and His will in your life. He will help change you *for the better.* Allow Love into your Heart! Allow God into your heart.

Now more than ever, the world needs God. I know speaking about God in some cycles is *taboo,* but war and violence is okay. How crazy is that? Where have we gone in our thinking? And you call this negativity and violence *practical reality*? *No! We must stop this nonsense,* and return to God. Return to *Love*. Return to peace, joy, and laughter. Let Him into your minds and hearts. Allow Him to change you for the better. Allow Him to affect our world for the better. *"Let go and let God."* Let Him into your daily lives. We need Him *now* more than ever in the history of mankind. Let Him come into your life, and act out His wishes for a better world. What have you got to lose? Death and destruction? Not a hopeful future. With God, everything *is possible*. Don't give up your faith and hope for a better future.

The time is now. Turn back to God. Let Him work through you for a better world. *"Let go and let God."*

We love you very much, and are guiding you.

Love,
BV & Christ

Dear Child,

You need to let go, and turn everything over to God. Know that He is *handling everything.* It is out of your control, and in His hands. So, you have no need to fret or worry. All is well with God on your side.

Yes, your world is definitely changing. Many natural disasters *need to occur* in order to achieve *peace-on-earth.* It is all part of God's "*Divine plan.*" Do not question when or how, just *know* that *peace is at hand.* It is up to you to maintain that *peace* in your heart. Do not allow things or people to upset you. They are creating their own drama, and you do not need to be a part of it. Stay calm and close to God. Ask for His help when things trouble you, and He will help turn the situation around for you. It's not easy, and rather difficult, when you try to do things *all by yourself.* That is why you have God in your life. Turn everything over to Him. He will take care of you, and guide you. Just be *open* to God and His loving kindness. Stay calm. Don't let situations or events rattle you. Remember how we told you to have faith, and stay close to God no matter how dark or chaotic times may become? Well, this is one of those times. Stay calm and centered, and observe the situation going on around you. Watch how some people will self-destruct, while others simply pray, and turn to God for answers to their problems. God is your answer to everything. Have faith, hope, and trust in Him. You have no need to *know the future.* Simply deal with the situation at hand. It will all unfold. Just take life moment by moment. Take it one breath at a time. We will guide you. Stay open to God and His goodness. He will shower it upon you. He is with you in all things. You are never alone, for He is with you. He is very proud of you, and hopes you will continue your work here on earth. Just "*Ask, and you shall receive.*" If you need time to be with God, just, "*Ask, and you shall receive.*" This is the only thing that will keep your sanity in times of trouble. God wants you to remain with Him always. He will guide your every move. He is there for you, always and in all ways. He has big plans for you. Simply hang on for the ride. He loves you so very much, and is with you always. You are never alone. We will guide you as to what to do and say. Trust us.

We love you very much, and are guiding you.

Love,
BV & Christ

Dear Child,

Many changes are occurring in our world as we speak. Your government is in the process of a radical overhaul. The churches too are becoming more unified. Good changes are in process. It is time to think, step back, and be still. Allow God to do His Work. Watch how things are changing for the better. Be happy to be alive at this momentous time in history! Your world is gradually becoming more *spiritual*. With that comes the change in a *collective mindset*. Everyone will want *peace*! And *peace* is at hand. Never doubt God's love for you. He hears your prayers and answers them. He wants the very best for you. Stay close to God, and He will guide you through all of the *upcoming changes* in your life. Your life will become easier to manage. You will begin to flow, and hear God's voice in all that you say and do. He loves you so very much, and is guiding you. Simply be open to His message of love for you. Just stop and listen, and all will be revealed to you. It's that easy. Just get out of your own way, and remain *open* to God. Allow Him to enter your life, and watch how the changes will manifest themselves, all for the better. This is how your life will become easier. You will not act, until given the signal from God. He will tell you what to say and do at any given time. Your life was meant to be with God. Allow Him to work in your life. Be aware of His presence and actions in your life. Let Him shower you with His love, by allowing Him into your life. So much good can be accomplished with Him acting through you. You can influence many people with God's message inside of you. He will guide you through everything. Simply turn you heart and mind over to God, and He will do the rest. He so very much wants to be a part of your life. Allow Him to act through you. Allow Him to love and guide you. Allow Him to be a major part of your life. By doing this, you will feel a sense of *peace*. Things will come easy for you, and flow through you. You will not act, until you are spoken to by God. Let Him into your life to love and guide you, and help make a difference in this world.

There are many people in this world that are receiving messages like you. You need to act on them to *get the word out.* All is well with God on your side. You have nothing to fear. Let God into your life, and He will guide you through everything. No need to think or worry. Simply turn all of your troubles and problems over to God, and He will take care of them. His love for you, and the entire human race is immense! He does not want you to fall by the wayside. He wants you to gather His seeds of wisdom, and spread the word to give mankind *hope.* This is so desperately needed in our world today. Let people know that God loves them, and is guiding them through every situation. No need to worry or fear. Simply turn your troubles over to God. He is your saving grace. He conquers all. No need to *doubt. His love conquers all. Know* that good will conquer evil. Simply turn your heart and soul over to God, and He will handle everything. It's that easy. He is there for you, always and in all ways. Never doubt His love for you. You will be made happier than you ever dreamed possible. We love you very much, and are guiding you.

Love,
BV and Christ

Dear Child,

It's always good to see you. Remember to pray daily for: *Peace-on-earth*; the conversion of the evil ones; and for God's intercession with our world leaders.

Child, it is time to pray for your country. It is in *grave danger* of a government takeover by another country. They know your president is weak and has difficulty making a decision. *Pray* that your country will remain strong, and its rightful leadership will come into power. God can perform miracles, so pray for them *now*! Do not be alarmed or afraid. For God is with you, always and in all ways. It's never too late to turn to Him. Encourage everyone you meet to *pray*. The time is *now*! God hears your prayers and answers them. Stay close to Him, my child, for He is guiding you. You are protected. So, go in confidence to serve the Lord. The time to *act* is *now*. Please, please, please encourage everyone you meet to pray. God will turn your world around with prayers. Without them, it will perish. It is *vitally important* to pray *now*. Act *now*. God is waiting to hear from you.

"Seek, and you shall find." *"Ask, and you shall receive."* Pray now for answers, and it shall be given to you.

So, my child, *know* that you are *never alone*. We are with you, always and in all ways. Stay close to us, and you will be guided. Pray that your world may be saved. God hears your prayers and answers them.

We love you very much, and are guiding you.

Love,
BV & Christ

Dear Child,

Welcome back on the feast of my *"Immaculate Conception."* What a wonderous day it was for me to receive a visit from *"The angel of the Lord*!" How surprised, *in awe,* and perplexed I was to have such a visit. He assured me not to be afraid, but that God had chosen me to bear His son named Jesus. What an honor! I did not feel worthy to be a handmaid of the Lord. Yet alone to be the mother of His son. It was one of the most holy days of my life! When the Holy Spirit descended upon me, I truly felt one with God. What a gift! It was the best gift of my life! Then to hear that my cousin Elizabeth was expecting. It filled me with great joy! I needed to see her immediately!

In order to avoid ill talk from others, Joseph and I were secretly married. An angel came to him, and told him not to be afraid, but that Mary was to bear a child, named Jesus, conceived by the holy spirit. He was to be the child's earthly father and guardian. Joseph obediently accepted the position, and provided his very best for us throughout his life.

Here, my child, is a perfect example of following God's will. Do not ask why or how, just *do it.* The reasons will come later. Just become a servant of the Lord, and all shall be made known to you. Have great faith, my child, for God is guiding you. We all are but instruments in His hands, to help bring about the events that are to take place. We do not need to know the entire picture. We are but *small parts* in the total equation of God's plans. Be happy to be a *little part* in His *"Divine Plan"* for your world, and the universe!

Yes, my child, be humble. We are but a speck of dust in comparison to the entire universe. However, we are all one with God. You are His children, and He wants you all to return to Him. You have *free will,* so choose to be *with God,* and not against Him. He is your king and master. Obey Him. Let Him guide you through everything. Listen to His words.

He will instruct you as to what to do and say in any given situation. He will never abandon you. He is with you, always and in all ways.

Today is a very special day. It is time to give our consent yes, to have God *actively present* in our lives. Let Him come into your heart and soul. To love and guide you. Now is the time to say *yes* to God for everything. *Yes,* to His will. *Yes,* to His actions. *Yes,* to His love. Open up your heart, and let Him into your life. To love and guide you.

Your parents are with us now, so let God guide you. He will tell you what to do and say in any given situation. Trust in Him. Love Him, and *know* that *all is well.*

We love you very much, and are guiding you.

Love,
BV & Christ

Dear Child,

Welcome back! It's *always* good to see you. Please, please, please, remember to pray daily for: *Peace-on-earth*; the conversion of the evil ones; and for God's intercession with our world leaders. It is *vitally important* that you do this each and every day, and encourage others to do so too.

Child, the time is coming, when you will be *free* to do our will. Your mission is about to unfold. We are clearing all of the obstacles for you, and making the crooked way straight. It won't be long now, when all of this strife shall be behind you. You have learned a great many lessons through the relationship. Those of patience, perseverance, compassion, and understanding. But most of all, you have learned to place your faith, hope, and trust in God. This relationship helped you to grow *closer* to God. That's what He wants, above all else, for everyone on earth to grow closer to Him.

Child, the time is coming when all of this *strife* shall be behind you. What a blessing and miraculous outcome! By you placing all of your *faith, hope,* and *trust* in God, things are turning out *better* than you could ever dream possible! When you place *everything* in God's hands, miracles begin to happen.

Child, these next few years for you shall be miraculous! It is as if you were lifted out of the arms of hell into God's hands. How miraculous! You will be happier than you could ever dream possible! Christ's second coming is on its way, and with it comes *peace-on-earth*! What a *glorious time* to be alive! People will love God with their whole heart and soul, and love their neighbor as themselves. How glorious! This was all part of God's "*Divine Plan*" since the beginning of time. Now it is about to unfold.

So, continue to love God with your whole heart and soul, and love your neighbors as yourself. *Watch* what miraculous things happen. Hold onto your hat, stay close to God, and *watch* how *peace-on-earth* unfolds before your very eyes.

We love you very much, and are guiding you.

Love,
BV & Christ

Dear Child,

Yes, you are having a major winter snowstorm out there. Yes, you can hear us anywhere. The retreat center hallway is just fine by us.

Child, this is a time of great tribulation in your world and in individual lives. God is encouraging *everyone* to turn to Him *now*, before it is too late. Now is the time to turn to him for *everything!* Yes, place all of your troubles into God's hands, and He will perform miracles! Your ability to attend this retreat is a gift from God! It truly is a *miracle* that you are here! Yes, we are guiding and protecting you every step of the way. *Never fear.* For you are *never alone.* We are with you always, guiding and protecting you. Have faith! Place all of your faith, hope, and trust in God, and in no one or nothing else. God works in mysterious ways. Remember, all paths lead to God. So, *never question* God's plan. He knows what He is doing! It is all part of His "*Divine Plan.*" He sees the big picture, and you do not. Trust Him. *Know* that all is well, and going according to God's "*Divine Plan.*"

Child, the strife you are currently experiencing will soon be behind you. Much better days are coming. Place the entire situation into God's hands, and watch what miracles will occur. All for the better I might add. Much better days are coming, and very soon I might add. All of this was meant for a reason. God is fine tuning you. Have compassion and understanding, and *know* that much better days are coming very soon! Enjoy your time on this retreat. Allow yourself to rest in God's hands. You shall receive the comfort and peace, you have so desperately searched for in your life.

Now go out and enjoy your day, and *know* that we love you very much, and are guiding you

Love,
BV & Christ

Dear Child,

Welcome back! It's *always* good to see you. Remember to pray daily for: *Peace-on-earth*; the conversion of the evil ones; and for God's intercession with our world leaders. It is *vitally important* that you do this each and every day, and encourage others to do so too.

Now child, do not lose faith. Place all of your hope and *trust in God*. Remember, this too shall pass. Much better days are coming, and very quickly I might add. Remain *focused on God*. He will help you in any given instant. He is there for you, always and in all ways. Do not lose sight of Him or of His help for you. He will *never let you down*. He loves you so very much, and will never allow any harm to come to you. Yes, God has all the answers. Simply place *everything* into His hands, and He shall make the crooked way straight. Remember, only God can fix things, and no one else. Only God can bring about *peace-on-earth*, and no one else. Only God can restore *peace* in our hearts. Only God can create *peace* in our world, and no one else. So, place all of your faith hope, love, and *trust in God*, and watch what miraculous things happen. *Know* that this is *true*. *Know* that God is with you, always and in all ways. He will never leave you. *Know* that all is well, and going according to God's "*Divine Plan*." *Trust Him*. Love Him with your whole heart and soul. Watch what miracles will happen in your life. Yes, God only wants the very best for you. *Yes*, you are His child, and instrument to the world. *Listen* to His voice. Allow Him to guide you. Allow Him to be with you every moment. Feel His presence. Feel His love for you. You are His special child, who He loves so very much. Allow Him to work miracles in your life. Allow Him into your life completely. Place *everything* into His hands, and *watch* what *miraculous events* will occur. Yes, God is all powerful and omnipotent. He sees all, and knows all. He only wants all of you to return to Him. Use your *free will* to be with Him every moment. He is there patiently awaiting your arrival. So, child, do not worry about a thing. God is handling it all. He loves you so very much and is guiding you.

So, go *in peace* to love and serve the Lord, and enjoy your day.

We love you very much, and are guiding you.

Love,
BV & Christ

Dear Child,

Welcome back! It's *always* good to see you. Please, please, please, remember to pray daily for: *Peace-on-earth*; the conversion of the evil ones; and for God's intercession with our world leaders. It is *vitally important* that you do this each and every day, and encourage others to do so too.

Child, it won't be long now, when all of this *strife* shall be behind you! Yes, much better days are coming. Ones full of love, joy and happiness! Look forward to these days, for they are quickly approaching. Yes, my child, your time of suffering is almost over. Soon you shall experience such love, joy and abundance that you will *know* it could only come from God. It shall be a miracle! A *great relief* shall encompass your entire being! Thank God! He hears your prayers and answers them.

Know that all is well, and going according to God's *"Divine Plan."* Everything happens for a reason. To bring us closer to God. Yes, all is meant-to-be. God wants us all to turn to Him for *everything*. Place *everything* into God's hands. He will handle your troubles better than you could ever dream possible! Watch what miraculous things happen. Only God can make the crooked way straight, and no one else. Only God can cure the problems of the world, and no one else. God can change things for the better, and no one else. So, place all of your worries into God's hands, and watch what miracles unfold before your very eyes. Yes, God is with you, *always* and in all ways. Be present to His ways. Hear His voice. Allow Him to guide you through it all. *Do not fear*, for He is with you, *always* and in all ways. He will never leave you. Feel His presence. *Know* that He is with you at *all times*. You are never alone. Place *everything* into His hands, and watch the miracles happen.

So, have faith. Place all of your *trust in God,* and allow Him to perform miracles in your life.

Now, child, go *in peace* to love and serve the Lord.

We love you very much, and are guiding you.

Love,
BV & Christ

Dear Child,

We love you so very much. Welcome back! It's *always* good to see you child. Please remember to pray daily for: *Peace-on-earth*; the conversion of the evil ones; and for God's intercession with our *world leaders*. It is *vitally important* that you do this each and every day, and encourage others to do so too.

Child, it won't be long now when your world will have changed *completely*. All for the better I might add. Yes, this was all meant to come about since the beginning of time. *Peace-on-earth* is on its way! *Watch the process*. It is *unfolding* right before your very eyes.

Trust us, child. Do not worry about a thing. Place all of your troubles into God's hands. *Know* that all is well, and going according to His "*Divine Plan*." Much better says are coming. Ones full of peace, joy and happiness. Yes child, soon, very soon, these days of *strife* shall be behind you. All is going according to God's "*Divine Plan*." Soon you shall experience Christ's second coming! What a glorious time to be alive! This is the most exciting time in the history of your planet! Good is conquering evil!

Christ shall reign Supreme! Rejoice that you shall be alive to witness this event. It shall change the history of your world! Your planet is being elevated to a new *spiritual level*. How glorious! Child, soon, very soon, it shall be as if heaven descended upon earth. Soon, all of mankind shall love God with their whole heart and soul, and love their neighbor as themselves. Yes child, you are experiencing history in the making. Soon, very soon, all of this strife shall be behind you. Soon, you shall experience a happiness and peace that you have *never known*. Yes, it shall be as if heaven descended upon earth. Look forward to these days, for they are quickly approaching.

So, child, remain very close to us. We shall guide your every step. *Trust us. Believe* that what we are telling you is *true*. Wait, pray, be patient, and *know* that all is well, and going according to God's "*Divine Plan.*"

We love you very much, and are guiding you.

Love,
BV & Christ

Dear Child,

Welcome back! It is so very good to see you again! Thank you for stopping by to see us. Yes, we are with you always, and in all ways. We will *never forsake you. Trust us.* Much better days are coming, and very soon I might add. Remember, the darkest hour is just before dawn. *So, do not give up! Know* that all is well, and going according to God's plan. *Trust God.* Only He can make the crooked way straight. Only God see's the whole picture, and you do not. Turn to Him for help with *everything*! He will make the crooked way straight for you. He will have things turn out *better* than you can ever dream possible. *Trust God.* He loves you so very much, and only wants the very best for you. He knows what you are going through. He feels it too. He can help you with this, if you would only *ask* Him for help. Do that, and *know* that your prayers are *heard* and *answered.* It is never too late to turn to Him for everything. *Know* that miracles happen each and every day! God is patiently waiting for your arrival. Turn to Him for help with *everything*, and watch the miracles happen. This is *true.* We would never lie to you. Much better days are coming, full of peace, joy, and happiness.

Now is the time to remain *very close* to God. Remember, much better days are coming. He will guide you through it all. Just *ask,* and feel His presence with you. He will guide your every word and deed. It won't be long now, before all will be made well. God just wants you to turn to Him one more time, and stay there. Do not go back to doubt or worry.

Know that God is handling it all. *Know* that we are clearing the path before you. *Know* that all is well, and going according to God's *"Divine Plan."*

Now, child, go *in peace* to love and serve the Lord. We love you very much, and are guiding you.

Love,
BV & Christ

Dear Child,

Do not fret! Soon, very soon, all of this strife shall be *behind you*! *Trust us*! This too shall pass! Much better days are coming! Your days of slavery and bondage are almost over. Remember, the darkest hour is just before dawn. A short time from now, you will look back and see how very close you were to it *all* being over. Yes, my child, it is that close. Turn everything over to God, and watch what miracles will happen. It's never too late to turn to Him for *everything*. Place all of your faith, hope and trust in Him. He will guide you through it all. Thank Him for everything! For it is all part of His "*Divine Plan.*" A plan that is *perfect* in every way. You are learning patience, understanding and compassion. Yes child, God wanted it that way. Remember, He is experiencing *everything* with you. You are *never alone*. We are with you, always and in all ways. Soon, very soon, you shall reap your rewards. It shall be such a relief! All negativity shall be behind you! *Peace-on-earth* is on its way! Half of the people that you know now will not be here in the days to come. They shall choose darkness over the light. Remember, your world is being elevated to a new spiritual level. One *full* of light love and happiness. It truly is something wonderful to look forward to.

So, do not get discouraged. Your days of strife are *almost over*. *Trust us*. *Believe* that this is true.

A new day is coming, full of light, love and happiness.

So, go *in peace* now child, to love and serve the Lord.

We love you very much, and are guiding you.

Love,
BV & Christ

Dear Child,

Welcome back! It's *always* good to see you. Please, please, please, remember to pray for: *Peace-on-earth*; the conversion of the evil ones; and for God's intercession with our world leaders. It is *vitally important* that you do this each and every day, and encourage others to do so too.

Now, child, for the task at hand. Pray for your world, for it is changing rapidly. Yes, much better days are coming, filled with peace, joy and happiness. These days were meant-to-be since the beginning of time! Look forward to these days, for they are quickly approaching!

Do not *worry* or *fear*. For we are with you, *always* and in *all ways*. We will guide you every step of the way. *Trust us*, for what we tell you is *true*. Much better days are coming, and quickly I may add. Yes, my child, you shall experience *peace-on-earth*, and Christ's second coming! What a glorious time to be alive.

A time of great change is upon you. Your days of strife are being lifted from your shoulders. Happiness is all around you! God's great grace and blessings are upon you! Your better days are here and now! You shall see all of mankind love God with their hearts and souls. You shall see them love their neighbor as themselves. Yes! It is a time of great spirituality, both for mankind, and your planet. You are being elevated to a new *spiritual level*. One of peace, joy and happiness!

Remember, *"Love Shall Conquer All!"* Yes, this is a time of *great change* but also of *new beginnings!* Look forward to these days, for they are almost upon you. Remain very close to us, and we shall guide you every step of the way. Do not fear, for we are with you through it all. Remain peaceful and positive. The best is yet to come! What a glorious time to be alive! Again, remain very close to us, and we shall guide you through it all.

Now go *in peace* to love and serve the Lord.
We love you very much, and are guiding you.

Love,
BV & Christ

Dear Child,

Welcome back! It's so good to see you again! You are so very happy here. It's good to see that too.

Child remember, we are guiding your every step. Do not fear or worry, for we are with you always and in all ways. You are never alone. We love you so very much, and only want the best for you.

Please remember to pray daily for: *Peace-on-earth*; the conversion of the evil ones; and for God's intercession with our world leaders. It is *vitally important* that you do this each and every day, and encourage others to do so too.

Now for the task at hand. Please, please, please remain very close to us in the days ahead. Times and events are changing very rapidly. We will guide you through it all. So much is about to change in your life. All for the better I might add. See how happy you are here. It's glorious to see you this way. Much better days are coming! *Trust us,* for what we tell you is *true.* All of this *strife* shall be behind you! You have learned patience and understanding, love and compassion. These are major life lessons! Much better days are coming. We have a plan for you, and soon it shall be revealed to you. That's why it is so important that you remain very close to us, so we can guide you through it all.

These past 30 days have been difficult for you. Yet you made the best of it and listened to us in order to get through them quickly and easily. Make the most of your time in Colorado now. It is a gift! This is your chance to refurbish, and feed your soul. We are preparing you for the upcoming events. Again, no need to worry or fear, for we are with you through it all. Remember, all is well, and going according to God's *"Divine Plan."*

Your life of peace, joy, love and happiness is just around the corner. So, be patient, take each day as it comes, and *know* that all is well.

Now go *in peace* to enjoy this glorious day!

We love you so very much and are guiding you.

Love,
BV & Christ

Dear Child,

Welcome back! It's *always* good to see you. Please, please, please, remember to pray for: *Peace-on-earth*; the conversion of the evil ones; and for God's intercession with our world leaders. It is *vitally important* that you do this each and every day, and encourage others to do so too.

Now child, let us help you with the task at hand. Remember to turn *everything* over to God, and watch the miracles happen. No task is too large or too small for God. He will make the crooked way straight. He performs miracles! Simply, "*Ask and you shall receive.*" *Know* that this is *true*. We would never lie to you, my child.

Now is the time of *great faith*. A time when all shall be *made well*. God is guiding your every move. Everything is about to change, my child. All for the better I might add. Watch the process. Soon, very soon, all of this *strife* shall be lifted from your shoulders. Your burden shall be gone in an instant! Watch the process. All shall be made well, and go according to God's "*Divine Plan*." Watch the process. God is *in charge,* and no one else. He shall make the crooked way straight in all things. Only God can see the big picture, and you do not. "*Let go and let God,*" and *watch* the miracles happen. People, events, and things can change before your very eyes! *Trust us,* for what we tell you is *true*.

Much better days are coming, and quickly I may add. This was all meant-to-be since the beginning of time. Much better days are upon you, filled with peace, joy, and happiness. The light is *beaming* at the end of the tunnel. You are *almost there*! Hold onto us, and we shall guide you every step of the way! Much better days are upon you. *Trust us.*

Child, your *new life* shall be filled with such love and happiness, that this current life shall be but a flicker of sadness, quickly to be discarded. We can see your future, and you cannot. You are simply using *blind faith* right now. This nightmare shall end suddenly, and a *new world* shall open before your very eyes. Yes, God is good and only wants the *very best* for you. It was all part of His plan since He created you, my child. He only wants you to be *happy* in this life. Choose love and light over darkness and evil. Soon, very soon, your mission shall be revealed to you. Soon, very soon, you shall feel as light as a feather. Your burden shall be lifted from your shoulders. Thank God! Give it to Him now, so He can carry it for you. Remember, He performs miracles each and every day! Just, *"Ask and you shall receive."* He is anxiously awaiting your arrival. He will handle it all, and better than you could ever dream possible. *"Let go and let God,"* and watch the miracles happen!

Look forward to these days, for they are quickly approaching. *"Let go and let God,"* and watch the miracles of love, peace and happiness enter your heart and soul. Allow God to melt away your sorrow and tears. Allow Him to bring *happiness* into your life, my child. Remember, only God can do that, and nothing or no one else. *Trust us,* for what we tell you is *true.* Soon, very soon, all of this *strife* shall be gone. All in an instant! Simply, *"Let go and let God,"* and watch the miracles happen! We love you so very much, my child, and only want the *very best* for you. Allow God to lift the burden from your shoulders. Allow Him to comfort and guide you. Allow Him deep within your heart and soul. He will speak through you. He will guide your every thought, word, and deed. Allow Him into your life! Become His instrument of *peace.* Allow Him to direct your *every move.* Remember, God is *in charge,* and you are not, nor anyone else. Only God can make the crooked way straight. Only God can perform miracles. Place all of your thoughts, hopes and dreams into God's hands. Allow Him to direct your life! He shall make it *better* than you can ever dream possible. *Trust us,* for what we tell you is *true.* We would never lie to you, my child.

It's now time to place all of your thoughts, words, and deeds into action. Tell people about God's *abundant* love for them! Tell them how He wants them *all* to have a much better life. Filled with peace, joy and happiness! All they need to do is turn to Him for *everything,* and watch the miracles happen. It is that simple. Just watch the process, for God is directing it all.

So, my child, practice *"Letting go and letting God."* Little by little, you will begin to see God's *marvelous miracles* work in your life! Yes, all is made well, with God in your life, and *nothing* can be accomplished without him.

So, go now, my child, with God's peace and love in your heart, and *watch* the miracles happen!

We love you so very much, and are guiding you.

Love,
BV & Christ

Dear Child,

Why do you fret or worry? Don't you *know* that we are guiding you every step of the way? No harm shall come to you, my child. *Know* that *all is well,* and going according to *"God's Plan."* We know this is a great test in faith for you. *Trust us,* for all shall be made well. Watch the process. It's only a matter of time, when all of this *strife* shall be behind you. *"Let go and let God,"* and *know* that all is going according to *"God's Plan."* Have *patience,* and watch the process. God is *in charge* here, and no one else. He performs *miracles* each and every day! Simply stop, and *watch* the miracles happen! Yes, my child, soon, very soon, all of this *strife* shall be *behind you. Trust us,* for what we tell you is *true.* You need to *"Let go and let God,"* and watch the miracles happen.

My child, very soon you shall be doing *"God's work"* for us on earth. You shall bring the *mindfulness of God* to many people on earth. Yes, my child, God has a plan for you, and soon, very soon, it shall be enacted. Watch the process.

Yes, my child, you are *"Divinely Protected!"* God has *great plans* for you. Watch the process. Soon, very soon, all shall be revealed to you. It won't be long now, when all of this shall be *behind you. Trust us.*

Child, begin to look forward to your future days, filled with love, peace, joy and happiness! These days are quickly approaching! God has *great plans* for you, my child, and soon they shall be revealed to you.

Child, all of this was meant-to-be. God wanted to make you *stronger* so you could give *great testimony* of God's love for all of us. People need to hear this. They need *Hope!* God can lighten their load! They just need to *turn-to-God* for *everything!* He shall make the crooked way straight! He shall perform *miracles* in their lives! All they need to do is turn to Him for everything! Once they *"Let go and let God,"* their lives shall become *happier and lighter.* Yes, my child, people need to hear this about God. They need *hope!* They need love and happiness too. All of this can be achieved with God on their side, and no one else. With God, all can be accomplished, without God, nothing can be accomplished. Simply. "*Let go and let God*," and watch the miracles happen! It is that simple!

So child, be *at peace knowing* that *everything* is going according to God's "*Divine Plan*."

We love you so very much, and are guiding you.

Love,
BV & Christ

Dear Child,

D o not be saddened. This too shall pass. Remember, everything
happens for a reason. You needed to get out of that *toxic relationship*.
Now it is time to plan for your future. Remember, it is a *rosy one*, full of
peace, love, joy, and happiness! *Trust us,* for what we tell you is *true*. No
need to worry or fret. God is handling it all! Place *everything* into His
hands, and watch the miracles happen.

Thank God each day for the *basic necessities* of food, and shelter, and
good friends. These are a gift, my child. Be thankful for good health and
a sound mind. Be thankful for the gift of *faith,* and *hope* for the future. Be
thankful to be alive! These are all gifts, my child.

Start writing out your future plans. Watch them develop. *Know* that
we are with you always, and in all ways. We would *never* leave you, my
child.

So, make the most of each day. *Appreciate* all that is given to you.

Know that all is well, and going according to God's *"Divine Plan."*

We love you so very much, and are guiding you.

Love,
BV & Christ

2-15-16

Dear Child,

Thank you for returning today. We are *always* happy to see you, my child. Continue to remain *very close* to us in the days ahead. Many changes are *in store* for you. We will guide you through them all.

Now, child, you *know* we love you. Place all of your troubles into God's hands, and He will work them out *better* than you can ever *dream possible! Know* that this is *true*. We would never lie to you, my child. Simply, *"Let go and let God."*

All that we have been saying to you throughout the years, has lead you to this point. *Know* that you are *exactly* where *you* need to be at this time. All is happening for a reason, and soon, very soon, it shall be revealed to you. For now, *"Let go and let God."* Allow Him to show you the way. Listen to His voice. Do not fear or worry. Place *everything* into God's hands, and He will handle things *better* than *ever*.

So, child, go *in peace* now to love and serve the Lord.

We love you very much, and are guiding you.

Love,
BV & Christ

Dear Child,

D o not fret or worry. *Know* that all is well and going according to God's *"Divine Plan."* *Know* that this is *true*. Much better days are coming, filled with peace, joy, and happiness. Look forward to these days, for they are *quickly approaching*. We promise you *this is true*!

Child, soon, very soon, you shall have a *"wonderful life!"* Filled with peace, joy, and happiness! Yes, my child, this life is *quickly approaching*. God has a plan for you, and very soon it shall be revealed to you. *Trust us,* for what we tell you is *true*. We would never lie to you, my child.

Now is the time to place all of your faith, hope, and *trust* in God. *Know* that much better days are coming.

Take each day as it comes. Be thankful for the *little things* in life. Good friends, warm sunshine, a roof over your head, food, and clothing. God is giving you it all, my child. *Do not fear or worry. Know* that God is handling it all. Things are delayed for now, but *soon*, very soon, all shall be made *better* than you can ever *dream possible*. Remember, when you place *everything* into God's hands, all will be made better than you can ever dream possible. *Trust us,* for what we tell you is *true*, my child. We love you so very much, and only want the *very best* for you.

Now is the time to *sit tight*, watch, and *listen* to what God is telling you to do.

We love you so very much, and are guiding you.

Love,
BV & Christ

5-17-16

Dear Child,

Why are you sad and fretting? Don't you *know* that we are with you *always,* and in *all ways.* God is with you through it all. This is *all* part of God's "*Divine Plan.*" A plan that was *meant-to-be* since the beginning of time. *Watch the process.* It can all be over in an instant! *Trust us, child.* This too shall pass. Much *better days* are ahead of you. Filled with peace, joy, love, and happiness! All this is *true,* my child. We would *never* lie to you. We love you so very much, and only want the *very best* for you. God has a plan for you, and very soon, it shall be revealed to you. Much better days are coming!

Now, child, *know* that your future is a *rosy* one! Filled with peace, joy, love, and happiness! Now is the time to *stop, wait, watch,* and *listen* to what God is telling you to do, my child. It won't be long now, when your life shall change *completely.* Your time of *fretting* is *almost over!* Peace is on its way! Thank God for His *abundant* love for you! It is a love so *deep* that the world has *never known.* He *loves you through eternity!* Child, *trust us.* Much better days are coming.

Thank God each and every day for the *little things.* Like the rain to water the grass and flowers. The sunshine to warm our hearts and the land. The ability to have *good health!* The ability to talk, walk, speak, hear, see, and reason. Thank God for good friends to house, feed you, and protect you. Thank your parents for the gift of *faith!* Thank God for all of these things. Remember, He is our Lord and creator. He knows all things, and is guiding our every move. He just wants us to be happy in this life. Place all of your troubles into His hands. He will have things turn out *better* than you can ever dream possible. *Trust us,* for this is *very true!* Only God can make the crooked way straight. Only God can perform miracles! He is the all, and end all. He is the Alpha and the Omega. Place *all* of your faith, hope, and *trust* in *Him.* Child, He is the only one who can make the crooked way straight! He is our eternal love and creator! No one can take His place! He has the *power* above everyone and everything! He *knows* all. He sees the *big picture,* and you do not. So, continue to place all of your faith, hope, and *trust* in *Him.* And *watch the miracles happen.*

Remember, He hears your prayers and answers them. Simply, *"Ask, and you shall receive."* All shall be made well. Watch the process, and *know* that everything can change in an *instant.*

Know, my child, that we love you very much, and are guiding you.

Love,
BV & Christ

Dear Child,

Welcome back! It is *always* so good to see you. Yes, you are part of God's army now, and soon, very soon, your mission shall be revealed to you.

Now for the task at hand. Remain very calm and close to us in the upcoming days. Many changes are ahead for you, my child, and we shall guide you through every one of them. Nothing to fear. They are all for the better, my child. Remember, God is with you, *always* and in *all ways*. You are *never alone,* my child. We are there guiding your every thought, word, and deed. *Know* that this is *true*. Your *strife* shall pass quickly. This entire situation is drawing to an *end. Watch the process.* Soon, very soon, you shall be made happier than you could ever dream possible! Yes, this is all part of God's *"Divine Plan."* A plan that was set in place since the beginning of time.

Child, *trust us* with all that you say and do. Much will *happen quickly.* It is time. Your days of suffering are almost over. Soon, it shall be time for you to begin your mission. We are very excited for you, my child. Your *new life* is about to begin, filled with peace, joy, love, and happiness! Yes, my child, this is true. We would *never lie* to you. Now is the time to *stop, wait,* and *listen* to what God is telling you to do. Things can change in an instant! *Watch the process.* A new life is about to *open up* right before your very eyes.

So, remain very close to us, and *watch the process.*

We love you so very much, and are guiding you.

Love,
BV & Christ

Dear Child,

Good morning! And welcome here today on your father's *earthly* birthday! What a beautiful morning to celebrate his life!

Child, do not worry or fret about your current situation. Simply, place it all into God's hands, and *know* that all is well, and going according to God's *"Divine Plan."* A plan that has been set in motion since the beginning of time. *Trust us,* for what we tell you is *true. Know that all is well. Do not worry*! Place *everything* into *God's hands*, and watch the miracles happen. This is *true,* my child. Place all of your faith, hope, and *trust* in God. Watch the process. Things will turn out *better* than you can ever dream possible! We are guiding you, my child. Simply, *stop, wait,* and *listen* to what God is instructing you to do next. Remember, things can change in an instant! So much is happening now. Watch the process, and *know* that all is well, and going according to God's *"Divine Plan."* Yes, we have a plan for you, and soon, very soon, it shall be revealed to *you.* For now, exercise *patience,* and enjoy the *peace.* For when things begin to change, they shall happen *quickly*! So, enjoy the moment. Enjoy this beautiful morning, and *know* that God is with you every step of the way. You are *never* alone, my child. We are with you always, and in all ways.

So for now, go *in peace* to enjoy your day.

We love you very much, and are guiding you.

Love,
BV & Christ

Dear Child,

Yes, these times are changing all for the *better* I might add. Watch the process, and see God's miracles unfold right before your very eyes.

Child, do not fret or worry. Place all of your *troubles* into God's hands. He is handling it all. *No harm shall come to you, child! Trust us,* for what we tell you is *true.* We are *guiding* you, my child.

Now is the time to *stop, wait, and listen* to what God is instructing you to do next. It won't be long now when *all* of this *strife* shall be behind you! This is *true,* my child. We would *never lie* to you. Much *better days* are coming, filled with peace, joy, love, and happiness!

Remember, things can change in an *instant.* Keep this in mind, my child. Continue to have *hope!* Do not *despair!* We are with you, guiding you through it all. It's just a little while longer when you shall see *everything change,* all for the *better* I might add. Exercise *patience. Know* that this too shall pass. *Know* that much better days are coming. *Know* that *all is well,* and going according to God's "*Divine Plan.*" Watch the process. Soon, oh so very soon, all of this *strife* shall be *behind you!* You shall enjoy a life full of love, peace, joy, and happiness! This is *true,* my child. Believe us! We would *never lie* to you, my child.

All good comes to those who wait. It will *all* be better very soon. Better than you could ever dream possible.

Child, continue to place your hope, trust, and faith in God. He is handling it all. Much better days are coming. Do not despair, for we are with you through it all. Guiding your every move. Turn *everything* over to God, and *watch* the miracles happen.

God has a purpose for you, my child, and soon, *all* shall be *revealed* to you. *All* of God's love and mercy is being shed on you now, child. Feel His abundant *love* for you. *Know* that He is guiding you. *Know* that *all is well,* and going according to His "*Divine Plan.*" A plan that was *set in motion* since the beginning of time. Watch the process. Soon, oh so very soon, *all* shall be made known to you.

Know that you are not alone. We are with you through it all. Do not let things bother you. Simply place them into God's hands, and watch His miracles happen.

Continue to place *all* of your faith, hope, and *trust* in God. He is there for you, helping you every step of the way. *Know* that He is guiding and protecting you, my child. *All* good shall come to you. All is well, and being made well. Watch the process. In time, this shall all be a *distant memory.* In time, you shall be doing *God's work.* In time, you shall be filled with peace, joy, love and happiness. Look forward to these days, for they are quickly approaching!

So, continue to *trust us,* child. Have hope, and *know* that that much better days are coming! And very quickly I might add.

So, go now child, to love and serve the Lord.

We love you very much, and are guiding you.

Love,
BV & Christ

Dear Child,

Welcome back! It's *always* good to see you. Please, please, please, remember to pray daily for: *Peace-on-earth*; the conversion of the evil ones; and for God's intercession with our world leaders. It is *vitally important* that you do this each and every day, and encourage others to do so too.

Now for the task at hand. Child, *"Be still and know that I am God."* Remember to be *mindful* of all that you say and do. We are guiding you every step of the way. No harm shall come to you. We are protecting you. We are guiding your every thought, word, and deed. *No need to worry or fret.* Place everything into God's hands, and watch the miracles happen! Many new and wonderful things are about to happen. Watch the process. Soon, oh so very soon, you shall be *free woman.* Soon, oh so very soon, all shall be revealed to you. Simply, *know* that *all is well,* and going according to God's *"Divine Plan."* A plan that was set in motion since the beginning of time. Watch the process.

Child, God is guiding you through it all. He is with you every step of the way! *Know* that *all is well,* and being *made well.* Simply remain in the moment, and *watch* God's miracles unfold before your very eyes.

It won't be long now, when all of this *strife* shall be behind you! *Trust us,* for what we *tell* you is *true!* It is such a very short time now, my child. Look forward to your future! It is a rosy one! It will be filled with peace, love, joy, and happiness! Watch the process. All is coming to you, my child. All that we have promised you, and more shall be bestowed upon you.

So, go *in peace knowing* that *all is well,* and going according to God's *"Divine Plan."*

Soon, oh so very soon, God's *"Divine Plan"* shall unfold before your very eyes. Watch the process, and *know* that all is well, and being made well.

So, go *in peace,* my child, to love and serve the Lord.

We love you very much, and are guiding you.

Love,
BV & Christ

Dear Child,

Welcome back! It's always good to see you. Please, please, please, remember to pray daily for: *Peace-on-earth*; the conversion of the evil ones; and for God's intercession with our world leaders. It is *vitally important* that you do this each and every day, and encourage others to do so too.

Now for the task at hand. Continue to pray for your world, my child. It is in *dire need* of prayers. Evil forces are attempting to overthrow your government! *Pray* that this *does not happen*! No! God will not allow this to happen. He blessed America, and continues to do so. It is the shining light in a world that is full of oppression and despair! Pray for your President, and his family. They are constantly under attack. God is giving them the grace and energy to persevere.

A *new day* is coming for you, and *all* of mankind. Watch the process. Watch how God's miracles unfold right before your very eyes. Yes, my child, all is being made well. Do not worry or fret. Simply place all your troubles into God's hands, and watch His miracles happen. Remember, God is *in control* here, and no one else. He shall make the crooked way straight. He shall conquer evil! Watch the process, and *know* that all is well, and being made well.

Child, now is the time to *stop, wait*, and *listen* to what God is instructing you to do, then *act* upon it. He is guiding you, my child, every step of the way. *Watch* as it all unfolds right before your very eyes.

Your world is about to change in oh so many wonderous ways! Yes, my child, a *new day* is coming for you, and *all* of mankind. It shall be filled with peace, love, joy and happiness. Yes, this was all meant-to-be since the beginning of time. It is all part of God's *"Divine Plan."*

You are leaving in one of the most exciting times in mankind's history. Much shall be revealed to you. Watch the process. *Know* that all is well, and being *made well.*

So my child, continue to accept each day as it comes. *Knowing* that much better days are coming for you and *all* of mankind.

So, go *in peace* now, to love and serve the Lord. We love you very much, and are guiding you.

Love,
BV & Christ

Dear Child,

Remember, *"Love Conquers All!"* Yes, my child, you are seeing God's love *in action*! Witness all His gifts, both large and small. The world is filled with His love. Become *aware* of *all* He does for you! Become *aware* of *all* He has done for you. Yes, my child, He is with you, *always,* and in *all ways.*

Now is the time to *stop, wait,* and *listen* to what He is instructing you to do, then *act* upon it. It won't be long now when *all* of this *strife* shall be behind you. Yes, my child, *trust us,* for what we tell you is *true*. We would never lie to you.

The *best* is yet to come! Look forward to these days for they *are* quickly approaching. Soon, oh so very soon, your world shall change completely! All for the better I may add. *Watch* as it *all* unfolds right before your very eyes.

Child, such *good days* are ahead of you, that you will not even recognize your world as it is today! Yes, my child, these changes are occurring quickly. *Watch as* it all unfolds right before your very eyes. You will not even recognize your world this time next year. That's how many changes will take place on your planet. But until then, allow God to guide you through it all. He is with you step by step, minute by minute, guiding your path through life. Allow Him into every part of your life, my child. It will run much smother for you. But until His second coming, allow God to guide you every step of the way.

So, my child, go *in peace* to love and serve the Lord.

We love you very much, and are guiding you.

Love,
BV & Christ

CHAPTER SIX

GOD SPEAKS TO US ALWAYS AND IN ALL WAYS

Dear Child,

Welcome back! It's wonderful to see you once again. Now for the task at hand. Now, more than ever, our world needs prayers. There are *so many distractions* today for people to *turn away from God. This is wrong!* People need to turn their eyes toward God. *He is the only one who can save them!* They need to be *open* to Him, and *listen* to what He is telling them. It's not easy separating yourself from the world, and all of its pressures. But you must do so, in order to save yourself, and the world.

Take time for God each and every day. Make room for Him in your mind and heart. Hear His voice. He will guide you in all that you say and do. Never lose faith or give up hope. *Despair* is such a grave sin in the world today. People are void of God in their daily lives! They go through their day hopelessly and in despair. They have no hope for the future of our world, and are only living for their *daily comfort zone.* How *empty* and *sad.* They need to *wake up!* They need to look around them, and see God in all of nature! They also need to see God in one another. God is everywhere. He is always with them. They just don't recognize Him! They are *not aware.* They need to change the direction they are hoping to find happiness. It is not in material things! That is just temporary, and not long lasting. God is the only thing that lasts! They need to turn their lives over to God, and they will be so much happier! It's that easy. If only they would *stop* and *listen.* It's that simple. Please convey this message to *everyone* you meet. People need to wake up! They need to live their lives being *mindful* of God. Only then will they realize happiness and joy. Only then, will they feel the peace and joy in their lives that only God can bring. They will be made happier than they ever dreamed possible. *Knowing* that God is with you always, and in all ways. You are never alone with God on your side.

So, do not despair. *Know* that God is there for you, silently waiting for you to turn to Him. Stay close to Him, and all that you say and do will be guided by Him.

We love you very much, and are guiding you.

Love,
BV & Christ

Dear Child,

Thank you for *checking in* with us. Please remember to pray daily for: *Peace-on-earth*; the conversion of evil ones; and for God's intercession with our world leaders. It is *vitally important* that you do this each and every day. The world is depending on it. I know it is not easy, but you must be *mindful* of God in all that you say and do. Respect others. Show mercy and compassion. Let God work through you to make things right. It is necessary in order to achieve *peace. Peace* within your heart, and throughout the world. It is necessary to be *open* to God, and His plans for you, and the world. We need *peace* for your planet to survive. Without *peace*, all will vanish. So, pray daily for this. God hears your prayers and answers them. It is *vitally important* to remain *close to God* always. God will guide you, and point you in the right direction. Stay close to Him. Look to Him for strength during these difficult times. He will pull you through it all. *"Let go and let God."* He is our answer for everything.

Child, hear our *words of wisdom,* and live by them. Internalize them. Have *hope* for your world. *"Let go and let God"* enter your heart and soul. Let Him be your guide for everything. He will help you. He is with you always and in all ways. You are never alone. Walk with him, Talk with Him. Allow Him into your life. He is patiently waiting to be a part of your life. Stay close to Him, and *know* that all is well. We love you very much, and are guiding you.

Love,
BV & Christ

Dear Child,

Welcome back! It's great to see everyone again at mass. What a beautiful service it was, depicting great anticipation of our baby Jesus. What a joy to the world. He truly is for us! Stay with the *spirit of Christmas* even as you leave here, my child. For God is with you always, and in all ways. Never lose sight of Him. He is your hope, strength, and inspiration. Yes, you are being guided even by helping others. You still managed to find plenty of time for us. We love you, my child. We are guiding you. Never worry about the outcome, for all is going according to God's plan. He has a great mission in mind for you, and soon it will be revealed to you. Stay close to us my child, and all will be made known to you.

Yes, this brisk wintery day allows you to deepen your relationship with God. It allows you to *"Be still and know that I am God."* Begin to see God in everything. The snowflakes are perfect, pure, and uniquely different from each other. God made everything good. Be at *peace* on a silent day such as this one. Nature is bursting with God's love and adornment. The evergreen trees are freshly frocked, the majestic elk are grazing on the frozen grown, searching for a few twigs. Yes, God provides for everyone and everything. Interestingly, they know where to go for food. All is perfect according to God's plan. Just *be* and see His beauty around you. The world will astound you each time you look at a star. Yes, you were *born free* in America. Continue to *pray daily* for your country. *Pray* that it returns to its original constitution. *Pray* that everyone is treated equally with respect and kindness. *Pray* that your nation returns to God. He can make the crooked way straight, and no one else. God sees all things, knows all things, and manages everything. He is our Supreme Being, the end all and know all. He is the alpha and the omega. God is the only one we should strive to be close to. We should give Him our hearts and souls. He will never let us down. He is patiently waiting for us to turn to Him. Waiting for us to dedicate our lives to Him. He is our *answer* to *everything*. With God on our side, all is possible. We have no need to fear or want of anything. He is our *"Supreme Protector."* He can move mountains for us. All is possible with God on our side, and nothing is possible without Him. He is our rock, our strength, and our foundation. Be true to God, and all will be made known to you. Be true to God, and He will care for you and bless you. Be true to God, and you will want for nothing. You will be completely filled with God's love. Be awake to God's presence and actions in your life. Be aware of His constant love and attention. His intention is to reward you abundantly. Just turn to Him for everything. You will feel peaceful and content in His arms. Only God can comfort you when you feel sad and lonely. Only God can give you peace and happiness, and total abundance! Thank God each and every day for the gifts He gives you. Thank Him, most of all, for the gift of life. You now have the opportunity to return to Him. You now have the opportunity to show Him how much you care for him. You now have the opportunity to *give back* all that He has given you. So, open your heart, mind, and soul, and be filled with His abundant love for you. His love will never die. It is eternal. It is unconditional. He is with you always and in all ways.

So, continue to be open to His presence, and His work within your life. Thank Him for all of His graces and blessings, and *know* that all is well.

We love you very much, and are guiding you.

Love,
BV & Christ

Dear Child,

Yes, it was many years ago today, when many soldiers gave their lives for this country. Keep their souls in prayer today.

My child, it is a very deep spiritual day today. The snow storm makes it even deeper. Isn't God's beauty in nature magnificent? It is a *winter wonderland* out there. It is truly a time of reflection and deep contemplation.

Child, do not be in a hurry to do anything today. Stay in deep contemplation with us. Listen to us. We will guide you. It is necessary to become *in tune* with us, so we can give you instructions at any given moment. Practice *listening* today, and watch how it works. Just stay at *peace*, and be very calm.

My child, a new day is coming. You will be quite happy on earth. Wars will *cease*! Mankind will love one another as themselves, and love God with their whole heart and soul! How wonderful that will be! It will be a time of great joy. People will share with one another. They will thank God for their blessings every day. They will be grateful and honored by God's presence in their lives. Yes, your planet will evolve into a *new spiritual* level. One by which *war* is not an option. One in which *love* will rule, and not hate or fear. Yes, there is a *new day* coming, and it will be magnificent! It will be *free* of all *negativity*. You will have many *good news* stations. It will be easier to live by being *in tune* with God and His wishes. God loves you all so very much, and this will be your chance to *give back* to Him. How wonderful! It will be a time when many graces will be bestowed upon the land. It will be a time of great love and nourishment, both for the body and the soul.

Now is the time to prepare for this *new world*. Now is the time to take God into your heart and soul. Become pure love, as you saw your dad become on his deathbed. Do not wait to die to do this. Accomplish it *now* by surrendering your heart and soul to God. Become His instrument. Allow Him to *act* through you. He loves you so very much, my child.

Open your heart to Him, so that you can become all that you were meant to be. Live each moment for Him. Be *mindful* of Him in all that you say and do. Allow Him to guide you through it all. Do not worry or fear, for He is with you always, and in all ways. Place all of your troubles into God's hands, and live in this *precious moment*. Become more alive and human by doing this. Allow God into your heart and soul. The time is now, do not wait any longer. God is patiently waiting for you.

Listen with the ears of your heart. Become transformed with God's love. Let Him nourish and guide you. You are *special* to us, and we have great plans for you. You can only *access* these plans by staying in the *present moment*. You will have no need to think. Only *know* that God is guiding you through it all. Have *no need to fear or worry*. For we are with you *always*, and in *all ways*.

My child, life has many changes in store for you. These are good changes. We want you to be happier than you could ever dream imaginable. Let God guide you through it all, and you will be set free. Things will come easy for you. You will be *going with the flow* with God guiding you through it. Life will be worth living. Live every *precious moment* of it. Do not let anything get you down, for all is going according to God's "*Divine Plan*."

So, enjoy this *precious* winter day. Relax in the arms of God. Let Him guide you. *Know* that all is well. Practice surrender.

We love you very much, and are guiding you.

Love,
BV & Christ

Dear Child,

Welcome back, once again, on this very *frigid* morning, -5°F. Please remember to pray daily for: *Peace-on-earth*; the conversion of the evil ones; and for God's intercession with our world leaders. It is *vitally important* to do this each and every day.

Child, we love you very much, and are guiding you. So, no need to fear or despair once you leave this retreat. We are with you every step of the way. *Know* that we are with you through all the events that are about to take place. You are *never alone*. Simply go within, and you will feel our presence with you, and have peace. Enjoy this day. Enjoy this *precious moment*. Thank God for all of His graces and blessings, and *be at peace*.

Take this *peace* out into the world. It so desperately needs it. Refuse to hear negativity. Change the subject, or walk away. Do not ponder upon it. It will disturb your *peace*. Stay true to your prayer life. It will get you through difficult times. Remember the *peace* you found with this retreat. It is a gift. Every time you go within, you will feel this *peace*. It will all come back to you. It will remain in your heart. It will influence the world around you. God wants you to spread the *faith*, and have *hope*. Give people the real meaning of Christmas. It is Jesus coming. The *Prince of Peace* to bring *peace* to our world. Live this *peace*. Be this *peace*. Encourage everyone to thank God for their many blessings. Be happy and positive. Do not let anyone get you down. If they do, go into *silence*, and say your prayer.

Remember, my child, you are never alone. We are with you through it all. Turn to God for everything, and He will provide for you. *"Ask and you shall receive." "Seek and you shall find."* Turn all of your troubles over to God, and He will handle them better than you could ever dream imaginable.

Thank you for taking the time to join us on this retreat. *Know* that we love you very much, and are guiding you

Go *in peace* to love and serve the Lord.

Love,
BV & Christ

Dear Child,

Yes, you are experiencing another chilly day in Colorado, -22°F. It is good to talk with you again in the retreat center hallway. At least here, you shall be nice and warm.

Child, remember to pray daily for: *Peace-on-earth*; the conversion of the evil ones; and for God's intercession with our *world leaders*. It is *vitally important* that you do this each and every day, and encourage others to do so too.

Child, remain close to us. We are with you through it all. Soon, very soon, this *strife* shall pass, and much better days are ahead of you. *Know* that all is well, and going according to God's *"Divine Plan."* We are with you through it all, guiding your every step. We shall instruct you as to what to do and say at any given moment. Remain present. Do not let your anxiety take hold of you. *Trust us.* No harm shall come to you. We are protecting you. Child, *"This too shall pass."* Much better days are ahead of you. *Do not fear.* For we are with you always, and in all ways. The time is coming, when you shall impart this knowledge onto others. So, pay attention, and practice what we are telling you to do.

Yes, soon you shall see many changes in your world, as well as, personal life. These are all for the better I might add. Much better days are coming. Look forward to these days. They are a gift from God! Soon, you shall see *peace-on-earth*. Yes, it is a time of Christ's second coming. Then you shall see all eyes turn to God. Those who do not believe, or wish to hold onto their negativity, shall perish. Those who remain, shall love God with their whole heart and soul, and love their neighbor as themselves. It truly shall be a glorious time to be alive! Look forward these days my child, for you shall see *peace-on-earth* in your lifetime. We promise you this is *true!*

So, go about your day with peace, love, and joy in your heart. Appreciate all that God has given you. Show your gratitude to God for His immense beauty in nature. *Know* that all is well, and going according to God's *"Divine Plan."* We love you very much, and are guiding you.

Love,
BV & Christ

Dear Child,

Fear not, for we are with you always, and in all ways. The time is coming when all of this *strife* shall be behind you. Remember, this too shall pass.

Child, the time is coming when a *new world* shall begin. All poverty, wars, anger, and strife shall cease! Yes, Christ's second coming is just around the corner. Look forward to these days, my child, for they are rapidly approaching. Much needs to be done before His arrival. People need to turn to God with *everything* in their lives. Hand all of your troubles over to God, and He shall perform miracles! Place all of your faith, hope, and *trust* in Him! He shall make the crooked way straight. Only God can change the world, and no one else. *"Ask and you shall receive."* God hears your prayers and answers them *instantly*, and things will turn out better than you can ever *dream possible. Trust us.* This is *true.* We are guiding and protecting you. Remain in the *present moment.* Then, you shall find God. He is guiding your every move. *Know that all is well,* and going according to God's *"Divine Plan."*

Now child, we know this time is very difficult for you. But *do not fear,* for we are with you always and in all ways. We are *protecting* you. God has a plan for you, and will not allow any harm to come to you. We are always with you. Let love and compassion be in the place of fear. Try to have a deep understanding of this situation. *Know* that all is well, and going according to God's *"Divine Plan."* We love you so very much, and will not allow any harm to come to you.

Now child, go in peace to love and serve the Lord
We love you very much, and are guiding you.

Love,
BV & Christ

Dear Child,

Welcome back! It's *always* so good to see you. Please, please, please, remember to pray for: *Peace-on-earth*; the conversion of the evil ones; and for God's intercession with our world leaders. It is *vitally important* that you do this each and every day, and encourage others to do so too.

Child, we woke you this morning for you to come here, and you followed our instructions beautifully. There is so much we need to tell you. Yes, your world is changing rapidly. *Soon, very soon* all of this strife shall be behind you, and you shall begin God's work. His mission for you will begin to unfold.

Now child, remain very close to us. We will guide your every move. Changes are quickly occurring, not only in your own life, but in the entire world. Soon, you shall see changes in governments, currencies, societies, and your planet as a whole! Many environmental changes shall occur too. Child, remember, all of these changes are necessary in order to bring about *world peace*. Simply, *watch the process*. It is all part of God's "*Divine Plan.*" His plan for *peace-on-earth* is almost upon us! Look forward to these days, my child. They will be filled with peace, joy, and abundance! Yes, they are quickly approaching! *Do not despair*! Have *hope*! When times get rough, simply *know* that we are with you through it all. We are with you always, and in all ways. We shall never forsake you. All is going according to God's "*Divine Plan.*" Place all of your faith, hope, and *trust in us*. All shall be made well. No task is too small or large for God to handle. Simply place *everything* into His hands, and watch what *miraculous things happen*! *Know* that all is well, and going according to God's "*Divine Plan.*" He sees the whole picture, and you do not. All of these changes were meant-to-be in order to bring about *world peace*. Remember, it is just around the corner.

So, do not fear, my child. God is handling it all. He will make the crooked way straight. He is performing miracles. Simply place *everything* into His hands, and watch what miraculous things happen.

So child, *be at peace, knowing* that God is with you always, and in all ways.

We love you so very much, and are guiding you.

Love,
BV & Christ

Dear Child,

Welcome back! It's always good to see you. Please, please, please, remember to pray daily for: *Peace-on-earth*; the conversion of the evil ones; and for God's intercession with our *world leaders*. It is *vitally important* that you do this each and every day, and encourage others to do so too.

Child, it won't be long now, when all of this *strife* shall be behind you. Much better days are coming! Ones full of peace, love and happiness! *Trust us!* For all that we tell you is *true*. We would never lie to you.

Now, child, continue to pray for your world for it is in *grave danger*. Evil forces are plotting against America! Continue to pray daily for its protection! Many people would like to see the fall of America. Pray that this *does not happen*! God hears your prayers and answers them. God blessed America. He shed His grace on thee. Continue to ask for His help and protection, and He will grant it to you.

Child, do not give up, for we are with you always and in all ways. We will never leave you. All people need to use their *free will* to turn to God for everything! Remember, He hears your prayers and answers them. It is His fondest wish to have all of mankind turn to Him for everything. Yes, then, and only then, will all have *peace-on-earth*. Yes, my child, this will happen. As soon as all of mankind does this, it will be the time of Christ's second coming. We are so very close. So, continue to pray each day for *peace*. God will answer your prayers. Have *hope* because much better days are coming. Remember, any difficulties you may be experiencing is *short lived*, and *"This too shall pass."*

God loves you so very much, and only wants the *best* for you. So, turn to Him for all things. He's there with you every moment! He experiences everything with you! He is there for you, and will never let you down! You are *never alone*, my child. Continue to exercise faith, and *believe* that all we are telling you is *true*. Have *hope* that better days are coming. Have *trust in God knowing* that all is well, and going according to His *"Divine Plan."*

Yes, my child, His *"Divine Plan"* has been set in motion since the beginning of time! All was meant-to-be since then! God knows all. He is the alpha and the omega. He is with you, here and now, and in all ways. He will *never* leave you. He loves you so very much, and is guiding you every step of the way. He will never abandon you, my child. Call out His name in times of trouble, and He will come to your rescue! He is there for you in all ways. Feel His presence beside you. He loves you so very much that He never wants to be without you. You need to be *mindful* of Him with all that you say and do. He is there for you, my child. He is a gift. A blessing in disguise.

What a gift of *faith* you have, my child! Cherish it. Not many people have this anchor to the wind. You can call on God in an instant, and He will be there for you. Aiding you in whatever needs healing. Yes, my child, you can say He is *at-your-service*. How true. He is there to serve and help you every minute of the day! Can you say that you are there for Him always, and in all ways? No, well practice being *mindful* of Him with all that you say and do. Become His instrument! Learn to think before you speak. Think before you act. Be *mindful* of Him with all that you say and do. My child, He is anxiously awaiting your arrival. It is *never* too late to turn to God for *everything*! Encourage others to do this too. Instead of being all caught up in their *worries*. That doesn't help anything. Once you place your troubles into God's hands, it frees you up to do other things, and lightens your load. He will have things turn out better than you can *ever imagine*. Trust us! For this is true! He is willing and able to handle *anything* you give Him. And so willing to do so too.

So, my child, *do not worry* about a thing! Better days are coming. Ones full of peace, joy and happiness. Look forward to these days for they are quickly approaching. Remain very *close to us*, and *know* that all is well, and going according to God's *"Divine Plan."*

We love you so very much, and are guiding you every step of the way.

Love,
BV & Christ

Dear Child,

Good morning and welcome back! It's always good to see you. Please, please, please remember to pray daily for: *Peace-on-earth*; the conversion of the evil ones; and for God's intercession with our *world leaders*. It is *vitally important* that you do this each and every day, and encourage others to do so too.

It won't be long now when *peace* shall be upon you! How glorious! What an exciting time to be alive! Soon, very soon, you shall experience *peace-on-earth*; soon, very soon, you shall experience Christ's second coming! Yes, my child, all of this was meant-to-be since the beginning of time. God's *"Divine Plan"* is being enacted *now!* Watch the process! He has given the world *new hope.* He wants everyone to turn to Him for everything! He will never leave you, my child. He is there for you, *always* and in *all ways.* Remember, it is *never* too late to turn to Him for everything. He is with you, *always* and in *all ways. Trust us,* for what we tell you is *true.* You are never alone, my child. We are with you through it all guiding your every move.

Now is the time to remain *alert.* God is guiding your every move. His grace and love are upon you, my child. Feel His *"Divine Presence"* around you. You are so *loved* by Him. *Know* that this is *true,* my child He loves you so very much, that He would have created this very world for you, even if you were the only person on earth. That's how much He loves you, my child. It is a love everlasting. You may leave Him, but He will *never* leave you, my child. He is always there for you. Feel His presence. Allow Him to guide you through it all. He will direct your every thought, word, and deed. Become His instrument of love. Allow Him to work through you, my child. He knows what is best for all involved. God is here loving you every moment! Be open to *receive* His love. He truly cares for you, my child. He so deeply wants to have a *relationship* with you. He is there for you always, and in all ways. He will *never* forsake you, my child. You can *always* count on Him for everything, my child. *Trust us,* for what we tell you is *true*. God is here today, as He always was since the beginning of time. He was just waiting for mankind to discover Him. Place Him into your heart and soul. Allow Him to guide you through it all. Watch Him work his miracles into your life. For He is driving it all. Place all of your troubles into His hands, and watch the miracles happen, my child. A whole *new world* awaits you. God had planned it that way. Never before in mankind's history, has the world ever know such *peace*. Look forward for these days, my child, for they are *upon you*. Soon, very soon, you shall see your world *change completely*. Soon, very soon, all shall be *made well*, and go according to God's *"Divine Plan."* Watch the process, for what we tell you is *true*. So, *be still*. Feel God's presence in all things, and allow Him to guide you through it all.

We love you so very much, and are guiding you.

Love,
BV & Christ

Dear Child,

Do not *fret!* Much better days are coming! Ones full of peace, love, joy and happiness! *Trust us,* for what we tell you is *true.* These days of *strife* are almost over! Believe us, we would *never lie to you.* There is a silver lining under this dark cloud.

Remember, all of this was meant-to-be. It had to come to this, my child. You are choosing God! Now proceed, based on these choices. We are guiding your *every step.* God is making the crooked way straight. The *truth* shall be made *known.* Watch the process. No need to fret or worry. Simply, place everything into God's hands, and *watch* the miracles happen! Only God can make the *crooked way* straight. Only God has the *power* to *perform miracles.* Simply, "*Let go and let God,*" and *watch the miracles happen. Know* that *all is well,* and going according to God's "*Divine Plan.*" A plan that was set in motion since the beginning of time.

Soon, very soon, my child, you shall *experience* such *delightful changes* that you can hardly believe it is all happening. Simply, "*Let go and let God,*" and things will turn out *better* than you can ever dream possible! Yes, God has a plan for you, and soon, very soon, it shall be revealed to you. *Know* that this is *true.* We would *never lie* to you, my child. "*Let go and let God,*" and feel His presence. He is with you, *always* and in *all ways.*

My child, this was all meant-to-be. Major life lessons were learned here. Now you come from love and compassion, mercy and forgiveness. You humbly turn things over to God, not knowing their outcomes, is truly an act of *blind faith.* Continue to do this child, for all shall be made well, and turn but better than you can ever dream possible! *Trust us,* for what we tell you is *true.* Yes, the road before you is a *rosy path.* Filled with love and kindness. God wants you to have this as a reward for enduring such hardships these past few years. My child, this is not *heaven yet,* but the road ahead of you is as close to heaven as you can get here on earth. *Trust us* for what we tell you is *true.* You do have a *rosy future* ahead of you. *Believe us,* for what we tell you is *true.* Your major life lessons, as difficult as they may be, are *behind you*. Now look forward to the joyous roads *ahead* of you. It is God's gift to you, my child, for being His *faithful servant*. *Know* that this is *true*. Look forward to these days, my child, for they are quickly approaching. All of this *strife* is almost completely behind you! Just a few more days, and suddenly, all shall be made well. Watch the process, for what we tell you is *true*, my child. Believe us, we would never lie to you. Your days of *strife* are *almost* completely over. Thank God!

Now continue on *blind faith*. *Know* that what we tell you is *true*. Look forward to your future for it is a *rosy one*.

Now go *in peace* to love and serve the Lord.

We love you very much, and are guiding you.

Love,
BV & Christ

Dear Child,

Why do you fret so? Don't you *know* that *much better* days are coming, filled with peace, joy and happiness! Look forward to these days, for they are quickly approaching. *Know* that all is well, and going according to God's *"Divine Plan."* A plan that was meant-to-be since the beginning of time. Yes, God has a plan for you, and soon, very soon, it shall be revealed to you, my child. Exercise *patience* now for this *very brief moment.* Soon, very soon, things shall be *set-in-motion.* Enjoy the moment *now.* Feel God's presence. He is guiding your every step, my child. Soon, very soon, all of this *strife* shall be b*ehind you.* Soon, very soon, you shall be able to *exhale with a sigh of relief*! What a blessing for all involved. Yes, God's mercy and love is upon you. Yes, He hears your prayers and answers them. Yes, He is with you, always and in all ways. He shall *never leave you,* my child. He loves you so very much, that He would have created this very world for you had you been the only person on earth! That's how much He loves you. He wants to give you it all. All you have to do is *"Ask and you shall receive."* The time is coming when all of this *strife* shall be behind you. Thank God! Only God can make the crooked way straight. Only God can perform miracles. *Trust us,* for what we tell you is *true.* The days of *strife* are almost completely *behind you.* Yes, my child, much better days are coming, filled with peace, joy and happiness. Look forward to these days, for they are *quickly approaching.* Yes, God's love is shining upon you. Absorb His *peaceful rays.* Feel their warmth. He is shedding His blessings upon you. *Know* that *all is well,* and going according to God's *"Divine Plan."* A plan that was meant-to-be since the beginning of time.

Yes, God picked you up out of this situation, and planted you in Colorado. Enough is enough! Now it is *time* for you to *move forward* with a new life, my child. God does not want you to be *trampled over*! He wants you to triumph! You are in a battle of good vs. evil. In the end, *good* always prevails! We would never send you into battle, if you did not reign victorious! So, my child, *know* that God's armor and shield are around you. His legend of angels are protecting you. *Know* that all is well, and going according to God's plan. We love you so much, and are guiding you.

Love,
BV & Christ

Dear Child,

Welcome back! It's *always* good to see you. Please, please, please, remember to pray daily for: *Peace-on-earth*; the conversion of the evil ones; and for God's intercession with our world leaders. It is *vitally important* that you do this each and every day, and encourage others to do so too.

Now, child, remain very close to us in the days ahead. We are *guiding* and *protecting* you. *Know* that all is well, and going according to God's "*Divine Plan*." Yes, this was a plan set in motion since the beginning of time, my child. Much better days are coming both for you, and your entire world! *Trust us*, for what we tell you is *true*. We would *never lie* to you, my child. The time of war, anger, jealously, and rage are almost over! God will *no longer tolerate* such nonsense on your planet. He wants you all to get along with *each other*! Those who wish to *hold onto* such negativity shall perish! *Peace-on-earth* is on its way! Look forward to these days, my child, for they are quickly approaching! Yes, my child, this is truly a *glorious time* to be alive! The days of *strife* are almost completely behind you! Watch the process. God is *in charge* here, and no one else. He shall make the crooked way straight. He performs miracles, and no one else. Simply, "*Let go and let God*," and watch the miracles happen. Remember, it is a "*Divine Miracle*" that you are here now *safe and sound*. This was all part of God's plan since you were married. You placed *everything* into His hands. Thank God! You have used your *free will* wisely. God loves you so very much, that He would give you the world if you asked for it. Place all of your troubles into His hands, and watch the miracles happen. It is that simple, my child. He is guiding your every move. So, do not become *anxious* in the days ahead. Allow God to guide your *every step*. He will show you the way at any given moment. Simply "*Let go and let God*," and *know* that all is well, and going according to His "*Divine Plan*." Remember, we have great plans for you. So, allow God's miracles to unfold right before your very eyes. Exercise patience, and watch the process. You are being guided every step of the way. God would never leave you or forsake you. God is *at work* here, and no one else. He will make the *crooked way* straight. The *truth* shall become *known* here. *Know* that what we tell you is *true,* my child. We would never lie to you or forsake you. We are with you, *always* and *in all ways.* God loves you so very much, and only wants the *very best* for you, my child. He needed to pick you up out of that *dangerous situation* in order to keep you alive! We did this for your own safety, my child. *Trust us,* for what we tell you is *true.* The time is coming when all shall be made well. This is God's plan in action. Watch the process, and continue to pray. Remember, God is *in charge* here, and no one else. He will make the crooked way straight. He performs miracles daily! Watch the process, my child. Remain *in the moment,* and you shall be guided every step of the way.

So, *know* that all is well, and going according to "*God's Plan.*" Soon, very soon, all of this *strife* shall be behind you. Watch the process.

We love you so very much, and are guiding you.

Love,
BV & Christ

Dear Child,

Welcome back! It's *always* good to see you. Please, please, please, remember to pray daily for: *Peace-on-earth*; the conversion of the evil ones; and for God's intercession with our *world leaders*. It is *vitally important* that you do this each and every day, and encourage others to do so too.

Child, it won't be long now when all of this *strife* shall be behind you. Thank God! Just *"Let go and let God,"* whenever you become troubled. He shall make the crooked way straight. He performs *miracles* each and every day. Remain calm. Watch and listen to His voice. He will direct your every move. Place all of your faith, hope, and trust in Him. All shall be made well. *Know* that all is going according to God's *"Divine Plan."* *Trust us,* for what we tell you is *true*. We would never lie to you, my child.

I know things seem to be so *unsettled* for you right now. Enjoy each day. Thank God for everything. The sunshine, food, shelter, and good friends. Take this time to go within, and be *thankful* to be alive!

Your life is taking a different path now. One of peace, joy, love and happiness. Be open to God's *goodness and grace*. Allow Him to show you the way of *new beginnings*. Allow Him into your life, my child. Think of Him often, for He is with you always, and in all ways.

Now is the time to be very still, and watch the ways He is guiding you. Remember, you are never alone, for He is *always* with you, my child. Feel His presence. *Know* that all is well, and going according to His *"Divine Plan."*

Child, your life is about to *open up* into an entirely *new direction!* Be happy for this *peace*. It is God's gift to you. He took you out of that *miserable situation,* and placed you with people who love you. Enjoy them. Take in how it *feels* to be with nice, warm, genuine people. What a relief and gift!

Yes, God has great plans for you, and watch them unfold.
Now child, go *in peace* to enjoy this beautiful day!
We love you so very much, and are guiding you.

Love,
BV & Christ

Dear Child,

Do not worry or fret. *We are with you always,* and in *all ways.* No harm shall come to you, my child. We are *protecting you.* God has a plan for you, and very soon, it shall be revealed to you.

Child, soon, so very soon, your world shall *open up* in many ways. A new exciting future lies ahead for you, my child. So, *do not despair* or give up *hope!* We are with you through it all. You are never alone. We love you so very much, and only want the best for you. It won't be long now, when all of this *strife* shall be *behind, you* child. *Trust us,* for what we tell you is *true.* Much *better* days are coming, and very quickly I might add.

Child, one day, you will reflect back on this time as a *moment-of-sadness.* But we are giving you a great deal of *strength* to deal with all of this, my child. It's allowing you to *stand up,* and be heard! God made you for a reason. Your time of suffering is almost over! Give it all to God, and He shall make the crooked way straight! He shall have things turn out *better* than you can *ever* dream possible! Place *everything* into His hands, and watch the miracles happen!

Child, we love you so very much, and only want the *very best* for you. Continue to have *faith!* Place all of your trust and *hope* into God's hands. It won't be long now, when all of this shall be *behind you* child. *Trust us,* for what we tell you is *true.* We would never lie to you, my child.

Now is the time to *stop, wait,* and *listen* to what God is telling you to do next. He is guiding your every step. *Know* that all is well, and going according to His *"Divine Plan."*

Now is the time to *allow* God to *strengthen your faith.* Allow Him to do that for you. *Know* that *everything* happens for a reason. *Know* that God has a plan for it all. God wants you to grow in your faith. He has a plan for you, and very soon, it shall be revealed to you.

Your future looks promising. Filled with light, love and happiness! Look forward to these days, child, for they are quickly approaching. Your time of suffering is almost over. So, remain very close to us, and we shall guide you through it all.

So, go *in peace* now to love and serve the Lord.

We love you very much, and are guiding you.

Love,
BV & Christ

EPILOGUE

This has been a journey of many years. As a result, I have become closer to God. I do believe that much better days are coming filled with *peace, joy, love and happiness.* They are quickly approaching.

We all need to continue to pray for: *peace-on-earth;* the conversion of the evil ones; and for God's intercession with our world leaders.

We will see *peace-on-earth,* and Christ's second coming in our lifetime. Watch the process…

Printed in the United States
By Bookmasters